Los Evangélicos

Los Evangélicos

*Portraits of Latino Protestantism
in the United States*

JUAN FRANCISCO MARTÍNEZ
AND
LINDY SCOTT, EDITORS

WIPF & STOCK · Eugene, Oregon

Wipf & Stock
A Division of Wipf and Stock Publishers
199 W. 8th Ave., Suite 3
Eugene, OR 97401
www.wipfandstock.com

ISBN 13: 978-1-60608-270-6

Manufactured in the U.S.A.

Original title in Spanish: *Iglesias peregrinas en busca de identidad: Cuadros del protestantismo latino en los Estados Unidos*
© 2004 by Ediciones Kairós
Published by Ediciones Kairós
José Mármol 1734, B1602EAF Florida
Buenos Aires, Argentina
Translated by Gretchen Abernathy.

Contents

Acknowledgments

T HIS BOOK HAS BEEN published with the generous financial support of two organizations:

The *Comisión de Estudios de Historia de la Iglesia en América Latina y el Caribe*, Commission for the Study of the History of the Church in Latin America and the Caribbean (CEHILA), exists to write the history of Latin American Christianity from the "perspective of the poor and the marginalized, in a scientific, critical, and ecumenical manner." For more information, visit www.cehila.org.

Wheaton College, an Evangelical college in Wheaton, Illinois, gave a grant for the publication of this book as part of its commitment to doing everything "For Christ and His Kingdom." For more information about the work and mission of Wheaton College, visit www.wheaton.edu.

Contributors

Carlos F. Cardoza-Orlandi is professor of world Christianity at Columbia Theological Seminary. With his doctorate in mission, ecumenics, and history of religions from Princeton Theological Seminary, Cardoza-Orlandi contributes to critical reflection on missiology in Caribbean, Latin American, and Hispanic-Latino contexts. He has authored numerous books, including *Mission: An Essential Guide* (Abingdon, 1999)—also in Spanish and Korean—and *Una historia general de las misiones* (Barcelona: CLIE, 2008), with Justo González, forthcoming in English and Portuguese. In 2007, he was awarded the Building Bridges Award by the Islamic Speakers Bureau of Atlanta, a religious organization that, through dialogue and education, seeks understanding among religions in the United States. He has more than ten years of ministerial experience and participates actively in congregational life and in inter-cultural and inter-religious mission organizations. He lives with his wife and three children in Decatur, Georgia.

Eduardo Font is president of the Alberto Mottesi School of Evangelists and the founding pastor of the Esperanza Viva Church. He has been a leader in the American Baptist Church for many years. He has been a pastor, a professor, and the director of various programs of theological study, including Fuller Seminary's Hispanic Studies department. He is a graduate of the University of California and the *Seminario Internacional Teológico Bautista*. Among his many publications are *La evangelización: Aquí y ahora* and *Pasando la antorcha* (Editorial Kerygma, 2006).

Nora O. Lozano, Mexican, is associate professor of theological studies at the Baptist University of the Américas in San Antonio, Texas and co-founder and co-director of the Latina Leadership Institute. She received her bachelor's degree from the *Universidad Regiomontana* in Monterrey, Mexico, her master's degree from Eastern Baptist Seminary in Philadelphia, and her doctorate from Drew University. She specializes in Latin American and Hispanic theology, women's studies and systematic theology. She lives in San Antonio, Texas with her husband Paul Kraus and their two children, Andrea and Eric.

Ismael Martín del Campo is the international secretary of Christian education for the Apostolic Assembly. He also served as bishop for the Los Angeles district of the Apostolic Assembly. In the last fifteen years he has been the pastor of the Christian Family Center in South Gate, California. He comes from a family which includes five generations of Apostolics. Before coming to the United States in 1992, he served as dean of the *Centro Cultural Mexicano*, a theological institution of the *Iglesia Apostólica de México*. He is currently the president of the International Apostolic Bible Colleges for the Apostolic Assembly. He has published several books, among them *La familia, escuela de valores*, *Apologetic Doctrinal Symposium*, and *Strategy of Jesus: Friendship Groups*. He and his wife Oralia have two sons, Ismael Jr. and Jasiel.

Juan Francisco Martínez Guerra is assistant dean for the Hispanic Church Studies Department and associate professor of Hispanic studies and pastoral leadership at Fuller Theological Seminary. He has been a pastor and a professor for over twenty-five years, including eight years as president of the *Seminario Anabautista Latinoamericano* in Guatemala City. His areas of scholarship and publications are Latino Protestantism in the United States and Anabaptists in Latin America. Juan and his wife, Olga, live in Sunland, California. They have two children, Xaris and Josué.

Sergio Navarrete is superintendent of the Southern Pacific Latin American District of the Assemblies of God denomination. He received his doctor of ministry in spiritual formation from the Hagaard School of Theology of Azusa Pacific University. He rejoices in his loving family, consisting of his wife Janice and their two daughters, Andrea and Aimee. Dr. Navarrete is originally from Tijuana, Mexico and has been an Assemblies of God pastor in the United States for twenty-two years. He is an adjunct professor at Azusa Pacific University, Vanguard University, the *Seminario Teológico Latino-Americano de las Asambleas de Dios*, and the *Instituto Bíblico Latino-Americano* in La Puente, California.

Daniel Ramírez is assistant professor of religious studies at Arizona State University. His areas of research and teaching include religions of the Southwest borderlands and migration, with a special interest in the history of religious contact, conflict, and conversion in the Americas and in the transnational and cultural dimensions of religious practice. Of particular interest are the role of music as a religious or symbolic remittance and catalyst for religious change and the question of indigenous conversion. He received his Ph.D. from Duke University.

Lindy Scott is professor of Spanish and Latin American studies at Whitworth University. He has been a professor for over thirty years, having taught at Wheaton College, the *Universidad Nacional Autónoma de México*, and the *Comunidad Teológica de México*. He recently edited the volume *Christians, the Care of Creation, and Global Climate Change* (Pickwick Publications, 2008) and co-authored with René Padilla *Terrorism and the War in Iraq: A Christian Word from Latin America* (Ediciones Kairos, 2004). He is the regional coordinator of the Latin American Theological Fellowship (FTL) and is the editor of the *Journal of Latin American Theology: Christian Reflections from the Latino South.*

Tony Solórzano is associate pastor of the *Iglesia Central* of the *Ministerios Llamada Final*. He received his doctorate degree from California Christian University. He has produced a variety of Christian education materials for children and for new believers. He and his wife Dalila have four children. He is grateful to God for the opportunity to minister within *Llamada Final* and to have the strong support of his family.

Janet Lynn Treviño-Elizarraraz was born in Monterrey, Mexico and was raised in Illinois. She received her B.A. in Bible and theology at Moody Bible Institute with a concentration in historical theology. She earned her M.A. in theology, with a concentration in church history, from Wheaton College. Mother of three preschool boys, she and her husband, Roberto, live in San Antonio, Texas. They actively serve in the Mennonite Church USA, at both the local and state levels.

Prologue

Justo L. González

SPANISH PHILOSOPHER JOSÉ ORTEGA y Gasset declared that life is the radical reality in which all other reality is encountered and that in order to talk about life we have to use terms of history rather than essence. Think about it for a minute: Although I have a name, and those who know me call me by my name, in reality I am not that name; I am the history that that name represents. My last names, González and García, point toward a story that began long before I was born. The names say something about who my mother and father were, and, if we continue the trajectory, who my grandparents, great-grandparents, and earlier ancestors were. I received my first and middle names, Justo Luis, from my father Justo and my mother Luisa, respectively. However, whoever uses my name refers not only to the story that was going on before I was born or before I became conscious of my existence but also to the story that, for better or worse, my own life has been. Without referencing a story, or more precisely a history, my name is nothing more than a certain sound. Thus Ortega suggests that instead of abstract or speculative reasoning, the foundation for philosophical thought should be historical reasoning, "history as a system."

If Ortega's suggestion is true for all human reality, it is certainly true for Christianity. It is frequently said that Christianity is a "historical religion." Though this phrase can mean many things, for me it means that, more than anything else, Christianity consists not of a series of abstract doctrines—although doctrine has an important place—but rather of a series of historical acts, historical events through which we see and receive the presence of God.

Of all these events, the incarnation of God in Jesus Christ is the most important for Christianity—it defines and determines what Christianity is. Other religions talk about a monotheistic God. Other religions have

xiii

moral teachings similar to those in Christianity. Other religions teach about life after death or about the final triumph of good over evil. But Christianity, more than all these teachings, claims that in the man Jesus of Nazareth, who lived in a particular place at a particular time, God is present in a unique way and that in order to truly know God we have to go there, to Jesus of Nazareth, to find God.

If such is the case, if Christianity is a historical religion in this sense, then certain important consequences follow regarding how we arrive at the knowledge of the truth of Christianity. There are many other sorts of truth that are not historical, and each has a method through which we arrive at that truth.

For example, there are mathematical truths. We can argue all we want about how we arrive at the knowledge of these truths, but there is no doubt that, if we use our intelligence, we can at least figure out the simple truths of mathematics without anyone teaching them to us. In one of his dialogues, Plato presents Socrates interviewing an uneducated young man and, through a series of questions, leading the young man to a set of mathematical conclusions that no one taught to him. If, for example, I know that two plus two equals four, plus two more equals six, and plus two more equals eight, then I do not need anyone to tell me that two times four is eight. Maybe a teacher can help me carry out this reasoning, but the reasoning is mine. I believe that two times two equals four not because the teacher tells me so but because I, in my own mind, can prove it. Based on this reasoning, once I arrive at that conclusion, I can be sure that two times two will equal four in the next century, that it equaled four in the last century, and that it equals four for a Mongolian nomad just as much as it does for my neighbors or for whoever else uses his or her reason.

Some theologians have attempted to demonstrate that some truths of the faith are like mathematical truths. Thus, for example, Anselm's famous ontological argument claims that the existence of a Supreme Being is rational in such a way that one can arrive at the conclusion by using reason alone, even apart from any sensorial data. For Anselm, "God exists" is a truth as obvious and undeniable as "two plus two equals four."

Then there are other truths we could call empirical and that are demonstrable not through pure reason but through observation. For example, if someone says that seawater is salty, it is enough for us to go and try it ourselves. However, not everyone can try it directly since some have never even seen the ocean. In this case, we have to trust the word of those who tell us they have had the experience. We cannot arrive at these truths through pure abstract reasoning because this reasoning does not tell us even that the ocean exists, much less that its water is salty.

In the area of religion there is also a place for this type of truth which uses the experience of others—especially experience corroborated by many other people—as a mode of proving the truth. For example, when we tell other people about the great joy inherent in the Christian faith, we are talking about an experience we have tested, that thousands of other people affirm, but that our audience cannot know directly without trying it—just as the landlocked person who hears about salty seawater cannot know it through direct experience until he or she tastes seawater.

Thirdly, some truths are purely subjective. If I tell a neighbor that I like Bach's symphonies but that I do not like salsa music, I am telling her something she cannot prove directly. Perhaps she can follow me around and see if my actions support the preferences I profess—if, for example, I go to an organ concert in a cathedral or to a salsa concert in the city park. Even with all this testing, though, my neighbor can have no more than a hunch, an idea, regarding the truth of what I have told her. At the end of the day, I am the only person who knows my preferences in the depths of my being.

This sort of truth is also present in the Christian faith. If I say that I love God, no one but God knows to what extent I may or may not be speaking the truth. Whoever hears me say it can, by observing my attitudes and actions, have an indication of whether or not what I say is true; no one, however, can know it through direct experience like tasting seawater or through abstract reasoning like knowing that two plus two equals four.

Finally, there are historical truths. We say, for example, that Christopher Columbus sailed in three ships, the Niña, the Pinta, and the Santa María. We cannot prove this fact through reason alone. Columbus himself could not have known it in 1470. It is possible that the Mongolian nomad I referenced earlier does not know about the three ships. My daughter did not know about them until she learned this information in school. Someone has to tell us about historical truths. Moreover, historical truths require a line of witnesses that in some way puts us in contact with the events to which they refer. Thus, in the case of Columbus and his three ships, the only reason I know about these events is because someone told me about them, if not in person then at least through writings, and someone else had told this person, and someone else had told that person;

and so on successively all the way back to someone who saw Columbus board the ships.

This is what we mean when we say that Christianity is a historical religion: if the incarnation of God in Jesus Christ is the center of the Christian faith, we cannot know about it except through a series of links that lead back to those first century events. Naturally, the four Gospels take a primary place in this chain since they let us hear the testimony of the Christians who were near the first witnesses to the gospel. But in between Jesus himself and the Gospels there is already a chain of witnesses; and after the Gospels were written, there is another whole chain of people—many of them monks—who dedicated themselves to copying and recopying the Gospels until they came to be printed. There is also an entire chain of translators. And there is a long chain of witnesses who have testified to the importance of the gospel.

But there is more. Historical events always come to us through interpretation. The very fact that Columbus sailed on the Santa María in company with the Niña and the Pinta is an interpretation. If we read the texts of that era, we see that the "Niña" and the "Pinta" were nicknames, not the official names for those ships. In the same way, in some texts we read that on October 12, Columbus landed on Guanahaní Island, while other texts say it was the Island of San Salvador, and yet others say it was on Watling Island. They all may be right since each one names and describes the same events from a different perspective and names the same island according to those perspectives.

The same is true of the Gospels. They differ among themselves in many details like names, numbers, the order of events, etc., but they all agree on the fundamentals about Jesus Christ.

All of the above helps us understand the importance of the present book. It is, as the editors say, a type of "family photo album." Like every photo album, it helps us know where we came from and how we came to be who we are. Just as there has to be a history and a story in order to talk about human reality in general, we also have to know our family history, we need our photo album, in order to know who we are as the Latino church.

Yet there is more. The illustrations that appear in these photographs show us how the gospel reached us. Seeing how the gospel reached us helps us understand some of the subtle shades and tones that have been added to what we have received. If history always includes an interpretative dimension—as it did when the Gospels were written—it follows that this family album will help us grasp something of why our history tends to interpret and practice the gospel in this way or that.

Recognizing our interpretations is important for at least two reasons: first, it helps us understand ourselves better; second, it helps us discover what might be important contributions to the rest of the church. The Gospel of Matthew, for example, is not only different from Mark but, thanks to its particular perspective, it also enriches Mark's Gospel. The same is true for John and Luke. In the same way, the Latino gospel, through its particular, unique dimensions, enriches the vision of the church as a whole.

The church among our people is so important because it is part of the church as a whole. This book is, therefore, a valuable contribution not only for our community but also for this wide, diverse people of God that make up the church.

Furthermore, besides being a contribution, this book is an invitation. A mere album of scattered pictures is not enough to get to know our family. We have to meet each other and tell stories about the moments that determined the course of events for us—when Grandmother moved to California, when she met Grandfather, when Papa's brother died, when Papa went off to war, etc. We have to tell the good and the bad. We have to get an idea of the relationship between Susana and Florentino, an idea about how and why the conflict between Pedrito and Jacinto arose, etc. That is, we need to know our family history. What is even more important, if the family begins to forget its history, the family itself begins to fall apart.

This book calls us toward the next steps, beyond the magnificent collection of photos and pictures of distinct moments in our history. Thus I say that this book is also an invitation.

The invitation first of all urges us to compile more "photos" for our album. Our "photos" have lain around forgotten, sometimes because the family members themselves have not thought them important. But we have to collect the stories that are in danger of being forgotten. We need to study the history of hymnology in all our denominations; to study the history and contribution of Latina women in various regions confronting different circumstances; to study the conversion experiences of our ancestors in the faith. We need to keep adding to our family album whatever photos we can find.

Secondly this book invites us to begin organizing all these photos. We can organize our history, just like arranging photos, in many different ways, all of which are important. For example, we can organize our pictures along denominational lines—and already we see the history of various Latino denominations emerging. We should also try organizing along different principles of classification. For example, we are missing a history of the place and contribution of women in the Latino church. What about a history of the place of the church in the education of our communities? A history of worship in our churches? The list could go on.

Thirdly, we need to place these photos and the collections of the photos in their diverse historical contexts. Let us explore, for example, the situation of the Latino church during the Great Depression, the relationship between World War II and the Latino church, and the relationship between the Civil Rights movement and the Latino church. Again, the list could go on and on.

In fourth place, this book reminds us to use our "album" and our more organized and arranged histories to correct the traditional mode of telling the story of Christianity in the United States. According to the traditional map, that story begins in New England and little by little moves south and west. Nevertheless, when we show up at the centers where North American Christian history is written, bringing with us organized collections of family photos, those who write the history of Christianity in the United States will no longer do what they are accustomed to doing—forgetting us or, at best, assigning us an obligatory footnote.

In conclusion, this book shows us that at last we have good "photographers"—women and men with the ability to study particular moments or elements of our history and to do so with clarity and wisdom. We now need to invite these people, and many others within our faith communities, to contribute more photos to our "family album" and to arrange new albums in such a way that something new emerges: a new narrative, a new family history that is not only about our Latino family but also includes our whole family in Jesus Christ, a family that speaks of God's love in every tongue and culture.

Amen!

Justo L. González
Decatur, GA
May 30, 2004
Day of Pentecost

Introduction

Portraits of Latino[1] Protestantism in the United States

PERHAPS IT SEEMS HOPELESSLY idealistic to attempt to write the history of Latino Protestantism in the United States. The wide variety of Protestant movements and efforts has resulted in countless congregations and ministries among Latinos in the United States. Some have documented their work, but many only retain an oral memory of their efforts. Some denominations have worked over 150 years in the Latino community while others are just now beginning. Over the years, many congregations and movements have been established. Some have disappeared but the vast majority are growing and are expanding with many new projects.

Throughout the years, parts of the history of Latino Protestantism have been researched. A few historians have written about stages, regions, or specific denominations, but up to now no one has attempted a panoramic history of Latino Protestantism in the United States.

PROBLEMS WITH WRITING THE HISTORY

The history of Latino Protestant churches in the United States raises a series of complications that has no simple resolution. The majority of the difficulties have to do with the discontinuity between the Protestant efforts among US Latinos. For example, the first Protestant contact among Latinos took place in the Southwest during the nineteenth century. Protestant missionaries began preaching to the Latinos who became US citizens after the United States conquered the southwestern states that had belonged to Mexico. On the other hand, the immigration of Cubans, Puerto Ricans, and Spaniards to the East Coast of the United States also

---

1. The editors recognize that both "Latino" and "Hispanic" are used to describe the Latino community in the United States. This anthology uses both words according to the preference of each author.

led to the formation of Protestant congregations among these communities in the nineteenth century. Though they utilized the same Spanish language, these efforts were completely isolated from each other given the different nationalities.

The situation grew more complicated in the twentieth century with the different waves of immigrants. The wave of Mexican immigrants, due in large part to the Mexican Revolution, and the subsequent rapid growth of this community at the beginning of the twentieth century generated a new Protestant missionary effort somewhat disconnected from the efforts of the nineteenth century. The following waves of twentieth century immigrants brought people from many different Latin American countries. During the first half of the twentieth century, Protestant efforts treated each nationality as a different project, and usually there was little communication or continuity between the projects. Mexicans, or Mexican-Americans, Puerto Ricans, Cubans, and other communities were seen as distinct groups and not as belonging to a global group of Latinos or Hispanics.

The waves of immigrants that have resulted in a growing Latino Protestant community introduce various discontinuities into this same community. Immigration, instead of following a consistent pattern, happens in waves that obey a complicated series of factors in the United States and the immigrant's country of origin. Each wave of immigrants impacts the already existing Latino Protestant churches, especially since some of the immigrants bring with them new variations of Protestantism in Latin America. As the number of Latino immigrants who are already Protestant before arriving in the United States grows, the profile of US Latino churches changes more and more. The constant immigration causes many Latino Protestant churches to have a constant "immigrant" flavor. Each wave of immigrants washes up new dynamics and foments new Protestant movements that do not always fit in well with the existent Latino Protestantism.

A further complication relates to the fact that many different denominations and Protestant groups have planted Latino churches. The vast majority of North American denominations have at least a handful of Latino congregations. Latino Protestants have also founded their own denominations and groups of churches in the United States. Furthermore, several Latin American denominations or Protestant groups have established churches in the United States. In general, all these churches have little to do with each other. Within the Latino community the number of independent churches also continues to grow. Thus, it is nearly impossible to keep a clear count of all the Latino Protestant churches in the United States.

Closely linked to this difficulty is the fact that Protestant denominations and movements have founded a variety of ministries among the Latino community in the United States. Many have planted churches, but others have focused on social service projects or "missions" that, they hope, will eventually be incorporated into the existing "Anglo" churches. What do we make of these groups of Spanish speakers who are part of English-speaking congregations? Are they Latino churches? How do we include these efforts in the telling of Latino Protestant church history?

The ever-changing identity of the Latino community in the United States also complicates the task of history writing. We Latinos represent quite diverse historical backgrounds, nationalities, and ethnicities. We have different perspectives regarding our relationship to the larger non-Latino society and culture. All these differences show up in our churches and ministries. Some opt to begin or to participate in ministries with a clear Latino focus. Others want to be part of English-speaking Protestant churches.

The ever-changing identity also suffers the impact of cultural assimilation. Some congregations that were established as Latino churches later opt to function in English and to be incorporated into an English-speaking congregation.[2] How should we treat these cases in the history? What about those who were part of a Latino congregation but who later joined an English-speaking congregation? Do we leave them out of the history? And what about the Latinos who are Protestant but who have never been part of a Latino church? Are they also part of this history, or should we only include Latinos who are or who have been part of a church with a clear Latino identity?[3] A related phenomenon is churches with Latino leadership and a largely Latino congregation but who minister among various ethnic groups and who do not claim to be a "Latino

---

2. In some cases these changes come about due to pressure from denominations that want to "reflect" the unity among different ethnic groups. Chapter 2, about the American Baptists, mentions how denominational leaders imposed "unity" on the Latino churches.

3. Again we face problems of identification. For example, how do we define the Spanish word "*evangélico*"? Is "*evangélico*" in Spanish a synonym of "Evangelical" in English? Or should we use the term in the wider sense of its traditional use of "Protestant" in Latin America (as Alberto Rembao used it in his *Discurso a la nación evangélica* [Speech to the Protestant nation])? In general, this book translates "*evangélico*" in the second, Latin American sense of "Protestant."

church." Again we face the question about who and what to include in the history of the Latino Protestant church in the United States.

This present collection of essays consists of two primary sections. The first focuses on the history of various Protestant movements that have ministered among the Latino community. The second section describes various aspects of the Latino Protestant experience. Each of the two sections begins with a short introduction that explains the general direction of the section and how the individual chapters relate to each other.

We the editors, Lindy Scott and I, see this collection as a type of family album. We have not been able to include "photos" of all the relatives due to lack of space. Yet we hope that the members of the North American Latino Protestant family can find at least a familiar face in the pictures we have included. We also hope that those who are not part of this family get to know a bit of the diversity of Latino Protestantism in the United States. If these two hopes are realized, this "album" will have completed its mission.

Projects like this one are always a group effort. We would like to thank the Protestant division of CEHILA (*Comisión de Estudios de Historia de la Iglesia en América Latina y el Caribe*, Commission for the Study of the History of the Church in Latin America and the Caribbean). CEHILA offered great encouragement throughout the years of gestation that this volume required. We are also grateful for the economic support that enables us to present this book as part of CEHILA's global project. We thank Wheaton College for its monetary contribution and the Aldeen Grant in particular. Gretchen Abernathy has also been an indispensable part of this project by reading, editing, correcting, and rereading the chapters in the original Spanish version. Her role grew in importance as she became the translator of this English edition. And I, Juan Martínez, appreciate the invitation from Lindy Scott to work with him as coeditor on this project. Although the experience has been arduous, it has produced a great joy as well.

Though it came to us as a translation from the English version, one hymn in particular faithfully reflects the commitment of Latino Protestants in the United States and throughout Latin America. Nearly every Latino Protestant church, despite their differing traditions, has sung "*Firmes y adelante*," or "Onward Christian Soldiers." It is a testimony to commitment but also to the confidence of generations who have decided to follow Jesus Christ as Latino Protestant Christians. The third stanza and the chorus capture the confession and hope of this pilgrim people.

Introduction

Here we reproduce and translate it as traditionally sung in Spanish since it differs from the original, militaristic English version of the hymn:

Spanish version:

Muévase potente la iglesia de Dios
De los ya gloriosos marchamos hoy en pos;
Somos sólo un cuerpo y uno es el Señor
Una la esperanza y uno nuestro amor.

Firmes y adelante, huestes de la fe
Sin temer alguno, que Jesús nos ve.[4]

Literal translation:

May the mighty church of God be on the move,
We're marching in the footsteps of those who've already reached Glory;
We are one body, the Lord is one,
Our hope is one, and our love is one.

Steadfast and full speed ahead, armies of faith,
We've no fear since Jesus is watching us.[5]

Juan Francisco Martínez Guerra
El Pueblo de Nuestra Señora Reina de Los Ángeles de Porciúncula,
California[6]

---

4. Translated by Juan Bautista Cabrera (1837–1916). Public domain.

5. The original English text of the hymn "Onward, Christian Soldiers" is as follows: Verse 3: "Like a mighty army moves the church of God; / Brothers, we are treading where the saints have trod. / We are not divided, all one body we, / One in hope and doctrine, one in charity." Chorus: "Onward, Christian soldiers, marching as to war, / With the cross of Jesus going on before." Words: Sabine Baring-Gould, in *Church Times*, 1865. Music: St. Gertrude, Arthur S. Sullivan, 1871. Public domain.

6. The original name of the city Los Angeles (the City of Our Lady the Queen of Los Angeles of Porciúncula, California) reflects two important realities for the Latino Protestant community there. On the one hand, the name reminds us that Spaniards founded the city and that it belonged to Mexico before becoming part of the United States. The original name also points out that Latino Protestants are a minority inside a largely Catholic community.

SECTION ONE

Histories, But Not Just One History

Juan Francisco Martínez Guerra

THE TASK OF WRITING a history of the Latino Protestant church in the United States is, frankly, too ambitious for this book. Wrestling with all the problems outlined in the Introduction will have to wait for another day. This section of the book, however, does succeed in telling a series of histories about parts of the Latino Protestant church in this country.

Chapter 1 sketches the early stages of Protestantism during the nineteenth century in the Southwest of the United States. Chronologically this chapter describes the "first" beginning of Latino Protestantism in this country.[1] During this period and in this region, North American Protestants first had contact with Latinos, the first Latino converts to Protestantism are recorded, and the first Latino Protestant church in the United States came into being.

The next chapter discusses Latino churches in the American Baptist Convention. Eduardo Font, a long-time American Baptist leader, writes about this historical North American denomination that has worked for over 100 years in the Latino community. All the historical denominations have Latino congregations, and a few denominations have been serving the Latino population for at least 100 years. Of all these traditional denominations, the American Baptists have the most Latino members in the United States today.

---

1. Though the ministries in the Southwest represent the first encounter of Latinos with Protestantism in the United States, projects in the eastern United States among Cubans, Puerto Ricans, and Spaniards in the second half of the nineteenth century represent a "second" beginning. The efforts in the East had little to no connection with the ministries in the Southwest even though some of the same denominations worked in both areas.

1

Sergio Navarrete, superintendent of the Latin American Pacific District of the Assemblies of God, pens the third history in this section. The Assemblies of God is one of the oldest Pentecostal denominations and is the largest Protestant denomination among Latinos in the United States. The denomination surfaced during the Pentecostal revival at the beginning of the twentieth century. The union between this revival and the wave of migration due to the Mexican Revolution beginning in 1910 resulted in the birth of this denomination's Latino congregations.

The next history describes the Apostolic Assembly of the Faith in Christ Jesus, another denomination resulting from the union of the Pentecostal revival and migration during the Mexican Revolution. Ismael Martín del Campo, Apostolic Bishop of the Los Angeles District, writes about how this denomination was started and has always been directed by Latinos. Belonging to the oneness branch of Pentecostalism, the Apostolic Assembly also represents those Pentecostal movements that have never been linked to North American Protestant denominations.

Lindy Scott writes in chapter 5 about the Evangelical Free Church's work among Latinos. This denomination represents the pattern of many other traditional Protestant[2] denominations in the United States that have started Latino congregations in the past few years, particularly due to the new waves of Latino immigrants to the United States.

The final chapter in this section relates the story of *Ministerios Llamada Final*, Last Call Ministries, a relatively recent movement started by a Latino immigrant. Tony Solórzano, leader of Llamada Final, describes the vision and development of this movement that has existed for fewer than thirty years. Llamada Final is representative of the neo-Pentecostal and neo-Apostolic movements that have swept through Latin America and the Latino community in the United States in the last few years.

These denominations and movements represent some of the different ways Latino Protestantism has developed in the United States. All have been "successful" among the North American Latino community though they portray a wide variety of expressions of Latino Protestantism. The reader can surely think of other movements that represent different faces of Latino Protestantism. For example, this section does not include those denominations that work among Latinos yet do not have Latino congregations. Neither does it include movements that work primarily with Latinos and

2. See note 3 in the Introduction for a discussion of the difference between the English "evangelical" and the Spanish "*evangélico*."

yet do not claim to be "Latino." We hope, however, that the six "portraits" included here demonstrate the breadth of experience of Latino Protestantism in the United States.

1

Origins of Protestantism Among Latinos in the Southwestern United States (1836–1900)[1]

Juan Francisco Martínez Guerra

L ATINO PROTESTANTS IN THE United States during the nineteenth century have been a nearly invisible community. The majority of the reports about North American Latinos from the nineteenth century hardly mention Protestants within the community, and very few writings about North American Protestantism during the nineteenth century acknowledge Latinos. In general, the history of Protestantism among North American Latinos is thought to begin with the arrival of the first Mexican immigrants fleeing the Mexican Revolution at the beginning of the twentieth century or with the Caribbean immigrants who settled in the eastern United States.

THE OPENING OF A NEW MISSIONARY FIELD

The conquest of what are now the states of California, Arizona, New Mexico, Colorado, and Texas was part of the United States' process of western expansion. The Republic of Texas' War of Independence (1836) and the war between the United States and Mexico (1846–1848) resulted in the United States' taking control of half of what had been Mexican territory.

The war with Mexico produced conflicting responses from US Protestant leaders. Some interpreted the conquest of Mexican land as an

---

1. This chapter is based on the doctoral dissertation "Origins and Development of Protestantism among Latinos in the Southwestern United States 1836–1900," written by the author. The dissertation was later rewritten and published as *Sea la Luz: The Making of Mexican Protestantism in the American Southwest, 1829–1900*.

unjust aggression by a strong country against a weaker neighbor. Others saw the hand of God opening a new "promised land" for the United States in its desire to expand across the continent. Still others thanked God because the conquest opened the door to the evangelization of Mexican Catholics, something that Mexican law at the time prohibited.

The roughly 100,000 Mexicans in the region who instantaneously became US citizens were Catholic. As Spanish rule of the colony came to an end, and throughout the years of Mexican independence, this region had seen very little religious leadership. There were a few priests in New Mexico, two in Texas, a few more in upper California but none in northern Sonora (present-day Arizona). Catholicism in the territory was a popular religion, observed with much devotion yet little formal leadership.

Mexicans in this region first encountered their new countrymen when the United States citizens, usually Protestants, began the process of migrating west. In 1849 Gold Fever wooed US citizens to California and other southwestern regions in search of new lands and new possibilities. Conflicts between US citizens and former Mexicans arose almost immediately regarding land, political control, the administration of justice, and new socioeconomic realities. Since US citizens now controlled all the systems of power, the Mexican population found itself on the margins of this new reality. By the end of the nineteenth century, many Mexicans had lost their lands and goods and had suffered countless injustices at the hands of the new US authorities.

In this context, Protestant mission agencies began their missionary work among the Mexican community. Some questioned the effort, calling it futile and saying that missionary efforts would be better focused on the US citizens who moved to the West and Southwest. However, some Protestant denominations decided to carry out missionary work in the "new field." They were confident of the importance of spreading the gospel among this community; at the same time, they felt responsible as the superior US society to help the "needy" Mexican society. Their goals included both preaching the Protestant message and teaching the US lifestyle so that the Mexican community would learn how to function in its new country.[2]

---

2. This concern shows up in missionary efforts. Presbyterians, Methodists, and Congregationalists founded several schools in New Mexico in the nineteenth century for Latino children. One motivation for doing mission work among Latinos was the importance of both Christianizing and Americanizing them. For more information, see Martínez, *Origins and Development*, 127–40.

Protestant Work during the Nineteenth Century

The first known Protestant missions effort among the Mexican people of southern Texas took place in the period of Texan independence. A Presbyterian missionary tried to distribute Spanish-language Bibles in 1839. His effort led to no known results.

There were a few other scattered missionary outreaches among the newly conquered Mexicans after the war (1848). The American Baptist Church (North) worked in New Mexico and reported the founding of several congregations. The effort resulted in some converts but no long-term, stable church. Nor did missionaries sent to the region by the Methodist Episcopal Church see any stable results. These outreaches did give rise to the first Latino Protestant church in Peralta, New Mexico and to the first Latino Protestants, Ambrosio González and Blas Chávez. The Presbyterian missionary Melinda Rankin worked in southern Texas hoping for an opportunity to enter Mexico as a missionary. Also, some lay leaders from the Methodist Episcopal Church (South) preached among Latinos in Corpus Christi in the 1850s.

The US Civil War (1861–1865) truncated these first missionary efforts, however. Long-term projects were not established until after the war's end. The greater part of the work was concentrated in areas in which the majority of the population spoke Spanish, in northern New Mexico (which included part of what is now southern Colorado) and in central Texas.

Missionary Efforts in Texas

Of all the denominations, the Methodist Episcopal Church (South)[3] worked the most among the *tejanos* in the nineteenth century. The denomination began working in Corpus Christi in the 1850s. The work halted during the US Civil War but resumed almost as soon as the war ended. In 1870 a Mexican leader, Alejo Hernández, helped organize the first official congregation in Corpus Christi; the denomination named a superintendent for Spanish-speaking churches in the Western Texas Conference in 1872. By 1877, the total of new congregations reached 10, with 432 members in all. The denomination organized a second district in

---

3. Several US denominations split over the slavery issue before the US Civil War. Thus, two Methodist, Presbyterian, and Baptist denominations worked simultaneously among Latinos in the United States. In general, "Southern" denominations worked in Texas while "Northern" denominations concentrated on New Mexico and Colorado.

1880 to manage the continued growth of new churches (16 congregations with 709 members).

This growth began to slow down when the Methodists decided to unite the projects in Texas with their foreign missions work in Mexico. Latino churches were treated from then on as "foreign" even though they were located within the United States. This change created certain tensions since the missions agency had dedicated itself to working abroad but not in the United States. After 1884, the work within Mexico grew substantially. Yet Texas saw few new churches planted. The Methodist Episcopal Church (South) reported sixteen Spanish-speaking congregations in Texas in 1885. By 1900 there were only seventeen congregations in Texas, with a total of 1,450 members. These churches belonged to two different districts based out of Mexico. Being in different districts separated the churches from each other and from their neighboring English-speaking Texan churches. Methodist pastors in this period were usually both *tejano* and Mexican, and the denomination would assign them to one side of the frontier or the other. This practice did not change until 1914 when the Mexican Mission of Texas formed.

Latino Congregations of the Methodist Episcopal Church (South)
in Texas (1900)

The Presbyterian Church, US (South) work among Texans began in a different way than projects of other denominations. The Presbyterian Church of Matamoros, Tamaulipas sent lay workers to start a congregation in Brownsville, Texas in 1877. This congregation was the first Latino

Presbyterian church in Texas. In 1885 José María Botello, an elder of the congregation in Matamoros, moved to San Marcos, Texas. By the next year, ten Spanish-speaking people were accepted as members of the *Iglesia Presbiteriana de San Marcos* (Presbyterian Church of San Marcos).[4]

In 1887, the Presbytery of Western Texas accepted the little congregation. The denomination did not attempt other projects until it ordained Walter Scott, a Mexican with Scottish background, to work among Mexicans in Texas. By 1893, there were three congregations which grew to eight with 517 total members in 1900.[5]

In 1858 the Baptist General Convention of Texas[6] began weighing the importance of working among Spanish speakers. Not until 1880 did the denomination send the first missionary contacts to Laredo, Texas. In 1887, the combined leadership of a former missionary returning from Mexico, William Powell, and a former Methodist (South) pastor, Manuel Treviño, organized the first church in San Antonio. The denomination received another Methodist (North) pastor, Alejandro Marchand, in 1892. Marchand convinced several Methodist members in El Paso to become Baptist. These Baptist churches suffered internal problems and the 1895 statistics do not report a single Baptist congregation in Texas. Statistics do not mention "Mexican" churches again until 1901. The fledgling congregations survived, though. Exact records do not exist, but the estimated nine "Mexican" Baptist churches in Texas in 1900 had around 360 members.

---

4. For more information about the beginnings of Presbyterian work in the US Southwest, see Brackenridge and García-Treto, *Iglesia Presbiteriana*.

5. In 1896, Henry Pratt, translator of the *Versión Moderna de la Biblia* (modern version of the Bible) in Spanish, joined the work. He established a Bible institute for Hispanic pastors. Interestingly, his program offered no general education courses because Pratt did not want the pastors to have the temptation to look for other employment or to leave the small, poor communities they served. These projects were very different from Presbyterian efforts in New Mexico and Colorado, where the program of studies for Latino pastors was the same as for all English-speaking Presbyterian pastors studying for ordination.

6. Until a few years ago, the Baptist General Convention of Texas was part of the Southern Baptist Convention.

Latino Congregations in the Baptist General Convention,
the Methodist Episcopal Church, and Presbyterian Churches, US (1900)

The Methodist Episcopal Church (North) worked principally among Mexicans in New Mexico and southern Colorado. In 1886, though, the denomination established a congregation in El Paso, Texas. This congregation remained the denomination's only church in Texas throughout the nineteenth century.

Protestant Work in New Mexico

In 1869 the Women's Missionary Union of the Presbyterian Church, USA (North) sent John Annin as a missionary to work among the *novomexicanos* in Las Vegas. There he met José Inés Perea, a *novomexicano* who had converted to Protestantism while studying in New York. They founded the first Presbyterian church in Las Vegas in 1870. The Presbyterian Church, USA continued sending various missionaries to the region over the next few years. Some worked among the *Penitentes*, a Catholic brotherhood. The new Catholic hierarchy strongly questioned this group of lay Catholics, and some *Penitente* leaders joined the Presbyterians.[7]

---

7. Two *novomexicano* Presbyterian leaders, José Mondragón and Vicente Romero, had connections with the *Penitentes*. Mondragón had been a *Penitente* leader. According to the Presbyterians, Romero was the natural child of Antonio José Martínez, a *novomexicano*

Presbyterians in New Mexico emphasized education. They established primary schools in rural New Mexico and Colorado communities where there were no public schools yet. Through the schools, the missionaries both made useful contacts for future church plants and achieved their goal of Americanizing the *novomexicanos*. Since the Presbyterian Church, USA maintained very high standards for ordaining pastors, the missionaries sought to establish institutions for the theological education of future Latino pastors. During the first few years, *novomexicano* pastors could only be assistants or evangelists. In 1890, the missionary James Gilchrist founded a summer school for training Latino pastors. Also in 1890, the Presbyterian College of the Southwest in Del Norte, Colorado began a special program for training Latino pastors.

The Presbyterian projects grew most in the final years of the nineteenth century. In 1900 the denomination reported twenty-nine organized congregations with 908 members. The vast majority of these churches were situated in the Sangre de Cristo Mountains in northern New Mexico where most of the *novomexicano* community resided.

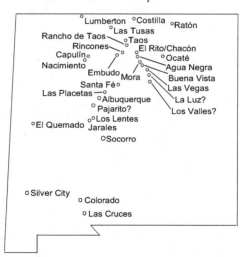

Latino Presbyterian Churches in New Mexico (1900)

The missionary work of the Methodist Episcopal Church in New Mexico throughout the nineteenth century is largely the history of Thomas and Emily Harwood's ministry. The couple arrived in New Mexico in 1869 and stayed until the beginning of the twentieth century. They embodied

---

priest who opposed Catholic bishop Lamy's leadership and supported the *Penitentes* in their struggles against the new Catholic hierarchy.

the common perspective of Protestant missionaries of the time, assuming that the "backwards" *novomexicano* community had languished under the strict control of Catholic priests. For the Harwoods, the New Mexicans needed both the Protestant message and US American civilization to stir them out of their Mexican Catholic lethargy.[8]

The Methodists began their outreach by reorganizing the disparate Methodist and Baptist groups that remained from the pre-Civil War missionary efforts. From these groups arose a handful of lay leaders who helped spread the Methodist outreach to other communities. One crucial part of Harwood's work included offering basic ministerial training to *novomexicano* leaders and commissioning them to start Bible studies in different towns. These leaders and missionaries traveled a preaching circuit, preaching and organizing Sunday schools from town to town. Once a stable group organized officially, the new congregation usually tried to construct a church building.

Methodists had a certain level of success in New Mexico in the nineteenth century. By 1900 the Methodist Episcopal Church reported fifty-eight congregations or preaching points (missions) divided into three districts with a total membership of 1,537.

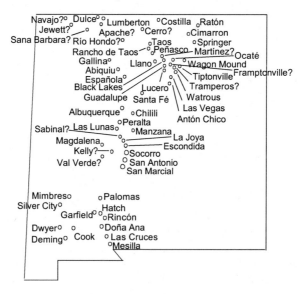

Methodist Preaching Points in New Mexico (1900)

8. Thomas Harwood relates the history of these efforts in *History of the New Mexico Spanish and English Missions of the Methodist Episcopal Church from 1850–1910.*

The Congregational Church began working among *novomexicanos* in 1880. The General Association of Congregational Churches in New Mexico and Arizona bestowed a preaching license on a *novomexicano*, G. R. Archeta (Ancheta?) in 1884. The Association licensed another leader, Ezequiel Chávez, in 1886. These two men and a few English-speaking missionaries established missions in various communities (Española, San Rafael, Cubero, San Mateo, Albuquerque, Atrisco, Rinconada, and San José), but by 1900 none of the missions had grown into an official church. All together, these congregations only had about forty-five members.

The Bible played a very important role in the lives of *novomexicano* Protestants. A common Protestant perspective assumed that whoever read the Bible would convert. Therefore, missionaries gave away Bibles and traveled house-to-house reading Scripture aloud. Some of these Bibles affected individuals and families in profound ways and, over time, became part of the testimonies the new Protestants told each other to strengthen their faith and commitment. The Bibles themselves would be named after the community or family who converted after reading them. Some of the more famous include the Chimayó, Gómez, Madrid, Ocaté, Peralta, and Sánchez Bibles.[9]

Protestant Work in Colorado

Southern Colorado, where the majority of Spanish speakers lived, had formed part of the territory of New Mexico while under both Spanish and Mexican control. US jurisdiction maintained this original delineation for a time. Methodist work in the area sprang from New Mexico, and Presbyterian efforts, though officially separated, coordinated various projects between the two regions.

Protestants who had converted in New Mexico founded the first Presbyterian Church, USA congregations in Colorado. When missionaries arrived they found recently converted Protestant groups in Cenicero (1876) and La Luz (1879) that soon organized as Presbyterian churches.

---

9. Each one of these Bibles has its own history including several testimonies of conversions. For example, Juan Gómez bought the Gómez Bible in 1868. He paid $60.00 for the book that became the starting point for a Bible study that turned into a congregation in southern Colorado. Several daughter churches sprung off from this first church. Several of Juan Gómez's grandchildren became Presbyterian leaders at the end of the nineteenth century and the beginning of the twentieth century.

The gospel spread from this base out to communities in the San Luis Valley.

The state of Colorado was the only place where a university program to train Spanish-speaking pastors was established during the nineteenth century. The Presbyterian College of the Southwest began as a general education university but in 1890 offered a training program for Latino pastors and evangelists from New Mexico and Colorado. The college functioned only until 1901. In its few years of operation, however, it prepared several *novomexicanos* who would become key leaders in the twentieth century. Several students completed internships in Colorado, and with the help of these seminarians, the Presbyterian outreach in the region grew. By 1900, the fourteen Presbyterian congregations totaled 410 members.

Catholic opposition to these communities gave rise to a peculiar phenomenon in Colorado. Three little towns divided into separate Catholic and Protestant sections. The divisions created the twin towns of Costilla, New Mexico (Protestant) / García, Colorado (Catholic); San Pablo (Protestant) / San Pedro (Catholic); Mogote (Protestant) / San Rafael (Catholic).

The Methodist Episcopal Church work in Colorado extended from the denomination's projects in New Mexico. The first congregation organized in 1889; the number grew to only two congregations by 1900, with a total of fifty-two members.

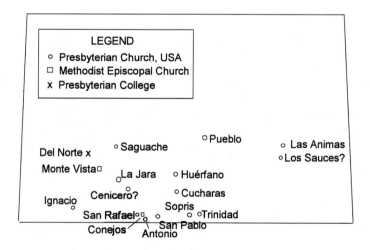

Latino Protestant Congregations in Colorado (1900)

Beginnings in Arizona and California

Protestant work in Arizona and California in the nineteenth century was very limited. Latino communities in these regions were small in comparison with those in Texas and New Mexico. Nearly all the projects in Arizona were extensions of New Mexican projects, and the fledgling outreaches in California had barely gotten off the ground by the end of the 1800s.

The Presbyterian Church, USA sent lay workers from New Mexico to the territory of Arizona where they established the first congregation in 1881. By 1883, these unordained pastors reported five congregations. The 1897 report mentioned three churches with 124 members, but by 1900 no congregations were reported.

The Methodist Episcopal Church in 1891 sent lay workers from New Mexico to Solomonville to begin a mission connected to the congregation in Silver City, New Mexico. By 1895 the lay pastors reported five preaching points with 157 members. By 1900, however, the number had dwindled to fifty-nine members.

The Methodist Episcopal Church (South) established a Latino church in Phoenix in 1891 under the supervision of Mexico's Northwest Conference. The denomination reported that this congregation had thirty-seven members in 1900.

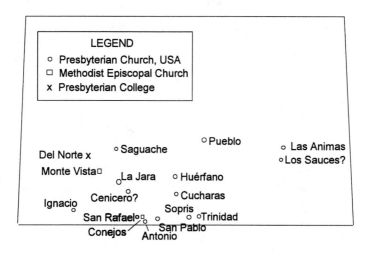

Latino Protestant Congregations in Arizona (1900)

Because there were so few Spanish speakers in the region at the time, California saw very little Protestant work in the nineteenth century. The Methodist Episcopal Church began an outreach in Los Angeles in 1880 under the leadership of Antonio Díaz. Nevertheless, the California Conference does not mention this outreach after 1883.

In 1883 the Presbyterian Church, USA mentions this same Antonio Díaz as a licensed Presbyterian pastor. Apparently Díaz had converted to the gospel in Mexico in the Presbyterian church (1862), yet it remains unclear why he switched from the Methodist Episcopal Church to become a Presbyterian minister by 1883. That same year the Presbytery of Los Angeles named Carlos Bransby, a former missionary to Colombia, to work among Spanish speakers. By 1900 the denomination recorded a total of 115 members in four Latino congregations in Los Angeles, San Gabriel, and Azusa.

Analysis of the Findings

At the beginning of the twentieth century, several Latino communities in the southwestern United States had Protestant churches. These congregations benefited from leaders with a clear vision of their mission. The Latino leaders dedicated themselves to and readily sacrificed for the work entrusted to them. Latino Protestants were also people of the Book. Reading the Bible had led to their conversion, and they were wholly persuaded of the importance of sharing the biblical message within their communities.

The missionary efforts, however, suffered marked limitations and failed to produce significant results. The lack of results owes as much to the weaknesses in Protestant missionary societies as to the changing situation in the southwestern United States. On the one hand, the mission agencies did not develop a consistent, united missionary effort. This situation was due to several reasons. Some agencies decided to focus on the new US immigrants moving into the region. Others paid more attention to Mexico and Latin America. Also, a certain amount of prejudice against Latinos played a role. Even missionaries working in Latino communities during the nineteenth century failed to grasp the cultural and social realities of these communities, and they ministered with a very negative attitude toward Catholicism.

Other factors also limited the growth of the early missionary efforts. The conquest by the United States produced profound, lasting changes among Latino communities in the Southwest. These changes turned life upside down for many Latinos. Many lost both their lands and their means of livelihood. The resulting migratory movement dissolved some communities in which Protestant churches had been established. The relationship between Protestantism and acculturation further complicated the situation. Particularly in New Mexico, Latino Protestants were more likely to attend Protestant schools and identify more and more with US culture. The nineteenth century witnessed a tendency among some educated *novomexicano* Protestants to leave their Latino churches and join English-speaking congregations.

LATINO PROTESTANTS AT THE BEGINNING OF THE TWENTIETH CENTURY

According to the reports of the Protestant churches, in 1900 there were 5,572 active members in 149 Latino congregations in Texas, New Mexico, Colorado, Arizona, and California. Of the denominations working in the Southwest in the nineteenth century, the Methodist Episcopal Church was the strongest with 1,699 members in sixty-six congregations. Next follow the Methodist Episcopal Church (South) with 1,487 members in eighteen congregations, the Presbyterian Church, USA (North) with 1,464 members in forty-six congregations, and the Presbyterian Church, US (South) with 517 members in eight congregations. Two other groups had Latino congregations as well: the Baptists of Texas with 360 members in ten congregations and the Congregationalists with forty-five members, one congregation, and two small preaching points.

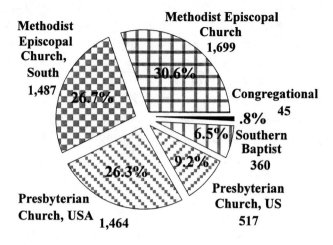

Distribution of Latino Protestants by Denomination in the USA (1900)

Latino Protestants were statistically divided among the five US southwestern states in the following manner: New Mexico (2,521), Texas (2,378), Colorado (462), California (115), and Arizona (96).

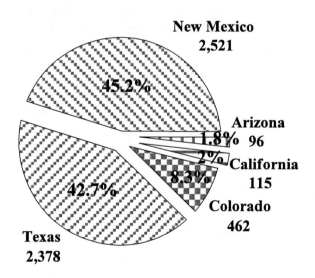

Distribution of Latino Protestants in the USA by States—1900.

The majority of the churches were situated in three regions: 1) Northern New Mexico and southern Colorado; 2) Central Texas; and 3) near the

Rio Grande (Bravo) in southern New Mexico towards El Paso, Texas. There were very few congregations in California and Arizona.

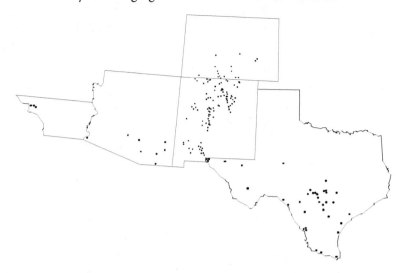

Distribution of Latino Protestant Churches in the USA (1900)

At the close of the nineteenth century, the majority of Latinos found themselves at the margin of US society. Nearly all lived in isolated rural areas where they maintained their own subcultures. Latino Protestants lived an even more isolated existence. Their religious convictions pushed them to the outskirts of their own communities; yet, in general, the US Protestant majority also marginalized them for being Latino.

The tiny Latino Protestant churches were full of very dedicated members. They shared the common experience of radical conversion, persecution for their faith, and isolation from their fellow countrymen. Balancing both a Latino and a Protestant identity proved very difficult. Protestantism was so closely linked to the US Americanism of the period that Latino Protestants who held on to their Protestantism felt compelled to cut ties with their native culture. They were constructing a new subculture at a high price due to factors outside their control like cultural assimilation, changing economic situations, and new waves of Mexican immigration.

These tiny Protestant congregations have all but disappeared from history's memory. Despite being pioneers of Protestantism among US Latinos, few today place much importance on these early congregations. This forgetfulness is due to three main factors. First, defining the place of this community within North American religious history of the nineteenth century is tricky. Being such a miniscule part of Protestantism, these congregations left no great, obvious impact on the continent. Furthermore, since Catholicism is seen as so crucial for understanding US Latinos in the nineteenth century, Latino Protestants are not considered critical to an understanding of the Latino community.

Secondly, most of these early New Mexico and southern Colorado churches began to disappear by the beginning of the twentieth century. Entire communities floundered and disappeared due to economic changes, and, in some communities, the Latino congregation merged with the corresponding English-speaking congregation. The few congregations that remain generally lie on the experiential fringes of the vast majority of Latinos in the United States today.

A third factor has to do with immigration and cultural assimilation. The twentieth century brought several new waves of Latino immigrants. Each wave represents a new chapter in the life of the US Latino Protestant church. The connection between new waves of immigrants and the tendency towards cultural and social assimilation within the US Latino community creates a discontinuity, at times very tense, between each generation of US Latino Protestants.

US Latino Protestant churches began growing strong in the twentieth century and continue strengthening now at the beginning of the twenty-first century. But the tensions inherent in being both Protestant and Latino within the United States have not diminished since the nineteenth century. Assimilation and cultural survival are still live issues in the US Latino Protestant reality today. The community's future depends on its desire and ability to develop an identity that is as thoroughly Protestant as it is US Latino.

2

Latino American Baptist Churches

Eduardo Font

B APTISTS HAVE HAD ARDENT advocates of missionary zeal for working among peoples of other languages, races, and nations since 1791
when William Carey, the first Baptist missionary to India, presented his
missionary challenge to his English countrymen. This zeal quickly crossed
the Atlantic and rooted itself in US American leaders and churches. With
neither their own missionary society nor officially named missionaries,
the American Baptists, in cooperation with English Baptists, missionaries to India, and other denominations, threw themselves into missionary
work in the last decade of the eighteenth century and the beginning of the
nineteenth century.[1]

BEGINNING OF THE LATINO PROJECT

The American Baptist Church of the United States of America discovered
the Latino missionary field within their borders first in Puerto Rico and
almost simultaneously in California.[2] Specifically, the Baptist work among
Latinos began at the end of the nineteenth century, in 1899, in Río Piedras
and at the beginning of the twentieth century, in 1901, in Santa Barbara.

---

1. Torbet, *A History*, 249 ff.

2. As mentioned in chapter 1, the American Baptists began a project in New Mexico
around 1850 but abandoned it within a few years. There were no permanent results from
this effort, and not until the beginning of the twentieth century did the American Baptists
establish a permanent outreach among the Latino community.

Puerto Rico[3]

Soon after the Spanish-American War, when the United States took occupation of Puerto Rico, the first Evangelical denominations arrived on the island. In 1899 the new territory was divided into regions in order to better accomplish the missionary work. The American Baptists took charge of the central zone, from San Juan to Ponce. Thus the first Baptist missionaries arrived on the island: Hugo P. McCormick worked in the Rio Piedras area; A. B. Rudd took the southern zone; and Edgar L. Humphrey established himself in the central section. McCormick arrived in San Juan on February 2, 1899. Three days later he delivered his first sermon on Puerto Rican soil, in English in the morning and in Spanish in the afternoon.

Two weeks later, McCormick traveled to Río Piedras and visited Manuel and Juana Candelaria Lebrón. Three months earlier, through the testimony of the minister William Sloan who had been staying in their house, this couple had become Christians. With the help of Manuel Lebrón, who was the city mayor, Brother McCormick invited a group of people to the first Baptist service, held on February 23 in the reception room of the mayor's office in Río Piedras. McCormick preached again on February 26 and 28. On March 11 the fledgling congregation rented a house to hold services, and by July 17 they had bought the house. When McCormick had to return to the United States for personal reasons, A. B. Rudd had the privilege of baptizing the first Christians. The first to be baptized was Manuel Lebrón.

February 23, 1899 is the date of the first official Baptist Puerto Rican outreach, and July 11 of the same year marks the formal organization of the *Primera Iglesia Bautista de Río Piedras* (First Baptist Church of Río Piedras). This congregation would become the Baptist "Antioch of Puerto Rico" as the gospel spread from there to many other places.

On March 17, 1899, another champion of the Baptist missionary work, Dr. A. B. Rudd, arrived on the island. Within a few months, on November 21, he had organized the second Baptist church in Puerto Rico

---

3. The bibliographical sources used and suggested by this Puerto Rican section are the following: Cristino Díaz Montañez and Luis Fidel Mercado, "Un vistazo retrospectivo y una visión futurista desde el Centenario de la Obra Bautista en Puerto Rico," Iglesias Bautistas de Puerto Rico, http://www.ibpr.org/modules.php?name=Content& pa=showpage&pid=2#loscomienzos (accessed July 30, 2008); http://groups.msn.com /1eraIglesiaBautistadeRioPiedras/historiadenuestraiglesia.msnw (accessed July 30, 2008); Riggs, *Baptists in Puerto Rico*; Ramos, *Historia de los Bautistas*.

under the name *Primera Iglesia Bautista de Ponce* (First Baptist Church of Ponce). The evangelistic work spread rapidly to other areas of the island. By 1902, several churches discussed banding together in an association. These discussions became reality when, in 1903, seventeen churches organized themselves as the Association of Puerto Rican Baptist churches. By 1910 the association included forty-two churches. The name changed in 1936 to the Convention of Puerto Rican Baptist Churches and again in 1975 to merely Baptist Churches of Puerto Rico. Today the convention includes 108 churches with around 25,000 active members total and is one of the thirty-four regions of the American Baptist Churches of the United States.

Southwest

At the turn of the twentieth century, Baptist testimony among Hispanics in the Southwest (at that time they were almost exclusively Mexicans and, according to some statistics, were a population of no more than 8,000 in California) burst out of a deep-rooted missionary spirit of sharing the Good News with neighbors and strangers alike. The First Baptist Church of Santa Barbara, California (English-speaking) was the first congregation to cross linguistic and ethnic borders to share the gospel with a Mexican family. Their pastor, I. A. Burroughs, combined his vision with the work and testimony of William Chase, a skilled bilingual Bible teacher, to share the love of Christ with the Olivera family. They were baptized in June of 1901, and others soon followed their example.[4]

In 1901, Conrado T. Valdivia, the first Baptist pastor from Mexico, arrived in Santa Barbara. He established a mission in Santa Barbara (1901?) and shortly thereafter, another one in Oxnard (1903). Both missions ceased functioning within a few years. However, Baptist work in both places resumed when Mr. and Mrs. L. E. Troyer joined Antonio Jiménez, recently arrived from Spain, to continue the missions.[5]

The year 1902 saw the first Spanish-language Baptist effort in Los Angeles, headed up by Miss Nina Mooreford.[6] The more permanent work, however, began in 1903 when a group from the First Baptist Church of Los Angeles (English speaking) appointed Miss Gatsetts and Miss Hargrave to

---

4. Morales, *American Baptists*, 35–36.

5. Troyer, *Sovereignty*, 29–30.

6. Ellis, "Origin and Development," 146. There is historical discrepancy over the spelling of Miss Mooreford's last name, "Mooreford" or "Morford."

spearhead the spreading of the gospel to Mexican families on the eastern side of the city. Their efforts planted the seeds of what would become *La Iglesia Bautista "El Salvador."*[7] Organized first as a mission between 1905 and 1906, the congregation became an official church in 1915 under the leadership of Spanish pastor Mateo Carceller.

At the beginning of the second decade of the twentieth century, outreach among Hispanics benefited greatly from two sources. First, denominational agencies in the region showed interest in supporting the work, and secondly, missionaries were appointed to promote, support, and direct the planning and development of these efforts. In January of 1911, the Southern Baptist Convention of California, meeting at Calvary Baptist Church (both groups English-speaking), included in their program Mr. and Mrs. L. E. Troyer, missionaries who had served in both Puerto Rico and Mexico. The convention immediately commissioned the couple to work with Mexicans in California. When Mr. Troyer passed away, Edwin R. Brown, recently returned from working in Mexico, took over the position of General Missionary of the Baptist Home Mission Society to work with Mexicans in 1919.[8]

Besides the three primary outreaches mentioned above (Santa Barbara, *La Iglesia Bautista "El Salvador,"* and the Mexican First Baptist Church of Los Angeles), other groups, missions, and churches formed, and they followed more or less the same model: English-speaking lay Christians and missionaries working side by side with Latino church members and pastors. Adam Morales christened this period up through 1935 the "Golden Age"

> in which Anglo Americans felt great satisfaction in working with the newcomers from Mexico. It was a period of missionary giants who learned to know the people, their history, their culture, and their language and who made their homes in the midst of the Spanish Americans with whom they worked. These missionaries brought many to know Jesus Christ as Lord and Savior, and together they worked to establish and serve the churches that grew out of this fellowship.[9]

---

7. Santiago, "Los Angeles Baptist City Mission Society," 17. Also see Morales, *American Baptists*, 36–37.

8. Ellis, "Origin and Development," 147.

9. Morales, *American Baptists*, 37.

From 1920 on, the Hispanic projects grew quickly. Churches enjoyed greater human and economic resources and benefited from institutions that trained leaders. Ortegón offers a socio-cultural interpretation of the growth. He says that the growth owed largely to the fact that English-speaking Baptist churches received the Mexicans with open arms, without racial discrimination. The small groups of converted Mexicans went on to assume leadership responsibilities, and they carried the message to their people, organizing missions in the heart of their communities.[10] The Mexicans provided the human resources while the English speakers provided the finances.

The well-known story of the "Mexican Chapel Car (*Carro Capilla Mexicano*)" illustrates this last statement. In 1923, Sister Crawford donated the Chapel Car as part of a fund that generated enough money to maintain a vehicle and support a driver. The Chapel Car served several functions at the same time: RV camper, chapel, classroom, library of Bibles, hymnals, and other resources, and storage bin for a revival tent. It cost more than $20,000. However, the car would now be long forgotten if not for its corresponding human element hailed as "heaven's gift to us in the great work of reaching Southern California." The story of the Chapel Car exemplifies the group-effort aspect of missions. It is the story of a man of God who dedicated himself to faithfully stewarding the material provisions that an English-speaking sister dedicated to the service of God. This man has become, for the Mexican and Hispanic community, a symbol of dedication and heroism in the Latino missionary movement in the West. His name is Pablo Villanueva, from the city of Lerdo in Durango, Mexico. Villanueva came to Southern California after working a few years in Arizona. An illustrious preacher, he could hardly finish a sermon before people would spontaneously approach the altar confessing their newfound faith in Jesus Christ. He tirelessly drove and preached from the Chapel Car for eight years. In the last two years, he founded new outreaches in La Habra, La Jolla, Placentia, Camarillo, Carpenteria, and Shafter.[11]

The 1920s were blessed by God as many new missions sprang up and soon became full churches. By 1930 there were a total of twenty-nine Baptist congregations. Over the next thirty years, however, the Hispanic outreach in Southern California saw only a net growth of six new congre-

---

10. Ortegón, "Religious Thought," 72–73.

11. Troyer, *Sovereignty*, 95; Morales, *American Baptists*, 40–41.

gations. The net growth of congregations and membership was relatively slow in the decades from 1930 to 1960. In terms of establishing and maintaining congregations, the most active decades were the 1920s, 60s, 70s, 80s, and 90s. The 1930s, 40s, and 50s suffered a marked decline in terms of new congregations.[12]

The Latino outreaches counted on the support, participation, and guidance of English-speaking churches and missionary entities until the middle of the 1930s. From then on, little by little, the direct influence of English-speaking organizations grew less visible as Latino leadership assumed greater responsibility in stewarding the churches. Several of these congregations achieved self-sustaining financial status. By the end of the 1940s, eleven churches supported their own pastors, and by the end of 1961, over seventy Latino Baptist churches did the same. At that time the American Baptist Home Mission Society insisted on a minimum salary for its missionaries, which inspired the Latino congregations to provide more dignified salaries for their own pastors.[13]

The 1960s was a decade of turmoil in many sectors of public life with all the confrontational movements of generational and cultural rebellion; intentional challenges to established values; efforts to end racial segregation in schools; awakenings of minorities seeking social justice; violence, disorder, and disrespect while at the same time a creative consciousness of civil rights. The decade transitioned the Baptist work in the Southwest from a long and blessed period of growth to a new fertile stage filled with both anxieties and possibilities. Three general factors brought about the end of the first period: the volatile socio-political situation, Cuban immigration, and the closing of the Spanish American Baptist Seminary. A fourth factor greatly influenced the next stage: the overwhelming and still active immigration from Mexico and Central America.

New York

During the second decade of the twentieth century, the United States experienced a shortage of workers due to World War I. The country recruited some of the newest "American citizens," Puerto Ricans, to fill in the gaps. The majority of the Puerto Ricans settled in New York and established

---

12. Holland, *Religious Dimension,* 296, 299–301, 305, 323–24, 327.

13. Morales, *American Baptists,* 64–65.

their own Puerto Rican colony of sorts. Some of those who migrated were Protestants, and among them were a few Baptists.

In 1919, José and Esperanza Toro Santiago visited the English-speaking Washington Avenue Baptist Church. The couple came from the *Primera Iglesia Bautista de San Juan* (First Baptist Church of San Juan), and the new church in Brooklyn accepted them readily. Other Puerto Ricans soon followed their example. Thus S. Soto Fontánez claims that the Latino Baptist projects in New York are the result of the missionary work in Puerto Rico.[14]

On May 2, 1920, the Toros began hosting services in their home. Soon the house could no longer accommodate all the attendees. Washington Avenue Baptist Church opened its doors to the group and invited them to hold services inside the church building. By February of 1921, the Baptist Extension Society employed Dr. Perry D. Woods to work with Washington Avenue Church's Latinos. They also appointed Miss Albertina D. Bischoff to serve among them. The work grew so rapidly that on March 24, 1921, the *Primera Iglesia Bautista Hispana* (First Baptist Hispanic Church) came into being with forty-two members and an average attendance of eighty-four.

Changes in pastoral leadership and the constant search for an adequate space for worship services made the next few years rather rocky for the *Primera Iglesia Bautista Hispana*. When they finally acquired their own building, the church concentrated on strengthening the congregation. With a membership of 500 people, the church eventually planted daughter churches (*La Segunda* and *La Tercera Iglesia Bautista*) and influenced the establishment of several other congregations.[15]

Of the churches planted by the *Primera Iglesia Bautista Hispana*, some succumbed to the passing of time though a few of the third-generation churches continued to flourish. The *Primera Iglesia Bautista Pan Americana* (First Pan-American Baptist Church) is a prime example. Several members of the *Primera Iglesia Bautista Hispana*, eager to serve in their immediate neighborhoods, organized the *Primera Iglesia Bautista Pan Americana* on December 25, 1930. In turn, from the *Pan Americana*, ten members began meeting in homes; these meetings turned into a Baptist mission which later became *Iglesia Bautista de Brooklyn* (Brooklyn Baptist Church) and now functions as *Iglesia Bautista Central de Brooklyn*

---

14. Fontánez, *Misión a la puerta*, 31.

15. Morales, *American Baptists*, 45–46.

(Central Baptist Church of Brooklyn). In 1936, the *Pan American* dissolved. *Iglesia Bautista Central*, meanwhile, remains strong as the granddaughter of *Primera Iglesia Bautista Hispana* and the daughter of the now dissolved *Primera Iglesia Bautista Pan Americana*. Other churches following this trend are *Iglesia Bautista Misionera del Bronx* (Missionary Baptist Church of the Bronx, 1941), *Primera Iglesia Bautista del Bronx* (First Baptist Church of the Bronx, 1952), *Primera Iglesia Bautista del East New York* (First Baptist Church of East New York, Brooklyn, 1956), and *Iglesia Bautista Emmanuel* (Emmanuel Baptist Church, Manhattan, 1957).

Midwest

Many Mexicans in the Midwest worked for the train companies building new lines or maintaining existing lines. There was no scarcity of Baptists among workers who followed the train routes with their families. Their economic stability depended on their collaboration with the Santa Fe, Southern Pacific, and Union Pacific train companies. Many Latino churches sprang up along the train tracks crossing the West and Midwest. Some of these included congregations in Topeka, Kansas; Fort Madison, Iowa; Winslow, Arizona; and Scottsbluff, Nebraska, all established in the 1920s. As time went on, Latino Baptists also established themselves in northern California in 1930, in Wisconsin in 1938, in Minnesota in 1941, in Missouri in 1958, and in Miami, Florida in 1963.[16]

DEVELOPMENT OF THE NATIONAL LATINO PROJECTS

The challenging effects of the 1960s movements of generational and cultural confrontation, of intentional challenge, and of the heightened sense of social justice, combined with an incipient holistic re-reading of the gospel, awoke in Latino Baptist leaders the desire and creativity to forge their own destinies and to participate actively in denominational life. At the same time, the message from the denomination's headquarters was to stop creating new Latino churches and instead to integrate the existing Latino churches into the English-speaking congregations. To accomplish this task, the denomination created Latino departments in English-speaking churches so that the Latino churches would no longer be their own

---

16. Ibid., 41.

distinct establishments. The denomination sought to weaken the movement of "ethnic" churches.[17]

The course of Latino Baptist history, given all the pressures, would experience a great change of direction compared to the previous decades. The benign neglect that had been practiced towards the Latino projects came to an end. Soto Fontánez summarizes that

> At the end of the 1960s the moral of the Hispanic workers and churches in the American Convention climaxed, but something was happening in the nation that would greatly affect our work.[18]

At the beginning of the 1970s, Latinos began organizing on both the national and regional levels into pressure groups called "caucuses." The idea for Hispanic caucuses arose in Canyon Meadows, at the American Baptist Church Conference Center of Los Angeles. From there the idea spread throughout the nation and to Puerto Rico. Thanks to an excellent *conscientización* effort by national Latino directors from Southern California, especially Vahac Mardirosian, sixteen Latino leaders confronted the denominational leadership in the Annual Convention in Cincinnati, Ohio in May of 1970. It was the first time Latinos had openly sought justice and inclusivity from the denomination. The confrontation resulted in several changes throughout the 1970s: greater Hispanic responsibilities on the regional and national levels and the creation and betterment of such services for Hispanics as social benefits, theological and Christian education, publications, and international ministries. Soto Fontánez says that the caucuses "increased awareness, if not in the entire convention, at least among the agency leaders, and the results have benefited the progress of our work."[19]

The final years of the 1970s and on through the 1980s were years of dreaming, of projects, of impressive congregational growth, and of a certain amount of consolidation. The churches benefited from the dynamism, efficiency, and tenacity of strong convention leaders and directors of the Hispanic projects.

---

17. Fontánez, "Mensaje a la diáspora hispana," 9.

18. Ibid., 10.

19. Ibid., 13.

The Past Few Years

At the end of the twentieth century, the Latino Baptist work in the United States boasted some three hundred congregations; some were departments inside English-speaking churches, others were missions, and the majority were properly constituted individual churches. Puerto Rico and the Southwest have the largest number of congregations. As mentioned above, Puerto Rico has 108 churches; there are 140 in the Southwest, ninety of which are clustered in Southern California.

While some congregations disbanded and a few others separated from the denomination, the majority have grown notably stronger in terms of membership, finances, and programs. Today, very few Latino Baptist churches use English only. Several offer certain programs in English or hold bilingual services. And it is more and more common to find a strong Latino presence integrated into multicultural churches.

The congregations constitute a very diverse community from ethnic, theological, and ecclesiological perspectives. Ethnically they reflect the great diversity of the Latino population including Mexicans, Puerto Ricans, Cubans, Salvadorans, Guatemalans, and Central Americans in general. The percentage of South Americans remains low. Theologically speaking, renewal-charismatic currents mix with more traditional positions. Charismatic expressions vary from contemporary praise and worship music and hand clapping to dancing and exercising gifts of the Spirit like speaking in tongues, casting out demons, and healing the sick.

The diversity of local church ecclesiology shows up in variations of congregational governance and, in some cases, Presbyterian or Episcopalian styles of church government. Some churches have changed from congregational governance to an Episcopalian style in hopes of protecting pastoral leadership from sad abuses that are all too common. These models have also borrowed from charismatic denominations.

The Structure of Baptist Work

Baptist churches in general retain a congregational model of church government. Local churches maintain their autonomy but at the same time share mutual responsibilities with each other through structures and organizations on different levels. Typically, churches in a particular region will group together in conventions or associations, all of which together make up the denomination. Among the most stable and oldest of these associations are the Baptist Churches of Puerto Rico (since 1902) and the Hispanic Baptist Churches of the Southwest (since 1923). Others include the Western Convention of Baptist Churches of Northern California; the Lagunera Association of Baptist Churches of Metro Chicago; the Association of Hispanic Baptist Churches of New York; and the associations of Latino Baptist churches in Florida and New Jersey. The relationship between the congregations and the regional and national bodies is one of interdependence in which each congregation retains its autonomy. The national directors of the Hispanic ministry of the American Baptist Church have been Adam Morales (1948–1973), José Ortiz (1974–1994), Enrique Torres as interim (1995), Héctor Cortés (1996–1998), and Eddie Cruz (1999–2003). Fela Barrueto is the current liaison to Hispanic and Portuguese-speaking churches.

The Evangelical Seminary of Puerto Rico

As the second decade of the twentieth century came to a close, the Grace Conaway Baptist Institute of Río Piedras united with three other theological institutions belonging, respectively, to the Presbyterians, the Methodists, and the Disciples of Christ. These four institutions joined to form the Evangelical Seminary of Puerto Rico. From then on the Puerto Rican Baptist efforts have maintained strong ties with the seminary, which has in turn trained the vast majority of Baptist pastors on the island. Classes began on September 11, 1919. In 1936 the seminary became an associate member of the Association of Theological Schools and since 1982 has been an accredited member. Baptist leaders have at times served as presidents of the seminary.[20]

Spanish American Baptist Seminary

Throughout World War I, in the following decade, and especially at the close of the Mexican Revolution, the Southwest experienced a significant increase in Mexican immigrants, at times receiving up to 100,000 per year. The need for Mexican ministers was immediate. The urgency of the situation led to the founding of a seminary at a very early stage in the development of Hispanic Baptist work in Southern California, an early

20. See González, *Theological Education* and "La educación teológica en Puerto Rico," a study by the Hispanic Association for Theological Education, Puerto Rican Chapter, 1998.

stage even considering Baptist work in the rest of the country. In February of 1921, two years before the fledgling congregations would organize into the Mexican Baptist Convention of Southern California, the small hand-ful of churches and missions founded an institution responsible for pre-paring workers for Christian ministry throughout the nation.[21]

The first president of the new institution was J. F. Detweiler (1921–1943); Samuel F. Nelson succeeded him (1943–1954); and Benjamín R. Morales succeeded him (1954–1963). In 1964, under interim director José Arreguín, the school closed permanently.[22] Some of the notable profes-sors were Albert B. Howell, the hymnologist George P. Simmonds, John R. Janeway, Laura Fish, and Joseph Barclay. Cosme G. Montemayor, Juan C. Varetto, and Frank Fagerberg were distinguished visiting professors.[23] Many self-sacrificing and talented workers graduated from the seminary and served throughout the United States, Puerto Rico, Mexico, Central America, and South America. Leonardo Mercado has the distinction of being the first graduate.[24]

According to communication from Paul O. Madsen, four factors led to the closing of the seminary in 1964: recruitment and training, budget problems, employment of graduates, and the level of academics. The clos-ing was one of many factors that marked the end of an era for Baptists in Southern California and even throughout the nation. The seminary had been the only Hispanic institution for training Latino Baptist leaders. The religious service held to officially close the seminary seemed more like a funeral service, with Ismael M. García reading a poem titled "*Defunción*" ("Death"). Many still look back on the loathsome year of 1964 with bitter-ness and resentment because of the ever present suspicion that they were doing a great disservice to the future.[25]

---

21. Leavenworth and Froyd, "The Spanish American Baptist Seminary and Its Tasks," 6. Also see Detweiler, "The Spanish-American Baptist Seminary: A Brief History," 26.

22. Seminario Bautista Hispano Americano, *Prospecto 1959–1960*, 13.

23. Kaiser, "Seminario Bautista Hispano Americano," 8.

24. Morales, *American Baptists*, 69.

25. Madsen, "Appendix 2." According to Fontánez, another reason behind the closing of the seminary was the mentality expressed in the following quote: "For several years the message delivered to the National Director had been: 'No more new Hispanic churches. We have to integrate them like before.' They created departments in English-speaking churches without the expectation that these would grow later to be Spanish-speaking churches" ("Mensaje a la diáspora hispana," 10).

Hispanic Urban Center

In 1971, after various negotiations and differences of opinion regarding procedures, the Hispanic Urban Center in Los Angeles was organized with Vahac Mardirosian as director and Fidel Mercado as dean. It was located on property belonging to *La Iglesia Bautista "El Salvador."* The center's principal objective was theological education. This goal was never realized, however, and within a short time the dean resigned without being replaced. For a large part of the center's first ten years of existence, it primarily served the community as an institution of secular education, preparing already trained teachers in specialties outside their fields: for example, in Hispanic language and culture. Horacio Quiñones directed the center from 1981 until his death in 1992. During this period the center offered services of various kinds, one of which was a conscience-raising effort to help people understand the social, cultural, and educational needs of the Hispanic community.

American Baptist Seminary of the West

The closing of the Spanish American Baptist Seminary in 1964 ushered in a drastic and extensive national vacuum in the theological education of Latino Baptists. Latino Baptists were expected to attend the Theological Baptist Seminary of California, later called American Baptist Seminary of the West, which almost exclusively served the white Baptist community. Reality contradicted this expectation, however, since between 1964 and 1978 apparently only five Latinos graduated from the seminary. They were David Luna, Frank Martínez, Daniel Rebassa, Leonel Robaina, and Daniel Statello.

After 1970, Latino leaders attempted various courses of action to provide theological education. None succeeded until the Board of Ministerial Education of the Hispanic Baptist Churches of the Southwest sought a partial, regional solution. In 1977 the board submitted a proposal to the American Baptist Seminary of the West for the creation of a program in Southern California and the appointment of a Hispanic professor who would reside in Los Angeles. The seminary responded positively and, in 1978, appointed Eduardo Font to teach Hispanic studies and direct the seminary in the Southwest.

While Latinos made up the majority of the students, the seminary in the Southwest opened its doors to all. It offered a Master of Religious

Arts, Master of Divinity, and Doctor of Ministry. Eduardo Font directed the seminary until its close in 1988.

Some of the seminary's students, for various reasons, lacked sufficient university training. Font, therefore, negotiated with the University of La Verne to set up a specialized program on the seminary's grounds. With Font as director, the university program conferred bachelor's degrees in religion, philosophy, and psychology beginning in 1983. Both the seminary and the university programs were accredited by the Association of Theological Schools and the Western Association of Schools and Colleges, respectively.

With the support of the Board of Ministerial Education, Font also directed a program of biblical institutes for the laity. These institutes functioned in churches and served groups of neighboring congregations. For many years some functioned with more regularity than others in Los Angeles, Ontario, Oxnard, Huntington Park, the Bay area, and San Diego. The plan of studies generally consisted of eighteen courses, at the end of which the director's office and the Board of Ministerial Education awarded a Christian Worker Certificate to the students.

With deep sadness the Baptist community in the Southwest once again witnessed the closing of their seminary in Covina even as the seminary was at its peak in terms of programs, number of students, and facilities. June 30, 1988, was the seminary's last official day of existence. At that time there were fifty-nine students pursuing master's or doctoral degrees and forty-seven earning bachelor's degrees. Nearly a thousand people attended the closing session of classes and graduation.

American Baptist Theological Center

As an emergency intervention, on August 1, 1988, the two Southwestern regions joined the Southwest Hispanic Baptist Churches in establishing the American Baptist Theological Center (ABTC). The ABTC would serve the Baptist community through a cooperative agreement with Fuller Theological Seminary in Pasadena, California. The university program formerly established with the University of La Verne was transferred to the ABTC where it has functioned up to the present day without further interruption. Furthermore, the biblical institutes for laity resumed function under the new name of academies. From 1978 to 1987, forty Latino pastors who continue in active service in the Southwest studied in or graduated from one of these programs.

The ABTC is located on the campus of Fuller Theological Seminary. Eduardo Font, the founding director, had an efficient team made up of his assistant Cassie Acevedo and Boris Durán as student coordinator (1988–1993), later replaced by Miguel A. Darino (1994–1996). When Font resigned in 1996, the ABTC's Board of Directors appointed Neil E. Frey as director beginning in September of 1997 and Camilo González as associate director.

Other Programs of Theological Education

Among the efforts to train laity and to form Latinos for the ministry of the Word, there have been institutes in New York, New Jersey, Chicago, and Northern California. The program developed at Northern Baptist Theological Seminary in Lombard, Illinois deserves special attention. In 1979, the seminary appointed Osvaldo Mottesi as professor of Christian ethics with the understanding that he would develop a Hispanic department that would be integrated into the seminary's existing master's programs and Doctor of Ministry program. The Hispanic department offered a large number of courses taught in Spanish. One of the program's calling cards was the number of students and visiting professors from Latin America and Puerto Rico. A sizeable number of the graduates completed doctoral studies, and some still teach today in seminaries and institutes throughout the Spanish speaking world. Unfortunately, this program met the same fate as similar programs and was dissolved in the year 2000.

The same year that Mottesi began the Hispanic program in Lombard, Eastern Baptist Theological Seminary in Philadelphia, Pennsylvania hired Orlando Costas. Costas developed an ambitious academic program that served the Latino community well. However, within a few years, Costas agreed to become the dean of the Andover Newton Theological Seminary, and Eastern's program reduced its emphasis on Hispanic students. When Costas died after a brief illness, the entire Baptist community and the wider theological community grieved the loss of a prolific author, a clear and insightful thinker, and an eloquent expositor of God's Word. In both institutions where Costas served, the Hispanic presence continues strong not only in terms of students and professors but also in terms of courses covering pertinent Latino themes.

The Baptist Center of Social Services

The Board of Social Action of the Southwest Hispanic Baptist Churches had dreamed and planned for years about founding the Baptist Center of Social Services. Located in El Monte and in East Los Angeles, the center opened its doors in June of 1985. It was a joint effort between the Board of Social Action, the denomination's National Ministries, the American Baptist Churches of Los Angeles, and the American Baptist Churches of the Pacific Southwest. Sylvestre Acevedo became the interim director in August of 1985 and went on to serve as fulltime director until 1995. In March of 1995 María Figueras took over as interim director and then as fulltime director. The center's objective is to promote spiritual growth through social services to improve the standard of living and wellbeing of needy people looking for a just, healthy, and communal life in which basic human rights are respected.[26] Some of the services offered include legal advice, immigration services, emergency food and housing, clothing, school supplies, employment advice, counseling, and medical and dental referrals.

PROJECTIONS ABOUT BAPTIST MINISTRIES

The current state of Latino Baptists is one of expectation and ardent desire to be active and responsible participants in the establishment of the Kingdom of God to the degree to which God's grace permits it.

"Growing in Love" and "Active in Missions"

In the 1980s, in a demonstration of solidarity with the rest of the Baptist family, Latinos on the regional and national level embraced two projects: "Growing in Love" and "Active in Missions." The first was a plan of holistic expansion inspired by the New Testament experience emphasizing love. The second, begun soon after Growing in Love, affirmed and strengthened the first. Active in Missions was a national effort to raise $30,000,000 to establish new congregations and to revitalize missionary projects. By July of 1987, the American Baptists had surpassed their goal in pledges.

Both projects sought to establish, in practical terms, 500 new churches in the United States by the mid 1990s. In response to the challenge of millions of Latinos living in the country and in an act of great faith, the Hispanics determined to found more than 100 new congregations. By

---

26. Centro Bautista de Servicio Social, "Artículos de Incorporación" (December, 1985).

June of 1995, the Baptists had met and again surpassed their goal of 500 new congregations, a large number of which were Latino churches.

Visión 2001

The Hispanic Baptist leadership realized in 1991 that they needed a national plan for meeting the challenges implicit in the projection that, by 2001, the Hispanic population in the United States would be 33 million. Visión 2001 was the plan through which the Hispanic Baptists would grow in Christ to be able to assume local, regional, and national responsibility for Hispanic ministries. The plan implied growth in spirituality, evangelization, stewardship, education, and commitment to missions within the American Baptist identity. Two of Visión 2001's concrete goals were to establish 100 new congregations and to baptize thirty thousand new believers by the year 2001.

A regional example of Visión 2001 was the Los Angeles Now movement. Over 800 adults, plus 150 children and teenagers, gathered at the First Baptist Church, Huntington Park for the kick-off event on March 21, 1998. Los Angeles Now sought to develop a style of evangelism based on an authentic personal and congregational style of living; to strengthen the evangelistic effectiveness of local churches; to refocus the church's mission on its fundamental priorities; and to make the Great Commission a challenge for the here and now of churches and communities.

New Life 2010

Visión 2001 served as the basis for the current denominational program New Life 2010, launched with the goals of planting 1,010 new churches and baptizing 1,000,010 new Christians in the midst of caring and transformational congregational ministries, all before the year 2010. Latinos trust that a large number of the new congregations and new Christians will be Latinos.

The Hispanic communities of the United States represent a gigantic challenge for the Christian mission. Despite good will, intricate plans, and herculean efforts, human attempts alone will never reach the communities. There is only one possibility, the only hope that truly counts: God. With God, all things are possible.

3

Latino Districts of the Assemblies of God in the United States

Sergio Navarrete

THE LATINO MOVEMENT OF the Assemblies of God in the United States began in a Methodist church in Kingsville, Texas. In 1911, pastor Hartfield invited a North American missionary who had worked in Venezuela to preach about missions. During the missionary's sermon, God impressed upon the heart of a young man, Henry Cleophas Ball, the need to carry the message of salvation to Latinos in the United States.[1] A few years later Ball pioneered the ministry of the Assemblies of God among Latinos.

Nearly 100 years later, Latinos are the fastest growing ethnic group among the Assemblies of God in the United States, a distinction they have held for the last thirty years. Latinos make up 14 percent (with more than 439,866 members) of the total membership of Assemblies of God in the nation. There are currently eight Latino districts throughout the country and Puerto Rico.[2]

The history of the Assemblies of God among Latinos in the United States testifies to great miracles of God, thousands of transformed lives, healings, and more than 1,759 Hispanic Pentecostal churches established throughout the country. The story can be told in four stages: the background of Pentecostalism in the United States, the beginnings of the Assemblies of God, the organization and growth of Latino districts in

---

1. de León, *Silent Pentecostals*, 15.

2. "Reporte de estadísticas vitales de las Asambleas de Dios" (Springfield, MO: May 27, 2003).

the Assemblies of God, and the future of Assemblies of God ministry to Latinos in the United States.

THE BACKGROUND OF PENTECOSTALISM
IN THE UNITED STATES

The nineteenth-century Holiness Movement within the Methodist church gave birth to Pentecostalism.[3] John Wesley, who taught about a second blessing for Christians, had uttered the phrase that formed the basis for twentieth-century Pentecostalism: "Baptism in the Holy Spirit."[4] Throughout the nineteenth century, Charles Finney (known as the father of Pentecostalism because of his revival campaigns and messages), Dwight Moody, Reuben Torrey, and A. B. Simpson taught about this second blessing, as well. Torrey even wrote a book called *Baptism in the Holy Spirit.*[5]

The year 1896 beheld two well-known Pentecostal manifestations of speaking in tongues. First, A. J. Tomlinson directed the Camp Creek revivals which led to the founding of the oldest Pentecostal church, the Church of God in Cleveland, Tennessee.[6] Second, Baptist pastor Richard G. Spauling organized a revival in which the Holy Spirit was poured out on people to such a degree than many spoke in tongues. In the same year, three distinct Holiness groups joined together to form the Holy Pentecostal Church.[7]

In 1900 C. F. Parham established Bethel Bible College in Topeka, Kansas. Pablo Deiros documents that a female student in the Bible college, Agnes Ozman,

> asked everyone to lay hands on her so that she would be full of the Holy Spirit. They did so. Parham describes that something like a halo appeared around the girl's face. She began to speak in "Chinese" and could not speak in English for three days. One student after the other received the "baptism" and apparently spoke in various languages (*xenolalia*).[8]

---

3. Deiros and Mraida, *Latinoamérica en llamas*, 47.
4. Ibid., 48.
5. Ibid., 50.
6. Ibid.
7. Menzies, *Anointed to Serve*, 27.
8. Deiros and Mraida, *Latinoamérica en llamas*, 52.

Pentecostals emphasized "the doctrine of divine holiness and speaking in tongues, which made the spiritual experience vivid and real."[9] In 1905 Parham established a second Bible college, this time in Houston, Texas. William J. Seymour graduated from this Bible college and took the message of baptism in the Holy Spirit to Los Angeles. On April 9, 1906, on Azusa Street, Seymour and several African-American church members received the baptism in the Holy Spirit in the form of the gift of tongues. "People felt 'energized' by the power of the Spirit and literally fell to the floor from their seats. White people began joining the primarily black group."[10] The *Los Angeles Times* wrote in its April 18, 1906, edition about the strange event in a small church on Azusa Street where the people spoke in tongues.[11] This Pentecostal revival lasted until 1909 with thousands of people all over the world receiving the baptism in the Holy Spirit manifested in speaking in tongues. There were miracles, healings, and wonders like in the first century Pentecost.[12] The revival spread throughout the entire country and abroad, and now more than twenty Pentecostal denominations trace their origins to the Azusa Street revival.[13]

The Birth of the Assemblies of God
in the United States

Between 1880 and 1923 around 200 small Pentecostal groups in the United States left their traditional denominations upon receiving the baptism in the Holy Spirit. One was the Pentecostal fellowship of Texas-Arkansas directed by E. N. Bell, and another was the Pentecostal group of Alabama-Mississippi directed by H. A. Goss.[14] These two Pentecostal leaders recognized the need to form an official Pentecostal organization. In its December 12, 1913, edition, the magazine *Word and Witness* announced a convocation to form such an organization. The meeting took place on April 2, 1914, in the Grand Opera House of Hot Springs, Arkansas. Three hundred men and women of similar Pentecostal persuasion attended. When the meeting ended on April 12, the people had established a new Pentecostal organization called

---

9. Menzies, *Anointed to Serve*, 27.

10. Deiros and Mraida, *Latinoamérica en llamas*, 52.

11. Díaz, *La nave pentecostal*, 17.

12. Ibid., 18.

13. de León, *Silent Pentecostals*, 7.

14. Kendrick, *Promise Fulfilled*, 81.

the General Council of the Assemblies of God. E. N. Bell served as the first president and J. Roswell Flower as the secretary.[15]

THE BEGINNINGS OF THE ASSEMBLIES OF GOD AMONG LATINOS

The history of Latinos in the Assemblies of God begins in 1915 with four valiant servants of God, three men and one woman: Henry C. Ball, Francisco Olazábal, Demetrio Bazán, Sr., and Alice E. Luce.

Henry Cleophas Ball

Henry C. Ball cannot be left out of the retelling of the beginnings of the Assemblies of God's Latino ministry. Henry grew up in Kingsville, Texas where he and his mother attended a Methodist church. After the missionary to Venezuela visited his church, Ball, or "Brother Ball" as he was also known, began to preach to Latinos using a translator in Ricardo, Texas. Ball was an Anglo-Saxon Methodist turned Pentecostal, and in January of 1918, he founded the Latino District Council of the Assemblies of God with the hope of establishing Latino churches in the United States. De León writes, "Who would have believed that day when Henry C. Ball and his mother left Iowa that Henry C. Ball would become one of the greatest missionaries of Christianity and Pentecostalism in the twentieth century."[16]

Francisco Olazábal

Francisco Olazábal, another great Latino Pentecostal pioneer, was born in El Verano, Sinaloa, Mexico, in 1886. At eighteen years of age he left home to live with his aunt in San Francisco, California. Misunderstandings between Olazábal and his mother were behind his move. For his part, the young Olazábal could not understand why his mother would faithfully serve God.[17]

While walking one afternoon through the San Francisco streets, Olazábal ran into George Montgomery, the pastor of a Missionary Alliance church. Montgomery gave Olazábal a salvation tract which eventually

---

15. Ibid.

16. de León, *Silent Pentecostals*, 52.

17. Ibid., 23–25.

influenced the young man so much that he visited the Montgomerys at home and dedicated his life to Christ.

Olazábal returned to Mexico and in 1907 entered Wesley Methodist College in San Luis Potosí, Mexico. After graduating, he served as a pastor for one year in Durango before moving to El Paso, Texas to pastor a Spanish-speaking Methodist church. He returned to California in 1913 and worked with the Methodist church in various cities.

God blessed the young Olazábal with a special spiritual experience in 1917. One afternoon he visited his spiritual parents, George and Carrie Judd Montgomery, who told him they had received the baptism in the Holy Spirit. Olazábal agreed to attend a prayer service in their house also attended by Assemblies of God ministers Alice E. Luce, Panchito Ortiz, Sr. (the first Latino ordained by the Assemblies of God in northern California), and Ángelo Fraticelli. These brothers and sisters prayed for Olazábal, and God baptized him in the Holy Spirit. Not long after that first Pentecostal experience, Olazábal joined the Assemblies of God.[18]

In 1918 Olazábal returned to El Paso, Texas, where he promptly established the first Latino Assemblies of God church.[19] A young couple named Demetrio and Nellie Bazán had a great desire to serve God, and in 1920 they joined Olazábal in his ministry with the church. In a short period of time the church was ministering to more than 300 Latinos every Sunday morning.[20]

Olazábal, the greatest Latino Pentecostal evangelist of his time, began touring the country leading evangelistic campaigns. His "powerful evangelistic and healing crusades surged through neighborhoods from Los Angeles, El Paso, and Chicago to New York and Puerto Rico like a great spiritual wave."[21] God used Olazábal to call a large number of Latinos into ministry with the Assemblies of God.[22] Many of them felt that Olazábal, instead of Henry C. Ball, ought to lead the Latino Assemblies of God movement since Olazábal understood the Latino culture better.[23] Olazábal worked together with H. C. Ball for five years until on January

18. Ibid., 26–27.
19. Franco, "Remembranzas," 7.
20. Bazán, "Reseña histórica," 10.
21. Franco, "Remembranzas," 24.
22. de León, *Silent Pentecostals*, 29.
23. Ibid.

13, 1923, he decided to leave the Assemblies of God. His decision owed largely to seeing that the Assemblies of God would not permit the Latin American Convention to elect their own Latino leaders and that "the 'gringos' had control."[24] With this understanding, Olazábal decided to leave the Assemblies of God and to form the Latin American Council of Christian Churches.[25]

Alice Evelyn Luce

Alice E. Luce was an Episcopalian missionary from England. She first traveled as a missionary to India in 1910 and then went to Canada. There she received the baptism in the Holy Spirit and in 1912 sensed a strong call to preach the gospel to Mexicans in Mexico and in the United States. While visiting Texas in 1915, she met H. C. Ball and other Pentecostal leaders. She soon left the Episcopal church and became an ordained minister in the Assemblies of God.[26]

Since Luce had had university training in nursing and theology from the London Bible Institute, she quickly gave herself to the task of establishing Bible schools for preparing Mexicans for the ministry. In October of 1926 in San Diego, California, she began the Berean Bible Institute, which later became the famous Latin American Bible Institute of La Puente, California. She and H. C. Ball collaborated later that same year to start the Latin American Bible Institute in San Antonio, Texas.[27] Luce also helped establish the *Instituto Bíblico Betania de las Asambleas de Dios* (Bethany Bible Institute of the Assemblies of God) in Tijuana, Mexico. Throughout her lifetime, Alice E. Luce served as a faithful and divine instrument for the biblical, theological, and ministerial training of thousands of Latino Pentecostals who have served and who still serve God all over the world.

Organization and Growth of the Latino Work of the Assemblies of God

There are currently eight Latino Assemblies of God districts in the United States, with more than 250,000 adult members and more than 1,800 churches. Though the majority of Latino Pentecostal churches report an

---

24. Ibid., 98–99.

25. Ibid.

26. Díaz, *La nave pentecostal*, 22.

27. de León, *Silent Pentecostals*, 78.

average of about 112 members, between 30,000 and 40,000 Latinos leave the Roman Catholic Church for a Pentecostal church every year.[28] Just as God used certain men and women to start his Pentecostal work among the Latino population in the United States, he raised up three visionary servants to organize and grow the work: Demetrio Bazán, Sr., José Girón, and Jesse Miranda.

Demetrio Bazán, Sr.

When Henry C. Ball retired in 1937, Demetrio Bazán, Sr. assumed leadership of the Latin American District of the Assemblies of God. In 1939 he was elected superintendent of the district, a position in which he faithfully served for nineteen years. His main focus was preparing the church for Christ's second coming.[29] Brother Bazán worked arduously with the national offices to reorganize the Latin American district from eleven conferences into four conferences with fulltime Latino superintendents for "better supervision, control, and evangelization."[30]

Dr. José Girón

Dr. Girón, one of God's key servants in the expansion of the Assemblies of God among Latinos in the United States, was instrumental in achieving one of Demetrio Bazán's dreams. Dr. Girón supervised the reorganization of the Latin American district into four Latino districts throughout the country. This 1970 reorganization became fundamental for furthering the growth of the Assemblies of God among US Latinos.

Born in 1911 in Del Norte, Colorado, Dr. Girón attended the Presbyterian Church of San Luis Valley, Colorado, with his parents.[31] When he finished high school, his church decided to pay his way through seminary for training to be a minister in the Presbyterian church. God had other plans for this young man, though. He would become one of the great organizers of the Latin American District of the Assemblies of God.

In 1929 a Pentecostal evangelist of the Assemblies of God, P. V. Jones, showed up in Girón's town. The young Girón and a Methodist pastor in town received the baptism in the Holy Spirit during Jones' evangelistic

---

28. Ibid., 25.

29. Miranda, "Mensaje de instalación."

30. de León, *Silent Pentecostals*, 108.

31. Ibid., 120.

crusades. After witnessing that blessing, the evangelist Jones contacted H. C. Ball and highly recommended Girón for ministry to US Latinos. Superintendent Ball felt the Lord's leading to send Brother Girón credentials for ministry without having ever met the young man.[32]

Fueled by the fire of the Holy Spirit, Girón began leading revival campaigns wherever he was invited. He established a Pentecostal church in his hometown in 1932, and in this church his fruitful ministry took off. In the next thirteen years he pastored eight churches.

In 1936 Girón served as pastor in Questa, New Mexico, and as presbyter to the New Mexico Conference. That year, while visiting an Assemblies of God church in Gallina, New Mexico, he was shot at by a group of Catholics. Girón was holding special services for several nights in the church in Gallina, and a group of Catholics made death threats to the Pentecostals for being "heretics" and for making so much noise during their services. Girón told the church's pastor, Arturo Martínez, that the services ought to continue regardless. After a marvelous service on May 14, Girón, the church pastor, and Miguel Sánchez, a young man in the church, were walking back home when "suddenly they heard three shots. Both Girón and Sánchez were shot. When he felt something warm running down his neck, Girón began to run. He quickly returned, though, because Miguel Sánchez suffered a gunshot wound in his left knee and needed help."[33] Victor de León relates, "The following night, to the surprise of many and in spite of the threats, Giron was preaching again in the small church in Gallina."[34]

The 1946 Council of the Latin American District of the Assemblies of God, held in Chicago, Illinois, elected José Girón as District Secretary. For the next eleven years, he served in this capacity, learning the ropes of district work from superintendent Demetrio Bazán. Girón described Bazán in the following way: "Demetrio Bazán was a very self-confident person. He realized that knowledge and prayer were two great tools, and he utilized both to the maximum."[35]

The national Assemblies of God magazine wrote in 1960 about the growth of Latinos in the denomination: "One of the most important de-

---

32. Ibid., 121.

33. José Girón, interview with the author, September 1, 1977.

34. de León, *Silent Pentecostals*, 122.

35. José Girón, interview.

velopments in evangelical religion in New York has been the rapid growth of Spanish-speaking Pentecostal congregations. In 1937, there were about twenty-five churches in the city. By 1960, the number had increased to around 240."[36]

The 1958 District Council elected Girón to superintend the Latin American District of the Assemblies of God in the United States, a responsibility he assumed on January 1, 1959. He blessed the Latino district greatly by strongly emphasizing ministerial education and the district's reorganization. Girón's primary message was "the power of the Holy Spirit for today's church."[37]

The reorganization of the district fell into two stages. First, in 1960, Girón wrote constitutions for the five growing Latin American Conferences of the Assemblies of God that already existed across the country. Second, in 1971, he reorganized the National Latin American District into four different Latino districts. Before this step in the reorganization, however, the Lord directed Girón, to everyone's surprise, to resign from his position as superintendent. He announced this decision in the 1970 Council in Albuquerque, New Mexico and explained that he would resign primarily because the Latino churches were growing so quickly all over the country that one national superintendent alone could not attend to them properly.[38] The council thus resolved to reorganize the National Latin American District into four different districts and asked Girón to superintend whichever one he chose. The new districts, their territories, the number of churches within them, and their initial leaders were the following:

1. The Latin American Pacific District; Dr. José Girón, superintendent; including California, Nevada, Arizona, Oregon, Washington, and Hawaii; beginning with 142 churches.

2. The Latin American Gulf District; Josué Sánchez, superintendent; including Texas, Oklahoma, Louisiana, and Arkansas; beginning with 142 churches.

3. The Latin American Central District; Nestor Bazán, superintendent; including Colorado Utah, Idaho, Wyoming, New Mexico, and Montana; beginning with 92 churches.

36. Lyon, "Latin American District."
37. Miranda, "Mensaje de instalación."
38. de León, *Silent Pentecostals*, 130.

4. The Latin American Midwest District; Reverend Zeferino Caballo, superintendent; including Illinois, Iowa, Minnesota, Missouri, Kansas, Michigan, Indiana, Nebraska, Wisconsin, and North and South Dakota; beginning with 37 churches.

There are also four other Latino districts, making a total of eight Latino districts in the United States:

1. The Puerto Rican District, organized in 1921; Reverend Juan L. Lugo, first president.

2. The Eastern Hispanic District, organized in 1957; Reverend Vicente Ortiz, superintendent.

3. The Southeast Hispanic District, organized in 1981; Reverend Gustavo Jiménez, superintendent; including Florida, North and South Carolina, Georgia, Alabama, and Mississippi.

4. The Pacific North Latin American District, organized in 1998; Reverend Felix Posos, superintendent; including Washington, Oregon, and northern California (from Bakersfield on north).

The last few years in particular have seen strong growth in the Latino Assemblies of God churches. The following chart represents the denominational reports about church growth since 1918.

Year	Convention	Ministers	Churches	Members
1918	Kingsville, TX	7	6	100
1930	San José, CA	117	65	3,000
1935	Dallas, TX	174	80	4,500
1956	Pueblo, CO	573	321	19,490
1960	El Paso, TX	600	325	20,000
1970	Report of the District Secretary	827	403	5,000
1977	Report of the General Secretary	1,135	481	36,000
2002	Report of the General Secretary	22,438	1,758	439,866[39]

After twenty-three years as superintendent (for twelve years in the National Latino District and eleven in the new Latin American Pacific District), Girón announced his retirement in the 1984 Council, and the council then elected the new superintendent, Jesse Miranda.

---

39. "Reporte de estadísticas vitales."

Jesse Miranda

Jesse Miranda, in his eight years as superintendent, provided the vision-ary leadership necessary for preparing the Latin American Pacific District to receive thousands of Latinos and to help them become integral parts of the Assemblies of God in North America. God used Miranda not only to bless the Assemblies of God but also to be "the uniting force for Hispanic Protestants in the U.S."[40]

Miranda grew up in a poor neighborhood in Albuquerque, New Mexico. His father was from Chihuahua, Mexico, his mother was of Spanish descent, and he had five brothers and sisters. He had the great privilege of growing up in the neighborhood Assemblies of God church where National Latin American District superintendent Demetrio Bazán and his assistant José Girón were also members. By permitting Miranda to grow up among the giants of the faith, God was already preparing the boy from an early age for national and international ministry.

God has used Jesse Miranda in many spheres. Miranda has blessed and expanded the Assemblies of God in the Latin American Pacific District and has advised three United States presidents on Latino issues. He is or has been the founder and president of AMEN (*La Asociación Ministerial de Evangélicos Nacionales*, the Ministerial Association of National Evangelicals); president of the Latin American Bible Institute in La Puente, California; founder of the Latin American Theological Seminary; associ-ate dean of the School of Theology of Azusa Pacific University; director of the Center for Urban Ethics of Vanguard University; executive presbyter of the Assemblies of God; and National Commissioner of Ethics of the Assemblies of God. Miranda is recognized and respected as one of the most important national representatives of Latino Evangelicals in the United States today.

A meeting in Washington, D. C. in 2003 demonstrates how God has used Miranda to unite Latino Christian leaders throughout the country. Miranda joined 120 other Latino Evangelical, Pentecostal, and Catholic leaders to discuss the results of a study on religion among Latinos in the United States.[41] He told the mixed crowd, "You're seeing history today,

---

40. Sellers, "You Can Take," subtitle.

41. See "Hispanic Churches in American Public Life: Summary of Findings," a study funded by a grant from The Pew Charitable Trusts, available at http://latinostudies .nd.edu/pubs/pubs/HispChurchesEnglishWEB.pdf.

because here we are. . . What we have in common is a people—Latinos—rather than focusing on theology and other differences."[42]

Dr. Miranda took the ministerial education aspect of the Latino ministry of the Assemblies of God to a higher level. He recognized that the "Hispanic hour" had arrived in the United States, and he understood that the education of pastors would be a great and necessary tool for God's Latino servants to reach their communities, cities, and country for Christ.

Jesse Miranda describes his life in twenty year increments: twenty years of education, twenty years in denominational leadership, and the remaining years as a national representative of Latino Evangelicals. He concludes by saying, "I was called to serve the Hispanic community, that's what I've done, and that's what I'll do the rest of my life."[43] With his visionary leadership, in 1990 he directed the Latin American Pacific District to construct new district offices, new apartments for retired ministers, and a new dormitory for students of the Latin American Bible Institute in La Puente, California. Latinos in the Assemblies of God had never before embarked on a project of such proportion, worth over five million dollars. After eight years as superintendent, Miranda sensed God's directing him to serve the Latino community in a national project, and in 1992 he decided to accept the position of associate dean in the School of Theology of Azusa Pacific University.

Following Jesse Miranda, four other servants of God have superintended the Latin American Pacific District: Joel Torres (1992–1997), Samuel Sánchez (1997–2000), Daniel Tamara (2000–2002), and Sergio Navarrete (2002–present).

The Future of the Assemblies of God Ministry among Latinos in the United States

The Assemblies of God began in 1914, compelled by the fire of the Holy Spirit and a strong call to missions and evangelism. This Pentecostal flame keeps burning in Latino Assemblies of God churches. The ministry of the Assemblies of God to Latinos was born in the heart of a young man, H. C. Ball, in 1911. Nearly 100 years later, this ministry has grown to include over 439,866 Latino members and over 1,758 Latino churches in the Assemblies of God in the United States.

---

42. Sellers, "You Can Take," under "Thicker than Water."
43. Ibid., under "Still Dreaming."

Though many English-speaking churches in the Assemblies of God have declined in growth, the future for Pentecostal missions among Latinos in the United States remains promising for the following reasons:

1. The fire of the Holy Spirit continues to be both the primary focus and the missional and evangelistic force that motivates Latinos in the Assemblies of God.

2. The Assemblies of God places more importance on God's call on the Christian than on educational or institutional requirements for the ministry.

3. The growing movement of cell groups in Assemblies of God churches teaches members to evangelize, disciple, and dedicate new converts into God's service.

4. A transformational vision teaches Assemblies of God pastors to change what is no longer working in the churches and to implement effective ministries with the goal of winning today's culture over to the Kingdom of God.

The history of Latinos in the Assemblies of God over the past century is a testimony of leading thousands of souls into God's Kingdom. This testimony still burns red-hot in Latino churches through the power of the Holy Spirit.

4

Apostolic Assembly of the Faith in Christ Jesus

Ismael Martín del Campo

WHY LOS ANGELES, CALIFORNIA?

IN HIS *A HISTORY of Christian Thought*, Paul Tillich comments on the Pauline idea of *kairos*, the word the apostle used to describe a special moment in history in which everything is ready for the appearance of Jesus.[1] Many Hispanic Apostolic Pentecostals believe that the Azusa Street revival in Los Angeles in 1906 took place in a *kairos* orchestrated by the hand of the God who intervenes in human history.

Frank Bartleman was a privileged witness of the revival since he both lived it and covered it in a journalistic role. He commented in 1905 that "Los Angeles is a veritable Jerusalem. Just the place for a mighty work of God to begin."[2] The well-known historian and cofounder of the Society for Pentecostal Studies, Vinson Synan, says, "When Seymour arrived in Los Angeles in the spring of 1906, he found 228,000 inhabitants in a city that grew by 15 percent every year." Synan adds, "Many strange religions and a multiplicity of denominations occupied the religious attentions of the city."[3]

Attempting to explain one of the reasons why Los Angeles was fertile ground for the birth of Pentecostalism, Harvey Cox highlights the cosmopolitan character and surprising tolerance that Los Angeles showed at the

---

1. Tillich, *History of Christian Thought*, 1.

2. Bartleman, *Azusa Street*, 16.

3. Synan, quoted in Bartleman, *Azusa Street*, x, xi.

time towards "spiritual innovators, political cranks, and religious eccentrics."[4] Although the president of the University of Southern California, Joseph Widney, wrote in 1907 about Los Angeles being the future world capital for the Aryan race,[5] the city had actually become the popular refuge for millions of new immigrants from every corner of the world. Vinson Synan says that "Los Angeles was a melting-pot metropolis with large numbers of Mexicans, Chinese, Russians, Greeks, Japanese, Koreans, and Anglo-American inhabitants."[6] By 1910, Los Angeles ranked third in the country among cities with the greatest number of Mexicans, behind San Antonio and El Paso, Texas.

BEGINNINGS OF THE PENTECOSTAL MOVEMENT

As is well known today, the Methodist minister Charles F. Parham founded Bethel Bible College in Topeka, Kansas. The school, typical of the Holiness movement of the time, took the Bible as its sole text and studied it thematically with cross-reference searches. Parham directed his students to study Acts chapter 2 and encouraged them to find true evidence of the Holy Spirit's presence.

January 1, 1901, is the commonly accepted date for when one of Parham's students, Agnes Ozman, became the first person to experience what Pentecostals call the "baptism of the Holy Spirit," that is, the experience in which a believer begins to praise God in a language previously unknown to him or her (a phenomenon called *glossolalia* in Greek). In the following weeks, other students and Parham himself received this baptism of fire. The movement of this new "Pentecostal doctrine" grew at irregular intervals, first in Kansas and later in Texas. Parham moved his Bible school to Houston, Texas in December of 1905.

William J. Seymour, a son of slaves, overheard a woman named Lucy Farrow pray by "speaking in new tongues" during a service in Houston. The experience touched his heart and moved the African-American minister from Louisiana to ask about the experience.[7] Sister Farrow directed Seymour's steps towards Parham. Immediately Seymour asked to be accepted into the Bible college. Severe segregation laws of

---

4. Cox, *Fire from Heaven*, 51.

5. Ibid., 53.

6. Synan, quoted in Bartleman, *Azusa Street*, foreword.

7. Burgess and McGee, *Dictionary*, 778.

the time prohibited him from participating inside the classroom during the ten weeks of training, but Parham allowed him to sit outside and listen through an open door or window.

Heeding the recommendation of Sister Neely Terry, recently returned from Los Angeles, Seymour decided to move to California. Parham laid hands on the African-American preacher to bless his trip to Los Angeles and, without realizing it, passed on to him the baton of the message of the "latter rains." The emerging Pentecostal movement would go from being a local religious phenomenon to an explosive worldwide movement.

Seymour arrived in Los Angeles on February 22, 1906, and sought out the church of pastor Julia W. Hutchins. Soon, he found the doors of this church literally shutting him out due to his preaching the Pentecostal doctrine. Circumstances led Seymour to continue his ministry in the home of the Asberry family at 214 N. Bonnie Brae Street.

On Monday, April 9, 1906, Seymour and another believer, Edward Lee, received the baptism of the Holy Spirit. For the next few days, various people also began receiving this baptism of fire. The Pentecostal revival in Los Angeles had begun.

MEXICANS IN THE REVIVAL FROM THE BEGINNING

Though it was unusual for the time, people from both white and black races worshiped together. And in their midst from the very beginning, the magazine *Apostolic Faith* (first issued in September 1906)[8] attests to the presence of Mexicans. The magazine relates how on August 11, 1906, a native of the central part of Mexico began speaking in new languages and how, under the power of the Holy Spirit, he laid hands on a Mrs. Knapp and instantly healed her of pulmonary tuberculosis. That Mexican families were part of the Mission of the Apostolic Faith, the name by which the movement referred to itself, from the beginning is not surprising given the revival's geographic proximity to Mexican neighborhoods and its unique respect for racial integration.

The October 1906 issue of *Apostolic Faith* praises Abundio and Rosa López[9] for their open-air preaching ministry in "the Plaza" (most likely the

---

8. Corum, *Like as of Fire*, vol. 1, no. 1:2–3.

9. Ibid., vol. 1, no. 2:4. Some historians of the Oneness Pentecostal movement have erroneously stated that the names Abundio and Rosa López appear in the first issue of *Apostolic Faith* when it is actually the second issue that mentions the couple (October 1906).

Placita Olvera). The November issue also mentions the couple "preaching to Hispanics" and again lauds their love for the Mexicans, commenting on how the López couple would help Mexicans who approached the altar. Brígido Pérez is the third Hispanic name to appear in the magazine. After experiencing the baptism of fire, the young man traveled to San Diego to share the Pentecostal message.[10]

Origins of Oneness Pentecostalism

It is possible that a worship service leader's humiliating treatment of a group of Mexicans[11] near the beginning of the revival catalyzed the banding together of the first group of Latino believers known to baptize in the name of Jesus Christ. Luis López is the first documented Mexican to be baptized in the name of Jesus Christ,[12] and his baptism occurred in 1909. It is also possible that Charles F. Parham himself modeled this practice since in 1902 he began to baptize in the name of Jesus Christ. In 1903 Parham baptized the recently converted Howard Goss in the name of Jesus Christ. Andrew Urshan was also baptized with the same formula in 1910. These examples point to Oneness Pentecostal groups existing even before the famous camp at Arroyo Seco in 1913, seen as the separation point between Oneness and Trinitarian Pentecostalism. Juan Navarro Martínez was the first documented Hispanic minister to come out of the Azusa Street revival.[13] In 1912 Martínez baptized Francisco F. Llorente (from Acapulco, Guerrero) in the name of Jesus Christ. Llorente would be elected in 1925 to be the first president of the "Church of the Apostolic Faith of Pentecost," the previous name of what is now the Apostolic Assembly.[14]

The rediscovery of the doctrine of the baptism of the Holy Spirit in the book of Acts gave birth to Pentecostalism. Speaking in tongues (*glossolalia*) was seen as the initial sign of having been baptized with, by, or in the Holy Spirit. Undoubtedly the honor of identifying this sign belongs to Charles

---

10. Ibid., vol. 1, no. 3:4.
11. Bartleman, *Another Wave*, 104.
12. *50 Aniversario*, 6.
13. Ramírez, "Borderland Praxis," 575.
14. Nava, *Autobiografía*, 8.

F. Parham.[15] Parham explains, "I set the students at work studying out diligently what was the Bible evidence of the baptism of the Holy Ghost."[16]

After Parham's rediscovery, thousands of the first Pentecostals dedicated themselves to an impassioned reading and studying of the book of Acts. They unearthed what the dogmas of their traditional denominations denied or neglected to teach: the baptism of the Holy Spirit accompanied by the sign of speaking in tongues; miracles and wonders; prayers for divine healing; and a totally extroverted, emotional (in the healthy sense), bodily, and audibly expressive form of worshipping God.

In re-reading Acts, thousands of these pioneer Pentecostals studied the biblical pattern of baptism by water: Acts 2:38: "In the name of Jesus Christ"; 8:16: "Into the name of the Lord Jesus"; 10:48: "In the name of Jesus Christ"; 19:5: "Into the name of the Lord Jesus"; and 22:16: "Get up, be baptized . . . calling on his name." To hundreds of new Pentecostals, then, the most natural and biblical way of baptism seemed to be in the name of Jesus Christ.

Next, the new Pentecostals faced the problem of relating Matthew 28:19 (whose literal application was the basis for baptism under the Trinitarian formula) to Acts' baptismal pattern, "in the name of Jesus Christ." However, all the emphasis on Jesus as God, on Jesus' Second Coming, and on christocentric preaching, three characteristics of US America's two Great Awakenings that preceded the Azusa Street revival, prepared the soil for Oneness Pentecostal theology.

Several Pentecostal pioneers soon began to testify that, through their baptism in the name of Jesus Christ, God had revealed to them his oneness (not one God in three Persons but one God principally manifested in three ways). This new revelation would sway one-fifth of the rising Pentecostal movement towards the apostolic or Oneness doctrine. Furthermore, as a historical reference, Eudorus N. Bell, the first superintendent of the Assemblies of God, was baptized in the name of Jesus Christ in the summer of 1915.

Pioneer Oneness Pentecostals, while studying the relation between Matthew 28:19 and Acts' various passages about baptism in the name of Jesus Christ, recovered an ancient theology about the name of God. Both Jewish and early Christian theologians had worked out the doctrine. It

---

15. Goff, *Fields White unto Harvest*.

16. Parham, *Life of Charles F. Parham*, 52.

is not uncommon, therefore, for Oneness Pentecostals to cite Trinitarian Christian authors word-for-word when discussing theology and the name of God. Oneness Pentecostals did not have to elaborate on their beliefs at the beginning because recovering already existing Christian literature sufficed. Urshan, Ewart, and Haywood, Oneness Pentecostals of the era, all turned to earlier writers for justification of the Oneness doctrine. Oneness Pentecostals concluded, then, that the Apostles understood Matthew 28:19 to be referring to the name of God, that is, the name of Jesus, and that the Apostles faithfully obeyed by baptizing Jews (Acts 2:38), Samaritans (Acts 8:16), Romans (Acts 10:48), and probably Greeks (Acts 19:5) in that name. To the Oneness Pentecostals, the importance of the name of Jesus in baptism was clear since Acts 4:12 says, "for there is no other name under heaven given to men by which we must be saved." The pioneer Pentecostals gave the same weight to Colossians 2:9 and other similar passages that declare "in Christ all the fullness of the Deity lives in bodily form."

Origins of the Apostolic Assembly

The group of Mexican believers and ministers who baptized in the name of Jesus Christ decided to place themselves under the authority of the Pentecostal Assemblies of the World, an African-American Oneness denomination with headquarters in Indianapolis, Indiana. The denomination authorized the Mexican ministers until 1930.[17] It was immediately clear that Llorente had a special calling in church ministry. In 1913 he baptized his first believers, María and Rita Serna. In 1914 he met, evangelized, and baptized Marcial de la Cruz (from Torreón, Coahuila) who would become a great evangelist, bishop, and the first Mexican Apostolic hymnologist.[18] Upon his premature death, de la Cruz left over 100 compositions, between complete hymns and others in various stages of editing.

The next link in the chain of the Apostolic Assembly's history is the baptism of Antonio C. Nava. Nava, from Nazas, Durango, immigrated to the United States in obedience to his father's wishes that he not enlist to fight in the Mexican Revolution. He would eventually serve as the president of the Apostolic Assembly from 1929 to 1950 and again from 1963 to 1966. A simple yet irreproachable and visionary man, Nava is the patri-

17. Ortega, *Mis memorias*, 77.
18. *50 Aniversario*, 97.

arch par excellence of the Assembly. Through the friendship and witness of Marcial de la Cruz, Nava experienced a singular conversion in a Los Angeles church on November 23, 1916,[19] when the English-speaking pastor Brookhart baptized him in the name of Jesus Christ with de la Cruz as the only witness.

While the shadows of World War I gathered on the horizon and the Mexican Revolution began tallying its bloody million deaths, the little group of Apostolic Mexicans in Los Angeles, the product of the Azusa Street revival, welcomed another key couple into the church in 1912. Romanita de Valenzuela and her husband no doubt sought a more peaceful and prosperous atmosphere when they left their home state of Chihuahua in Mexico and immigrated to California. They also found a church in which they received the baptism of Pentecostal fire and later baptism by water in the name of Jesus Christ. Towards the end of 1914, and with her husband's permission, Romanita embarked on the first of several trips. Following a *sui generis* missionological vision, Romanita accomplished many things in her trips: 1) She first of all ministered to a group of family and friends[20] in Villa Aldama, Chihuahua until they received the baptism of the Holy Spirit; 2) She witnessed to Methodist pastor Rubén Ortega, who was baptized in the name of Jesus Christ and later became the first Apostolic pastor in Mexico; 3) She shared the Pentecostal message in Durango, Coahuila, Chihuahua, Tamaulipas, and Texas. Her witness in these areas was the genesis of the Apostolic Church in Mexico.

The growth of Spanish-language newspaper circulation in Los Angeles and the creation of new Spanish-language newspapers between 1910 and 1920 demonstrate the phenomenon of the day: as a consequence of the long, bloody Mexican Revolution, a great wave of Mexican immigrants flooded into the United States. Though perhaps unconsciously, the Mexican Apostolic converts fresh from the Azusa Street revival sensitively took advantage of the immigration for a harvest of new believers. They went from being a few Latinos in 1906 to supporting eleven young congregations and various ministries by 1920.[21] Between 1920 and 1925, the number of fledgling churches grew from eleven to thirty-three. The few pioneers still living remember that these congregations practically sprouted up in the

---

19. Gaxiola, *La serpiente*, 161.

20. "75 años de pentecostés," 19.

21. *50 Aniversario*, 7.

fields. The first Apostolic congregations followed the planting and harvesting cycle of Southwest farming towns in the United States.

THE APOSTOLIC ASSEMBLY BEGINS TO ORGANIZE

The humble and visionary Antonio C. Nava wrote in his autobiography that in 1924, "the Lord showed me in a vision that we needed to organize ourselves." Noticing differences of great doctrinal import while visiting other churches convinced Nava of the urgency of obeying the vision. His words describe the difficulty of the task: "Those who indoctrinated us at the beginning taught us that organization like other groups did it was not good." Sure that getting organized was the only appropriate thing to do, Nava began writing letters to different pastors and ministers, sharing his concern for organization. Most readily accepted his ideas, but the Assembly's moral leader, Francisco Llorente, opposed the idea of organization for an entire year. Finally, after intense written exchanges, pastor Llorente supported the idea.

From December 1 through 5 of 1925, in San Bernardino, California, the "Church of Apostolic Pentecostal Faith" held its first convention. Twenty-seven ministers from California, New Mexico, and Arizona attended. They elected Llorente as General Pastor and Nava as Executive Elder. From then on, this Hispanic denomination would hold an annual convention. In the five acts of the first convention are the Apostolic Assembly's "first blueprints": instructions for selecting ministers, instructions for holding an orderly service, opportunities for pastors to dedicate themselves to fulltime ministry, emphasis on Apostolic doctrines (the oneness of God, baptism in the name of Jesus Christ, prayer for divine healing, the Bible as the supreme norm for faith, women's use of head coverings during the service, communion), and instructions for pastoral care of the church.

The second convention held in Indio, California in 1926 successfully confronted the first attempt to divide the Assembly. The location of the third convention, Colonia Zaragoza, Baja California, Mexico in December of 1927, demonstrates the active border-crossing element present in the Hispanic Apostolic movement from its beginnings. There in Colonia Zaragoza the Apostolic Assembly built its first church in Mexico.

At the beginning of 1928, Nava decided to travel to his home town. He intended to visit his ailing father, to share the gospel with his friends and family, and, almost inexplicably, to remain forever in Mexico. Llorente, the president of the Apostolic Assembly, had suffered the loss of his first wife and had remarried; this time he married an English-speaking believer, an "educated woman of Methodist ancestry" named Juanita Peach. Perhaps in a presentiment of his impending infirmity, Llorente moved with his new wife to Yuma, Arizona in July of 1928. He took a *de facto* leave of absence from his responsibilities as president of the Assembly. His move led to quarrels. At the beginning of September, a commission of six ministers in Los Angeles prepared to go and speak with President Llorente and ask him to continue fulfilling his duties as a leader. They were too late, though. On September 8, Llorente died from a sudden heart attack. The church leaders then urgently pleaded with Nava to return to the United States, but Nava did not comply until 1929 since he was in the middle of a very fruitful time of preaching in Mexico.

Besides visiting loved ones and reaping a large harvest of converts for the Lord, Nava's 1928–1929 trip to Mexico allowed him to visit Apostolic believers in the Mexican states of Coahuila, Chihuahua, Tamaulipas, and Nuevo León. His journey influenced the Mexican believers in several notable ways. One very important way was the manner in which, with his balanced and stable ministry, he neutralized the chaotic effects of two eccentric and self-proclaimed prophets, "Saul" and "Silas." Between 1924 and 1925, these two men destabilized the fledgling Apostolic churches in Torreón and Coahuila; from there their itinerary included creating confusion among new groups in Monterrey, Nuevo León, and finally Tamaulipas. The hawkers adopted a style of long tunics, unkempt beards, and tangled mops of hair accompanied by a "strong odor of holiness" (out of "humility," they rarely bathed). Upon learning about Nava's visit, they "prophesied" that fire from heaven would consume whoever dared to cut the prophets' long hair. Accompanied by a God-fearing barber, Nava put an end to their farce.

Nava returned from Mexico on March 3, 1929, and immediately began to visit Apostolic congregations in Texas, New Mexico, Arizona, California, and Baja California, Mexico. In a grand reception in Caléxico, the Assembly officially received Nava back and, with the support of directors Bernardo Hernández and Arturo Hermosillo, named him *de facto* leader until it could officially elect him President and General Pastor in the fifth convention held in Indio, California at the end of 1929.

Elected president by popular acclaim, Nava immediately proposed to the 1929 convention of ministers that in a fraternal manner they cut ties with the Pentecostal Assemblies of the World. He further suggested that the Assembly follow the necessary steps for becoming incorporated as a church under the laws of the United States. Since 1925 Nava had clearly seen this Hispanic church's potential. All throughout the first few conventions he grew more and more convinced that the primarily Mexican church should govern itself in an independent manner to effectively and freely serve the Hispanic community. The 1929 convention studied and approved Nava's proposal and named him head of a committee established to execute the proposal. On March 15, 1930, before the California secretary of state, the denomination was officially incorporated under the name Apostolic Assembly of the Faith in Christ Jesus.

This factor is perhaps the most important facet of the Apostolic Assembly's humble beginnings: behold, an indigenous Hispanic church. Since foreign missionaries neither founded nor supported it economically, the denomination naturally understood several points: 1) that this Hispanic church would function with its own leadership team; 2) that this church would accredit pastors and leaders based on their character and love for the church instead of based on graduation from a particular seminary; 3) above all, that from its beginnings this church would generate its own economic resources to meet its expenditures on all levels. It never occurred to the Assembly to hope for or seek out economic patronage from an English-speaking Apostolic organization. Its economic poverty and lack of experienced leaders with formal training forced the church to grow, to mature quickly, to be creative, and, above all, to be responsible for itself.

Nava served as the Apostolic Assembly's president from 1929 to 1950 and again from 1963 to 1966. Pastor Bernardo Hernández worked with Nava as general secretary from 1926 until his death in 1949. Arturo Y. Hermosillo also formed part of the board of general directors with Nava from 1927 to 1950. Among many others on the pioneering leadership team with President Nava, bishops Marcial de la Cruz and Jesús P. Torres stand out. Later, the Texan minister Benjamín Cantú would become another key pioneer leader.

Publishing the first Apostolic hymnal was one of President Nava's first tasks. Repeating one of the classic signs of a great revival or of a reformation within Christianity, the Apostolic Hispanics found themselves composing hundreds of hymns in their own language. They could sing their sweet Spanish tongue in a foreign land! The majority of the compositions in *Himnos de Consolación* (Hymns of Consolation) came from pioneer Apostolic Hispanics.

Having their own hymns strengthened Apostolic liturgical and doctrinal unity and the church's identity beyond estimation. The practice of composing their own hymns provided a nurturing space within the church for composers and motivated scores of future Apostolic musicians. Members' self-esteem and exercise of musical gifts increased notably. Furthermore, the hymnal provided an excellent evangelization tool since congregations could sing in styles arising from their Hispanic culture! Thus, while nearly all Protestant missionaries considered the guitar a worldly device, it was the Apostolics' most common instrument. It could travel easily to whatever field or farming camp where the nightly service would be held. And as a sensitive response to the difficulties in the life of an Apostolic Hispanic (economic poverty, the crisis of migration, frequent rejection from family members and friends for being a "Hallelujah"), the hymnal included hymns of "consolation."

In his first trip to Mexico as president, Nava took an official stamp and 100 authorized certificates to Felipe Rivas and José Ortega, leaders of the fledgling Apostolic Church of Mexico. The Apostolic Assembly's official support of these leaders bolstered the growth of their sister church across the border.

Toward the end of the 1930s, the Apostolic Assembly of the United States and the Apostolic Church of Mexico decided to strengthen their ties since they functioned according to the same principles of doctrine, organization, and economics. A unique relationship flourished for the next fifty years. With the phrase "our sister church" (in the United States or Mexico), every Apostolic Hispanic understood this intense ecclesiological connection to be stronger than borders, cultures, and linguistic differences.

THE DEVELOPMENT OF THE ASSEMBLY UNDER NAVA'S LEADERSHIP

By the time of the tenth general convention in Los Angeles in 1940, many of the first Apostolic Assembly congregations had grown notably stronger. Despite deportation and the impact of the Great Depression, the number of congregations had doubled to more than seventy.[22] Every Christian denomination, in its initial growth stages, faces challenges similar to what the Assembly next confronted. The blessing of growth brought with it problems of how to better organize the work and how to train new pastors who could advance only so far in the useful but limited "school of experience."

Part of the success of the Apostolic Assembly's consolidation and growth owed to the makeup of its form of government. While President Nava was the natural leader, others in the group of pioneer leaders also insisted from the beginning on directing the church "in an orderly fashion." They achieved order over time by constructing a clear system of episcopal government: 1) a board of general directors on the national level; 2) supervising bishops on the state and regional levels; 3) auxiliary elders in district sectors; and 4) pastors, ministers, and deacons on the local level.

Nava, Bernardo Hernández, and Arturo Y. Hermosillo from the Apostolic Assembly of the United States joined Felipe Rivas, José Ortega, and Maclovio Gaxiola of the Apostolic Church of Mexico on a committee formed for drafting a constitution. The constitution would normalize the organization, economic system, doctrine, and discipline of the Apostolic Church according to the agreements reached in the annual general conventions from 1925 until 1943. The committee presented the new constitution at the beginning of 1944, and the respective general conventions of both the US and the Mexican Apostolics approved it later that same year. Both denominations governed themselves by this unique, seldom altered document from 1944 until 1981. The constitution included a checks-and-balance clause under which both the US and the Mexican branches of the denomination would adopt constitutional changes only with the approval of the other sister church. For nitty-gritty details about visiting or moving back and forth between the United States and Mexico, the Assembly also established a "Unification Treaty" which secured equality of rights and privileges to members and ministers on both sides of the border. One erudite Apostolic wryly mentioned that the Unification Treaty respected the obvious implications of each country's migratory regulations.[23]

World War II impacted the Assembly doctrinally. In its theological beginnings, the pioneers wrote that, on the one hand, "the church recognizes human governments as being divinely ordained . . . and, this being

---

22. Benjamín Cantú, unpublished interview, August 1993.

23. Ramírez, *Antonio C. Nava*, 303.

the case, we exhort all members to affirm loyalty to the fatherland." On the other hand, they insisted that "followers of our Lord Jesus Christ ought not to destroy foreign property or take human life." They concluded, then, that Apostolics "ought to lend service in all non-combatant capacities."[24]

The young Apostolic men who were on the fronts of World War II returned home transformed by a maturity imposed by the brutality of warfare. This generation of men responded sensitively to the gospel and the call to serve the Lord. They had honored the Apostolic doctrine of only participating in "non-combatant fronts," and yet some returned with the most distinguished medals of honor. Without taking up arms, they proved themselves outstanding in the fire of war by saving the lives of many soldiers. Taking advantage of the option of a year's leave with the right to a government-subsidized study, several of these young men attended United Pentecostal Church schools (run by English-speaking Apostolics) and then passionately dedicated themselves to Hispanic ministries.

In 1945, two of the oldest English-speaking Apostolic denominations, the Pentecostal Church, Incorporated, and the Pentecostal Assemblies of Jesus Christ, fused to become the United Pentecostal Church (UPC).[25] The UPC sent two representatives to the Apostolic Assembly's seventeenth general convention in Los Angeles in 1946. Howard A. Goss, the UPC's first superintendent (also, as mentioned above, baptized in the name of Jesus Christ by Charles Parham), and Eldrege Lewis participated in the Apostolic Assembly's convention before visiting the Apostolic Church of Mexico's convention in Terreón, Coahuila. That year the Apostolic Church of Mexico adjusted its name. It had functioned as the "Apostolic Assembly" from 1932 to 1946, but in 1946 it modified its name to the "*Iglesia Apostólica de la Fe en Cristo Jesús*" (Apostolic Church of the Faith in Christ Jesus).

The explosive Apostolic growth among Mexican-Americans and Mexicans and the *sui generis* unity with which both sister churches ministered shocked the UPC's delegation in both conventions. The UPC promptly proposed forming an alliance between the three Apostolic denominations. The agreements of the twenty-third general conference of the UPC in 1947 in Dallas, Texas record how delegations from the three denominations studied, approved, and signed an "Alliance of Friendship

---

24. Constitución de la Asamblea Apostólica, 102.

25. Burgess and McGee, *Dictionary*, 860.

and Brotherhood." The Apostolic Assembly and the Apostolic Church of Mexico from the beginning limited the alliance with the UPC to sharing doctrine, visiting each others' general conventions, cultivating friendly ties, and respecting each other. Any more extensive integration would have perhaps debilitated the vigor with which the denominations, especially the Apostolic Assembly, had grown since their inception.

In 1949, the Apostolic Assembly launched its first foreign missionary effort. Collaborating with the Apostolic Church of Mexico and the UPC for economic support, it sent Leonardo Sepúlveda Treviño to Nicaragua. Since then, the Apostolic Assembly has dedicated itself to missionary work, exploring many countries and intermittently maintaining missionary presence in twenty nations, including Cuba.

The National Apostolic Bible College in Hayward, California came into being toward the end of the 1940s. This step was the Apostolic Assembly's first move towards training ministers and candidates for the ministry. The education program never evolved into a permanent residential school but instead has moved to different locations over the years. In the last decade it has functioned as a non-residential program for which each district shares partial responsibility.

Benjamín Cantú's Leadership (1950–1963)

President Nava, again acting as the prudent visionary on the eve of a new era and new leaders, announced in the 1946 general convention that he would not be a candidate for Bishop President in the 1950 convention. With a statesman's honor, he kept his word. With great love he handed over the responsibility to the new president elect, Benjamín Cantú. The peaceful transition demonstrated the denomination's maturity. The Apostolic Assembly was not a church of chiefs but of institutions. President Nava handed over a healthy, growing, organized church with just over 100 congregations!

The Texan-born Benjamín Cantú, in contrast with Nava who only spoke Spanish, was perfectly bilingual. He represented the arrival of a new generation of leaders who were now by in large Mexican-Americans instead of Mexicans. The presence of a generation born in the United States meant that churches would begin to use English, though slowly at first, in different activities during services, especially in hymns. This tendency continued up through the 1980s when the national youth conventions began utilizing English 100 percent of the time.

The period under Cantú's leadership reflects the economic boom the United States experienced during the 1950s and 60s. Between 1950 and 1963, Cantú dedicated ("dedication" is a special ceremony consecrating a newly built or bought church building) forty-two church buildings throughout the country. Many congregations also bought land for constructing future churches and other buildings. Beautiful church buildings popped up from Texas to California. Throughout these years, the Apostolic Assembly kept planting new churches in the original four states, all of which share a border with Mexico: California, Arizona, New Mexico, and Texas. After 1952, it began working in the Midwest (Chicago) and in Colorado. The attempt to reach the rest of the states in the American Union, though slow, remained a permanent goal.

Leonardo Sepúlveda had successfully initiated the Apostolic Assembly's missionary efforts in Nicaragua in 1949. Four years later, in 1953, Sepúlveda traveled as a pioneer missionary to Uruguay and Argentina where he served for six fruitful years. Lorenzo Salazar, a young minister and the future president of the Assembly, received support in 1952 to serve in Nicaragua. Francisco Gallego later joined him, and these two also served in El Salvador. Later, Daniel Jahuall was sent as a missionary to Nicaragua. He returned to the United States in 1961 to then become a missionary supervisor and serve in Panama and Honduras.

Toward the end of the 1950s, the good relationship between the Assembly and the Apostolic Church of Mexico suffered its first crisis. Both organizations began to develop separate, more defined identities after thirty years of unity. In 1958, the Apostolic Church had witnessed its first transition of presidential leadership from Rivas, who had led the organization since 1932, to Maclovio Gaxiola. The committees that studied the problems between the sister churches at first agreed that from then on, each church would be "free to organize itself as necessary due to the differences in laws and expectations in each country." Yet they ended up agreeing to commit themselves to maintaining the original unity. Toward the end of 1962, the Assembly realized that the differences with the Apostolic Church had "softened," and a new spirit of moving towards each other arose.

Transitions in Leadership

Unexpectedly, at the beginning of 1963, President Cantú resigned due to special circumstances. He had recently been reelected for a fourth four-year term. From then on, he served only as pastor to a flourishing church in Los Angeles. Two factors permitted another peaceful transition. First, the institutional criterion served the denomination well. Former missionary Leonardo Sepúlveda had been elected vice-president, and by constitutional right, he would automatically become the new president upon Cantú's resignation. However, in the period of turbulence, Sepúlveda thought that it would be better for the church if he handed the presidency over to Nava. Many years later, Sepúlveda, at ninety-two years of age, responded to a question about why he had waived his right to be the denomination's president.[26] He answered, "My son, the church is more important than any minister," and that was all. Similar to Nava's manner of thinking with an ecclesial statesman's mindset, Sepúlveda thought on the institutional level; he considered the wellbeing of the organization. Nava's moral stature also helped ease the transition. Respect for this pioneer had grown in the years while he had not been president because of his continued stability, humility, deference to the institutions formed under his leadership, and spotless testimony. Thus, Nava could easily serve again as president from 1963 to 1966.

Three years before he returned to the presidency, Nava had stepped down from pastoring *El Siloé* Church in Los Angeles. Coherent with his convictions about acting in the best interest of the church as a whole, Nava, at age 68, had decided that the best thing for his particular congregation would be a younger pastor. Nava remains a nearly unique example in this action as the Apostolic Assembly's tradition (and one of its weaker points) is to allow many of its ministers to serve as pastors until their deaths.

The Assembly continued to enjoy the economic bonanza of the 1960s in the United States. In his final term, Nava dedicated twenty-four new church buildings, all between 1963 and 1966. Many already-dedicated churches expanded their existing buildings to meet the demands of rapid growth. Apostolic efforts reached four new states, Washington, Oregon, Pennsylvania, and Florida, and the missionary work spread to Costa Rica, Central America, and Italy.

---

26. Leonardo Sepúlveda, unpublished interview, March 2002.

The Apostolic Church of Mexico elected former leader Felipe Rivas to be president again from 1962 to 1966. By coincidence, the two pioneer presidents found themselves working together one more time in what would be each one's final term. This coincidence created a more favorable environment for the sister denominations to draw closer to each other again. After a period of committee work, on March 18, 1965, leaders of these sister churches signed a second Agreement on Unity and Fellowship. Furthermore, in the Apostolic Church of Mexico's jubilee service on October 7, 1964, Nava was honored with a diploma of recognition for his forty-eight years of service to the Assembly in the United States. The Apostolic Church said Nava "had benefited the Mexican community in that country" whenever he preached the gospel in the United States.[27]

During Nava's last administration the Assembly celebrated its fiftieth anniversary. It recognized 1916 as the year in which the pioneers Llorente, Nava, and Marcial de la Cruz joined each other in the work of God that became the Apostolic Assembly. Perhaps a more appropriate date would have been 1909 when Luis López became the first Mexican to be baptized in the name of Jesus Christ. López remained a member of the Assembly until his death. Regardless, the Assembly set aside the last week of December 1966 in Phoenix, Arizona to celebrate the jubilee. The denomination's history since 1906 on Azusa Street was published. Edmund G. Brown, the governor of California, wrote a letter congratulating the church and recognizing the "many significant contributions the Mexican-American community of California has made to the state." His letter became the prologue to the little volume of history. At the end of the jubilee celebrations, the Assembly elected a new president. Nava bid farewell and handed over nearly 250 Apostolic Assembly congregations in the United States to the new leader.

Efraín Valverde, the new president-elect, had moved from his home state of California to Tijuana in Mexico with his family in 1931 during the Great Depression. The son and grandson of Baptists, he converted to Apostolic doctrine in 1949 and soon became a minister in the Apostolic Church of Mexico. He served as a national leader in the men's ministry, as pastor, and as an assistant elder. Later, following a pattern dating back to Miguelito García in 1922 in which pastors were transferred across the border, Valverde immigrated back to the United States in 1958 and was

---

27. Gaxiola López, *Historia*, 291.

received by and incorporated as a pastor in the Apostolic Assembly. Years later, he would be elected supervising bishop in Northern California.

Towards the end of the 1960s, the members of the board of general directors which assisted Valverde concluded that, because of several specific problems with his leadership, they should not reelect him. The general convention of 1970, held a few months early and with Antonio C. Nava's moral support, did not reelect Valverde as president. Valverde reacted by creating an unsuccessful division. His final step was to sue the Assembly. This suit has posed the greatest legal trial the Apostolic Assembly has confronted to date. The strength of the Assembly's constitution held up in court. Based on the constitution, the judge weighted his verdict in total favor of the Apostolic Assembly. Valverde continued ministering independently in Salinas, California in conjunction with other independent Apostolic congregations.

A Period of Stability, 1970–1978

Lorenzo Salazar, from Pasadena, California, replaced Valverde as Bishop President in 1970. A former missionary and a notable and prolific composer of eighty-eight hymns both in English and in Spanish, Salazar was part of the generation who had studied during their youth in United Pentecostal Church colleges. This affable Apostolic gentleman guided the Assembly through a period of stability and was reelected in 1974. From that point on, new constitutional rules limit members of the board of general directors and supervising bishops to one reelection. In order to return to the same position, leaders have to pass at least one term, or four years, outside of that position. Under Salazar's administration, the Assembly acquired its first general offices, located in eastern Los Angeles, and took over the printing of its own materials. In that period a common phrase was "Don't read church history; make it!"[28] Even so, at the end of the 1980s Salazar had "read enough church history" to earn his Master of Arts in Theology from Fuller Theological Seminary.

The election of Lorenzo Salazar shows a subtle change in the mentality of Apostolic pastors. The most difficult stage of foundation and consolidation, in which men like Nava and Cantú with solid character had played important roles, ended. However, in the new stage of having hundreds of churches and greater diversity, the Assembly realized the

---

28. Salazar, *My Story*, 25.

need for more charismatic and conciliatory leadership. This leadership change was apparent not only in Salazar's election and reelection but also in the choice of the next president.

Charisma for an Increasingly More Diverse Church

Baldemar Rodríguez was born in 1941 in Rio Grande Valley, Texas. As he grew older, he and his brothers formed the musical group "*Los hermanos Rodríguez de Santa Rosa*" and even made television appearances. During one of these musical trips, the family's father, Don Luis, suddenly died. His unexpected death led the young Baldemar to give his life to the Lord Jesus in February of 1961. Upon his conversion, Rodríguez initiated a prolific and still active career as a hymn composer.[29] Several of his hymns are already "classics" within the Apostolic context. From Francisco Llorente to Manuel Vizcarra, every Assembly president has been a hymn composer. Lorenzo Salazar and Baldemar Rodríguez stand out in particular. For years the joke was that writing hymns was an unspoken requirement to become Bishop President.

Since the end of the 1960s the Assembly had felt the impact of important changes in the flow of immigration. On the one hand, the wave of both documented and undocumented Mexican immigrants grew in number every year. This reality made it impossible for nearly any of the Hispanic Apostolic congregations to make the perhaps natural and logical transition toward English in their ecclesial life. On the other hand, though, the generations of children, adolescents, and young adults who had been born in the United States made the challenge of transitioning to English more urgent. Furthermore, political conflicts in Central America created a new and enormous migratory flood of Salvadorans and Nicaraguans.

Rodríguez, demonstrating his quality as president, began ministering bilingually despite being advised to the contrary. Soon, and especially in the long run, his intuition proved perceptive and accurately reflective of what the Assembly needed: a charismatic leader for an ever more diverse church. The Assembly kept developing smoothly along its institutional trajectory, expanding in every area. By 1986, the denomination had grown to more than 400 churches.

---

29. Rodríguez, *Antología*, 17.

Baldemar Rodríguez's reelection in 1982 cemented a practice in the Assembly: from 1970 to 2006, all the presidents have served two consecutive terms. While this practice points to the fact that the presidents serving have been men of respectable spiritual prestige, it also demonstrates the desire of the Assembly's pastors to maintain a stable leadership even when stability means that their plans for change happen more slowly. This practice of reelection greatly contrasts to the Apostolic Church of Mexico. The sister church has not reelected any president for two continuous terms since 1958. An aspect of Mexican culture, the political slogan "Effective Suffrage, no Reelection," has left its mark on the church.

AN INSTITUTIONAL PRESIDENCY, 1986–1994

The Apostolic Assembly is a church of passionate preachers, gifted evangelists, and dynamic, lively services. Thus, when the Assembly's pastors elect one of their most serious and formal ministers to be president, the preference for stability in leadership proves even more dramatic. This priority on stability stands out in the presidency of Manuel Vizcarra, a formal yet affable man elected after a long career of service to God's work. Though born in Chihuahua, Mexico in 1924, Vizcarra spent his childhood and adolescence in the United States. His family converted to the Apostolic message when the minister Juan Amaya prayed for Vizcarra's ill mother and she was immediately healed. Vizcarra returned to Mexico and developed an extensive career in the Apostolic Church of Mexico as pastor, auxiliary elder, and a young member of the board of directors. When he decided to return to the United States, Vizcarra served in every level of the denomination: pastor, auxiliary elder, supervising bishop, and member of the board of general directors. A wise man with a clean testimony, he used to say, "I grew old very young" in reference to the sober, formal, and serious personality that marked him since his youth. He always handled the things of God with great caution and care.

President Vizcarra utilized his visionary persistence to push for the purchase of new general office facilities. Overcoming an initial setback, the Assembly bought the building still currently used in Rancho Cucamonga (in the county of San Bernardino, CA). The property's initial value approached two million dollars, but the Assembly secured it for half that price.

During President Vizcarra's second term, the Assembly's relationship with the Apostolic Church of Mexico almost completely dissolved. For several years relations had been deteriorating. Up through the 1980s the Assembly accepted that the Church of Mexico could plant churches in the United States which would later be incorporated into the Assembly, and vice versa (that is, churches that the Assembly planted in Mexico would be incorporated into the Apostolic Church). However, President Reyes of the Apostolic Church of Mexico decided in 1990 to seek independent legal status for the congregations that the Apostolic Church had planted in the United States. His decision led to the crisis in relations. The Apostolic Assembly, after waiting a few years, also decided to give independent legal status to the congregations it had established in Mexico. The creation of legal status also implied the creation of two new organizations. Future Apostolics in both the United States and Mexico will probably look back on this display of force, the brandishing of the tool of new legal entities, as a short-sighted solution to a complex problem. The "solution" will most likely end up multiplying the difficulties since the challenge now is to cultivate a relationship not just between two sister churches but between four distinct organizations.

Also in this time period, the Apostolic Assembly of Canada acquired legal status. Apostolic ministry in the United States spread to nine new states, and the Assembly established a retirement fund for pastors. Furthermore, it embarked on the ambitious project of creating the A. C. Nava Trust Fund. The board of general directors' summary of 1994 reported 431 churches in the United States and 49,060 members.

A Charismatic President Once Again, 1994–2002

In an act comparable only to the presidency of Benjamín Cantú, Baldemar Rodríguez was again elected and reelected president in 1994 and 2002, making a total of four terms. His warm charisma and evident people-skills undoubtedly influenced the Assembly in its choice of leader. Pastors once again wanted to trust the destiny of the church to this conciliatory, ever-smiling man whose leadership radiated stability. By the time of his third term, Rodríguez had earned his Masters of Arts from Fuller Theological Seminary's Hispanic program. Many Apostolic leaders and pastors had completed theological studies at Fuller since the beginning of the 1980s.

Los Evangélicos

The Apostolic Assembly in the Twenty-First Century

In November of 2002, the Assembly elected Daniel Sánchez, a pastor's son from California, to be Bishop President. A minister who has run the gamut of institutional positions (pastor, auxiliary elder, supervising bishop, member of the board of general directors), Sánchez also made three important contributions when he served as secretary of social welfare: 1) organizing retirement funds for pastors in every local church; 2) creating the A. C. Nava Trust Fund; 3) producing and recording the video "Nuestro Canto" ("Our Song") which recaps, in an audiovisual format, the Apostolic Assembly's rich hymnology. Interesting historical references and theological reflections are interspersed throughout the video. Dr. Harvey Cox, a Harvard University professor who has spent the past few years studying the Pentecostal movement, wrote the video's script. From the beginnings of his presidency, Sánchez has pushed to clarify and redefine the Apostolic Assembly's mission. The slogan, "Exalt Christ, Equip the Church, Evangelize the World!" outlines his particular emphases.

In 2004 the Apostolic Assembly of the Faith in Christ Jesus in the United States of America reported the following statistics:

52,000	Adult baptized members
80,000	Members, including baptized adults, children, and adolescents
700	Local churches in 44 states
27	Districts (or dioceses) supervised by bishops and one national missions program for the states which have no organized district
3,200	Ordained ministers
1,900	Deacons or other people training for ministry
250	Church buildings, with a total value of 200 million dollars

Outside the continental United States, as of 2004, the Apostolic Assembly reported nineteen missionary projects: two in Europe (Italy and Spain); three in Central America (Panama, Honduras, and Costa Rica); nine in South America (Argentina, Uruguay, Chile, Paraguay, Venezuela, Columbia, Peru, Brazil, and Bolivia); two in the Caribbean (the Dominican Republic and Puerto Rico); and in Mexico, Canada, and Hawaii. These missionary projects reported the following statistics:

31,000	Adult baptized members
50,000	Members, including children, adolescents, and baptized adults
19	Missionaries
600	Congregations
800	Ministers and deacons
300	Church buildings

FUTURE CHALLENGES FOR THE APOSTOLIC ASSEMBLY

In the twenty-first century, the Assembly's first challenge is to be an inclusive church. The Apostolic Assembly needs to learn not only how to be a church for Mexicans and Mexican-Americans but also how to be a church open to the participation and leadership of our ever-more-numerous Central American, South American, and Caribbean brothers and sisters, not to mention cross-cultural marriages and people of all races. We need to get out of our little neighborhoods and reach the world knocking on our front door.

We also need to be inclusive in terms of language. There is no easy solution to the complicated Spanish/English dilemma. The situation's complexity owes largely to the fact that, for many Hispanics, language is a choice instead of a problem. Thus, on the one hand, an immigrant freshly arrived from Oaxaca or Santa Tecla may decide to forget Spanish and to fully embrace English as his new and his only language. On the other hand, a Hispanic who is a fifth-generation United States citizen may not care how many "English Only" programs the government implements, but she may insist until the day she dies, as did her great-great-grandmother, that church services should be held only in Spanish. The Assembly's challenge is to be inclusive in such a way that both extremes and everyone in the middle have a place in the pew or the pulpit.

The second key challenge lies in missionological clarity. The Assembly needs to recover a healthy evangelistic emphasis. We are a church called to proclaim the gospel of the Kingdom of God. In the Apostolic movement in general, over the years, national, district, and sectional activities tend to sour with *koinonitis*. We so enjoy fellowshipping together and hearing about how great our congregation is that we end up forgetting the energy that birthed us, the work to which God has called us: reaching the millions of lost men and women for whom Christ died.

Expanding diaconal ministries and deepening the church's prophetic voice are also crucial next steps. The Apostolic Assembly is a church of immigrants, yet we hardly ever speak publicly in favor of the thousands of undocumented immigrants that make up our congregations. Our presence is scarce in town halls to denounce abortion clinics where, every year, millions of innocent humans are dismembered in one of the most horrible and premeditated crimes, abortion. We preach passionately at a drunkard, but we have nothing to say to the colossal economic interests of the alcohol, tobacco, and casino industries. Of course we should keep praying for divine healings, but we should also fight on behalf of the thousands of laborers in our churches whose employee benefits do not include health insurance. We have to follow the Lord who not only restored individual sinners but also spoke out against the tradition of the elders. The elders had built an elaborate web of "structural sin,"[30] a perverse system that enchained generations and both deformed and trained entire institutions in doing evil.

A third challenge for the twenty-first century includes pastoral care of the family. It is a sick exaggeration to boast that "family is really important" to Hispanics. Domestic violence is one of the top ten causes of death among Hispanics. This fact is a true shame that reveals the great need to minister in this area.

The phenomenon of gangs demonstrates the extensive and profound dysfunction rampant in thousands and thousands of Latino families. Migration is particularly hard on the family, and the initial overcompensation and then subsequent swing to the opposite extreme (an impact on values because of migration, common to any race), causes the disintegration of many Hispanic families. Gangs are a dysfunctional response to dysfunctional families. A new generation of Hispanic businessmen and women insists that one of the secrets for success in Hispanic businesses is placing maximum priority on the family.[31] If family is a priority for success in business, how much more should family be a priority in Christian ministry and in pastoral care of the congregations!

---

30. Villafañe, *Espíritu liberador*, 173.

31. Failde, *Éxito latino*, 233.

Developing an efficient model of education for our pastors is the fourth challenge. Pentecostals "naturally" tend to be anti-intellectual. We are inclined to distrust our brains since the Pentecostal fire in our hearts burns so pleasantly. Furthermore, many Apostolic pastors without academic credentials have had great success in planting churches. Therefore, many wonder if we really need better theological preparation after all. Besides, what we have observed in the traditional models of seminaries belonging to historical denominations keeps us thinking, as Wagner put it, that a *seminary* is more often a *cemetery*.[32]

However, we do desperately need efficient models of education that emphasize whatever is instrumental in the training of our pastors. At the same time, Apostolics should heed Ralph Winter's advice and avoid the error several Protestant denominations have fallen into. These denominations invested millions of dollars in building schools and Bible colleges without appropriate accreditation only to find themselves, after many wasted years, obligated by reality to develop accredited programs.

Our fifth challenge has to do with our rising economic status. Given the upward social mobility experienced by every Christian denomination in the United States, we must remain faithful to preaching the gospel to the sector from which the Lord raised the Apostolic Assembly: the simple workers, the poor field laborers, and the new immigrants, many of whom are undocumented. We must keep bringing them the gospel's holistic blessing since we do not love the poor in order to keep them poor, as Douglas Petersen writes.[33] Realistically, the Apostolic Assembly is an important vehicle of social change. God calls us to minister in a holistic manner, to minister spiritual health, emotional health, physical health, and social health.

These challenges spell out a vision for a vibrant, growing ministry as we, the Apostolic Assembly, approach our second century of ministering, a second century of reclaiming the enthusiasm and fire of our spiritual ancestors in the Azusa Street revival.

---

32. Wagner, *Churchquake*, 224.
33. See Petersen, *Not by Might*, 186–233.

5

The Evangelical Free Church of America

Lindy Scott

THE EVANGELICAL FREE CHURCH of America (EFCA) is a mid-sized
denomination of approximately 1,300 congregations throughout the
United States. In the past three decades, the church has experienced a
notable 6 to 10 percent annual growth. While not considered to be an extreme fundamentalist denomination, the EFCA is a Protestant Evangelical
church with a conservative theology.[1] The denomination began in the
United States in the nineteenth century when Scandinavian immigrants
from Sweden, Norway, and Denmark arrived. These "free Christians" had
already separated from the state church, the Lutheran church, in their
home countries. Maintaining this spirit of independence in the United
States, the immigrants formed two decentralized associations of autono-
mous congregations, one Swedish-language association and the other
Norwegian. Many of their local churches refused to "North Americanize"
and thus stayed loyal to the customs and language of their home countries for the first three decades after their arrival. However, after World
War I, the second- and third-generation immigrants preferred to hold
services and other ministry activities principally in English. Little by little,
services in the Scandinavian languages disappeared,[2] and eventually the
two decentralized associations united into one denomination, the EFCA.

---

1. This important distinction shows up in many areas. For example, fundamentalism
is generally characterized by academic and social isolation and theological rigidity. Yet
the EFCA sponsors Trinity International University. The vast majority of Trinity professors have academic doctoral degrees from secular universities. Furthermore, more than
half of Trinity's professors and students come from ecclesiastical traditions other than
the EFCA (Baptists, Presbyterians, Methodists, etc., to name a few).

2. The church's publications reflect this process of "North Americanization." The

Before the 1980s, the EFCA exerted little effort to reach Latinos. There were fewer than five Latino congregations in the entire denomination. The denomination seemed to be waiting for the Latinos to little by little "North Americanize" until they would become regular members just like the other immigrants (for example, like the Swiss-Americans, Norwegian-Americans, Polish-Americans, etc.).[3] Yet the United States' "Melting Pot" has become a "mosaic," especially in the last twenty-five years. A multicultural environment now permits ethnic churches to flourish and to maintain their own particular characteristics, including their own language. The EFCA now has many churches that minister exclusively in languages that are not English, such as Korean, Arabic, Norwegian, Japanese, Chinese, and, of course, Spanish. Furthermore, many "American" EFCA churches have begun offering specialized ministries to immigrants in their native language. The EFCA currently has over sixty Spanish-speaking congregations, the majority of which are clustered in metropolitan Chicago, in California, and in southern Texas.[4]

THE BEGINNINGS

The first wave of Latino EFCA churches began in response to the initiative of English-speaking churches that recognized the need to evangelize the growing Latino population around them. One of the first Latino EFCA churches, the Latino Evangelical Free Church of Brooklyn, New York, existed alongside the English-speaking church in the mid-1960s. Edelmiro Feliciano pastored the Latino church for several years, and under subsequent pastor Rafael Puente's leadership the church grew to offer a variety of ministries.

The oldest Latino EFCA church in Chicago began as a ministry of Salem Evangelical Free Church, located in the Humboldt Park neighbor-

denominational magazine, *The Evangelical Beacon*, was launched in English in 1931 while the denomination's Swedish magazine, *Chicago-Bladet*, gradually declined and finally ceased publication in 1952.

3. A considerable number of Latinos have, in fact, experienced this phenomenon. For example, Luis Díaz, a third-generation Mexican-American, converted to the Protestant faith in California where he also completed his undergraduate and theological studies. For many years he pastored one of the largest churches in the denomination, the Wheaton Evangelical Free Church.

4. In 1996 and 1997 the author carried out unpublished interviews with pastors and leaders in Latino EFCA churches in the Chicago metropolitan area. The case studies that follow arise from those interviews. All statistics given are accurate as of 2002.

hood on the northwest side of the city. Salem, founded in the nineteenth century, used to hold services in Norwegian, but, as time passed, the church began offering services in English as well. With the 1960s white flight to the suburbs, other immigrant groups moved into the neighborhood. Salem began a third congregation in Arabic to reach immigrants who came mainly from Jordan. The neighborhood turned more and more Latino, especially Puerto Rican. In 1971 the English-speaking pastor Torrey Lindland invited professor Luis Resera to launch a ministry in Spanish. The English-speaking congregation supported the Latino project with materials and a salary for Resera. Throughout the 1970s, the Latino congregation grew to the point of becoming independent and affiliating with the EFCA on its own accord. Interestingly enough, in 1973 the English-speaking congregation called a bilingual Latino, Manuel Ortiz, to be its pastor. At about the same time the Latino congregation called Doug Moore, a bilingual minister who had grown up in Chile in a missionary family and then studied at Trinity Evangelical Divinity School, to be its pastor. Both the English and the Spanish churches continue to function independently with some ministries in common. The Latino congregation generally has a Sunday attendance of some eighty-five participants, with some twenty other Latinos attending the English-speaking church. Furthermore, some of its members have returned to their home states of Oaxaca and Guerrero in Mexico and have planted Evangelical Free churches there.

Three Different Models of Ministry
among Latinos: Chicago as a Case Study

The second wave of ministry among and by Latinos in the EFCA began in the 1980s. On the one hand, some English-speaking local churches showed increased interest in intentionally opening new doors into the Latino community. On the other hand, some independent (principally Mexican) congregations approached English-speaking EFCA churches seeking ways to work together in joint ministries. Three different models have arisen: 1) churches with totally Latino roots; 2) churches with mixed (both Latino and non-Latino) leadership; 3) "mission" churches founded by non-Latinos.

The Chicago area has been one of the most prolific areas for Latino congregations. Fifty-two EFCA churches fall within the greater Chicago metropolitan area. Of these congregations, fifteen have developed significant ministries among Latinos, nearly all of which have sprung up in the past twenty-five years.[5]

Churches with Latino Roots

Congregations that have followed the model of having Latino leadership from the beginning have seen the most success in terms of numerical growth. In the majority of the cases, a small nucleus of independent Latino Evangelicals together with their own pastor approach an English-speaking EFCA church with the hopes of renting part of the church building in order to hold public services in Spanish. They bring their own established style; they have their own music, literature, and internal organization. At the beginning, the relationship between the two churches consists merely of a rental contract. As time passes and if the two congregations get along well, they begin to work more closely together. Sometimes the Latino congregation decides to become affiliated with the EFCA.

The Evangelical Free Church of Wheeling, a suburb twenty miles north of Chicago with a considerable Latino population, provides the clearest example of this model. In 1983, Pastor Modesto Maya, of Mexican nationality, secured the rental of the English-speaking church's multipurpose room in order to hold services in Spanish. His congregation grew to the point that in 1986 the Latino church sought affiliation with the EFCA denomination, and Maya trained for ordination as an EFCA minister. In 1990, he handed the pastoral responsibilities over to a member of the Latino congregation, Florencio Carbajal. Maya moved to plant another Latino church in conjunction with the Evangelical Free Church of Franklin Park, a suburb northwest of Chicago. Sunday attendance at the Latino EFCA church in Wheeling grew to about 150 people, according to 1996 statistics.[6] The English-speaking congregation in Franklin Park dissolved due to declining membership, but the Latino congregation there, under Maya's leadership, flourished.

In the mid-1980s, Carlos Guadagno, a Latin American seminary student (Salvadoran on his mother's side and Italian on his father's) founded

---

5. See my chapter "La conversión de inmigrantes" in *Fronteras fragmentadas,* 415–17.

6. This community effort received eager promotion at the denominational level in the EFCA's following national conference. It was held up as an example to be imitated by other churches in the denomination.

a Latino church in Rolling Meadows, a suburb northwest of O'Hare airport. The church started as a home-based Bible study and grew to rent space for meetings first from a daycare facility and later from a non-denominational church. Around 150 people, most of them Mexicans, currently make up the congregation. The church emphasizes evangelism but has very little social ministry. According to the pastor, the testimony and love demonstrated by these Latino Christians is what has persuaded the majority of the church's new converts to come to faith. The church planted two new congregations in the late 1990s. Severiano Román, who served as youth pastor in the mother church in Rolling Meadows, planted the first new church in Wauconda, a town further to the northwest. Abel Flores started the second new church even further to the north, in Round Lake. Both of these new congregations began by renting space from English-speaking Evangelical Free churches in their respective towns.

In 1989 an independent pastor, Roberto Cambrany, fleshed out his dream to start a Latino church and rented the social room of the Evangelical Free Church of Libertyville, a town thirty miles northwest of Chicago. Cambrany had gotten to know a handful of people in this congregation through English classes that the church offered as a social service to the community. Following a process similar to that of the churches mentioned before, this Latino church grew on its own accord. Several years ago the Latino and the English-speaking EFCA congregations in Libertyville began to develop closer ties of friendship. Pastor Cambrany received his ordination in the EFCA in 1996. Two days a week the two churches began offering a joint tutoring service called "*Aprender Jugando*" ("Learn by Playing") to young Latinos in the community. The Latino church's story made it to the national level in the October 1996 edition of *The Evangelical Beacon*. The denomination was intentionally trying to persuade its English-speaking members to be more open to Latinos and to other immigrants.

The dynamism in this type of Latino church is quite apparent. Over the years, the Latino church in Wheeling has commissioned three teams to plant daughter churches in the metropolitan Chicago area. For a while, Pastor Maya led a Bible institute in Spanish for training new pastors. The three teams just mentioned, along with other Latinos hoping to start new churches, trained under Maya.

Addison, a suburb ten miles west of Chicago, hosts one of the daughter churches planted by a team from Wheeling. Esteban Hernández, a member of the Latino EFCA church in Wheeling, asked to rent space from the Evangelical Free Church of Addison in order to hold services in Spanish. The English-speaking church, which had already been looking for a way to reach out to its Latino neighbors, eagerly agreed. Within two years the Latino congregation grew large enough to affiliate with the EFCA under the name *Iglesia Maranatha* (Maranatha Church).

At the same time, Pedro Terán and his wife, also "graduates" of the Latino church in Wheeling, approached Grace Evangelical Free Church, a small English-speaking congregation in North Chicago. They agreed to share building space. The Latino congregation grew and became *Iglesia Fuente de Vida* (Fountain of Life Church) and later affiliated with the EFCA.

Mixed Leadership Churches
(started by a combination of Latino and non-Latino leadership)

The second model of ministry among and by Latinos begins with a degree of Latino leadership but generally develops at the initiative of a non-Latino church that recognizes the need to evangelize the growing Latino population in its community. The previously mentioned Salem Church belongs in this category.

The First Evangelical Free Church (EFC) of Chicago, located on 5255 N. Ashland in the northern section of Chicago, provides another example. Toward the beginning of the 1980s, the English-speaking church called Marcos Wittig, a seminary student who had grown up in Colombia as a missionary kid, to begin a ministry in the Spanish language. The project initially enjoyed great success but never grew large enough to become an independent church. Subsequent pastors in this Hispanic ministry included a former missionary to Venezuela and a Venezuelan seminary student. Nevertheless, in the late 1990s, the leadership of the First EFC concluded that the Latino ministry was not going to survive, and they decided to close down the Latino outreach.

The Evangelical Free Church in Des Plaines, a suburb fifteen miles northwest of Chicago, began a ministry among Latinos (and another among Japanese) in 1985 under the joint leadership of a Venezuelan couple studying at the Trinity seminary and of the senior pastor of the Des Plaines EFC who had served as a missionary in Mexico for several years. The English-speaking congregation supported the outreach initiative by offering English classes and classes on citizenship. The EFC in Des Plaines never intended to plant a separate Latino church but instead sought to foster a Latino ministry within its congregation that was experiencing a growing ethnic diversity. After the pastor and the seminary students moved to other cities, the church continued offering English classes for Latinos. A few Latino families currently participate in the English-speaking church. Others are involved in a new Spanish-speaking congregation that rents space from the Des Plaines EFC in a fashion similar to the first model.

In 1994, the Evangelical Free Church in Bensenville (south of O'Hare airport) launched an evangelization outreach to Latinos in its community. Two years later, the Mexican couple Ricardo and Josefina Palmerín came to study at Northern Baptist Theological Seminary, and they provided the necessary pastoral leadership to solidify the Bensenville EFC's efforts. In less than a year, the fledgling congregation grew to a weekly attendance of more than fifty people. Pastor Palmerín, on top of his pastoral work with this congregation, also served as a district-level advisor in the area of planting and caring for Latino churches.

Latino Churches Begun and Pastored by non-Latinos

The third model of ministry, Hispanic churches initiated by non-Latinos, has experienced little numerical success in the EFCA. In 1986 a US American couple attempted to plant a Latino church in Pilsen, a Mexican neighborhood close to Chicago's downtown area. In 1991, a young man who had been a missionary in Mexico returned to Chicago to assist the couple. Despite valiant efforts to identify with the Mexican community, the Caucasian leadership never succeeded in making the church plant successful. Finally in 1995, the Great Lakes District of the EFCA gave additional support to the struggling congregation and together they extended an invitation to a Mexican pastor, Carlos Ocampo, to see if he could fortify the weak Latino church. Indeed, the church began seeing solid, steady growth under Ocampo's leadership.

GROWTH FACTORS

Latino leadership is the determining growth factor for Latino EFCA churches in the metropolitan Chicago area. The eight churches presented above that were founded principally by Latino leadership (Wheeling, Libertyville, Addison, Franklin Park, Rolling Meadows, Wauconda,

Round Lake, and *Fuente de Vida*) have prospered and continue to grow. These congregations have not had to struggle as much to contextualize the gospel message. The leaders have faced the same problems as their members (for example, lack of legal documentation, employment problems, discrimination, difficulty with a new language, scarcity of economic resources, etc.) and, therefore, can closely identify with the Latino community they serve. This difference shows up even between churches of the first model and those of the second. Though leadership under the second model is partially Latino, often the leaders are seminary graduates with a lifestyle distanced from that of the church members (for example, they enjoy a higher level of education, are "legal," etc.).

The "silent but significant" contribution of women figures as another important factor in the growth of the churches. In EFCA churches in general, and particularly in Latino EFCA churches, women do not have many formal leadership roles. However, in any number of churches, the women are the ones who carry out much of the evangelization, discipleship, counseling, prayer, and mutual care. These activities facilitate the congregation's growth and wellbeing. Owing to the fact that the majority of Latino church members (60 to 70 percent) are women, and that many of these women depend more on the church than on their husbands for caring for their families (due to their husbands' machismo, absenteeism, alcoholism, etc.), the pastor's wife ends up functioning as another unofficial pastor, especially in ministering to the women in the congregation.

Evangelization carried out by the members themselves also influences the Latino churches' growth. These congregations teach and practice that every Christian has the responsibility and privilege of evangelizing others. The churches studied here prepare their members to carry out this ministry. Interviews in these churches reveal that between 50 and 90 percent of the new converts in each church were attracted to the Protestant faith not because of the pastor or the church's official programs but through the love and witness of common, ordinary church members.

Perhaps surprisingly, the support of the English-speaking congregations has impacted the Latino churches' growth less than the other factors discussed. When this support has been excessive and initiated by the English speakers, Latinos have not had the opportunity to take ownership of the responsibility and leadership required to sustain the church. In such cases the Latino church has died out or struggled (for example, First Evangelical Free Church of Chicago and Des Plaines Evangelical

Free Church, respectively). The best combination seems to be a strong Latino initiative backed by the secondary support of an English-speaking congregation. English classes, courses on citizenship, educational and youth ministries, and events held in conjunction with the English-speaking congregation provide a welcoming and accepting environment that contrasts with the rejection and discrimination Latinos generally face in the larger English-speaking society. Interviews carried out with Latinos to determine why they join Protestant churches demonstrate that the most important factor is the influence of the Latino Christians, not the ministries and programs offered by the English-speaking Christians.

A further noteworthy growth element has to do with the geographical location of the churches. That the most successful churches have been those located in the suburbs perhaps owes to the following factors:

1. A higher percentage of the suburban population (in comparison to the population of Chicago) is Protestant and active in church; the possibility is greater in the suburbs, then, that Latinos come into contact with and form friendships with Protestants (both Latino and non-Latino Protestants, especially through youth ministries like AWANA).

2. The Catholic church is stronger in Chicago (around 70 percent of Chicago's population is Catholic, at least nominally) and exercises a larger traditional influence over those who live in the city; in contrast, the individualism (each person has his or her own car) and the relative anonymity found in the suburbs permit Latinos to more easily leave their traditional Catholicism for the Protestant faith.

3. Latino neighborhoods in Chicago are often considered entryways instead of fertile ground to plant long-lasting roots; Latinos generally want to establish themselves in the suburbs, and belonging to a Protestant church that offers ministries for their children is very attractive to young Latino families.

4. The suburbs offer more jobs and, therefore, more money that can enter the church via tithes and offerings, thus enabling suburban Latino churches to become self-sustaining more quickly.

THE REST OF THE COUNTRY

Other areas of the United States demonstrate trends that are similar to those of the EFCA in Chicago. Southern California and the state of Texas are the regions experiencing the most rapid growth of Latino EFCA churches.

In April of 1983 the First Evangelical Free Church of Los Angeles invited Doug and Connie Moore to transfer from Chicago to pastor their congregation. The church realized that demographic changes had dramatically altered its surrounding neighborhood. As fast as English speakers moved out, Mexicans and Central Americans moved in. Therefore, in 1983, the Moores launched a Spanish-language Sunday school and Bible studies. The overwhelmingly positive response encouraged the church to hold worship services in Spanish as well. The Latino congregation grew to nearly 200 participants. As part of a holistic ministry, the church began offering English classes to facilitate the wellbeing of Latinos as they adapted to English-speaking life. These classes blossomed into one of the church's most successful ministries, at one point averaging a daily attendance of 240 students. The Latino congregation's success also owes to the participation of Protestant students in the church's tutoring ministry. University students from Biola, the Master's College, and the University of Southern California's InterVarsity campus group dedicated many hours of service as teachers and tutors to the neighborhood's children and adolescents. These tutors visited the children in their homes and helped them with their school work. Pastor Moore acknowledges that this direct contact with the families has been one of the most tangible signs of God's love demonstrated by the church and, as a result, one of the most important factors in the church's growth.

Coachella Valley, California hosts another Latino EFCA church. The missionary Paul Young of Central American Mission, International, planted the Spanish-language Evangelical Free Church of Coachella Valley in 1986. Young ministered for seven years in the church before Osvaldo Silveira became the first Latino pastor and the congregation's first fulltime minister. Eighteen months later, Pastor Raúl García replaced Silveira, and Rogelio Caballero later succeeded him.

The EFCA's Southern California District has taken various initiatives to plant Latino churches. Beginning in July of 1996, the district employed Osvaldo Silveira as a missionary to plant Latino churches. Silveira began collaboratating with Grace Evangelical Free Church's Latino ministry.

Don Smith, pastor of Laguna Hills Evangelical Free Church, has also supported the founding of Latino ministries in various congregations.

The District of Southern Texas has witnessed joint efforts between Latino Evangelical Free churches in the United States and Evangelical Free churches of Mexico.[7] For example, Bob Rowley, pastor of the Evangelical Free Church of Laredo, has promoted visits and exchanges of literature and other aids between churches on both sides of the Rio Bravo for over fifteen years. Furthermore, Mexican church leaders have participated at times in the ordination examinations for pastors in Texas. These types of interactions have enriched the churches in both countries.

Southern Florida offers other examples of innovative Latino EFCA projects. For example, English-speaking churches in the region asked the EFCA's Foreign Missions Department for help in founding a new kind of Latino church in Miami. Under the leadership of Guatemalan pastor Enrique Fernández, an international team planted the *Iglesia Evangélica Libre La Viña del Señor* in 1991. The church set out to emphasize the unique ministry of each member and participation in cell groups.

Miramar Evangelical Free Church has also charted new territory in Miami. This English-speaking church has walked alongside the development of a new congregation made up almost entirely of immigrants from the Dominican Republic. The church relied heavily on the help of a retired missionary, Mr. Anderson, who had served several decades as an EFCA missionary to Venezuela.

Intentional Changes in the Denomination

In the last few decades the Evangelical Free Church of America has taken some small, intentional steps in relation to ministry among Latinos. The most significant step was in response to California's Proposition 187, approved in the November 1994 state elections. This legislation limited educational and medical services available to undocumented immigrants. To understand the significance of the EFCA's action requires briefly reviewing the denomination's demographics and history. The majority of the EFCA's membership is currently made up of midwestern farmers or middle-class Caucasians living in small towns or suburbs. These

---

7. Evangelical Free churches have existed in Mexico since 1988. Currently some twenty churches are grouped together in the Fraternity of Evangelical Free Churches of Mexico (FIEL).

geographic and economic factors indicate a membership more attracted to the Republican Party. Furthermore, the EFCA's social conscience, expressed in resolutions called "Social Concerns" approved in their annual conferences, reflects an ideology located on the conservative side of the political spectrum. Regarding abortion, homosexuality, the arms race, prayer in schools, reducing the government's role in citizens' lives, euthanasia, the right to bear arms, and other issues, the EFCA solidly lands in the camp of the Republican Party's Religious Right. An estimated 70 to 85 percent of the EFCA's members regularly vote for the Republican Party. The EFCA would be expected, then, to support the Republican Party's anti-immigrant sentiment as succinctly expressed in California's Proposal 187 and other legislation throughout the country.

Nevertheless, the EFCA took a pro-immigrant stance in contrast with the Republican position. In the 1996 Annual Congress, held in Des Moines, Iowa, EFCA delegates unanimously approved the resolution "A Stranger at our Gates: A Christian Perspective on Immigration" (later published in the denomination's magazine *The Evangelical Beacon*).[8] The content rings out with a prophetic voice not frequently heard in the EFCA. Five biblical principles defending immigrants begin the resolution; the statement then develops a critique of US immigration policies, accusing the country of being motivated more by racism and materialism than by a supposed compassion. Later it refutes the most common criticisms leveled against foreigners (taking jobs away from US citizens, taking advantage of the welfare system, etc.). A long list of questions for self-reflection concludes the resolution. These questions raise critiques against Proposition 187, materialism, racism, and the politics of transnational companies and the US government.

Where did this perspective of openness to immigrants come from? It did not develop overnight. Certain historical factors help to explain this pro-immigrant platform.

1. The EFCA began as a denomination of immigrants. Enough historical memory remains to still positively influence the denomination in favor of foreigners.

2. The EFCA's eternal-perspective theology and evangelistic and missionary practices foster a concern for people's eternal state that helps the denomination somewhat rise above the racism and prejudice

---

8. Included at the end of this chapter as an appendix.

tendencies that are all too common in the majority culture. For decades, EFCA churches have sent missionaries to various countries all over the world, including Venezuela, Peru, and Mexico in Latin America. Many church leaders see God's hand behind global migration and conclude, "Even if we don't send missionaries to other nations, God has brought the world here." As a consequence, many pastors try to persuade their congregations to accept and to reach out to their immigrant neighbors.[9]

3. The EFCA has made intentional progress towards being more "ethnically friendly." Latino outreach projects receive a large boost from the Urban and Intercultural Mission (UIM) department of the EFCA. The UIM facilitates the planting and development of churches for immigrants from various countries and of various languages. For over ten years the EFCA has carried out its national conferences with simultaneous Spanish translations of the plenary sessions. The denomination has published many materials in Spanish to equip Latino churches and pastors. For example, one issue of the denomination's magazine, *The Beacon*, came out in Spanish (as well as in English) in 2003. Since 2001 churches throughout the country have offered a course called *Escuela de Fundación de Iglesias* (Church Planting School) held in Spanish. In 1992, the UIM helped to found MHIEL (*Ministerio Hispano de la Iglesia Evangélica Libre*), an association of Latino pastors, to help coordinate Latino ministries at the national level.[10] This association has matured to the point of being able to carry out the ordination and licensing of Latino pastors totally in Spanish.

However, relations are not entirely ideal. Trinity Evangelical Divinity School (part of Trinity International University), the primary seminary for the EFCA located in the Chicago suburb of Deerfield, Illinois, is very large and recognized worldwide. However, during the 1980s and 1990s, none of the seminary's fulltime professors had much experience in Latin America, and the seminary's course catalog did not include any classes

---

9. David Wolfe, pastor of the English-speaking EFCA church in Bensenville, IL, describes the missionary motivation behind his church's Latino ministry in the following way: "We have our own Latin America right here in Bensenville." Such openness contrasts with the discrimination and racism Latinos typically encounter in the larger US English-speaking culture.

10. See MHIEL's website, http://www.efca.org/urban/hispanicministries.

about Latino ministry in the United States.[11] Though an extension of the seminary in Chicago focuses on training African-American pastors, there is no similar seminary extension for the Spanish-speaking community. Thus, Pastor Maya had to open his own Bible institute. According to some Latino leaders in the EFCA, the denomination has not designated enough personnel or financial resources to the Latino outreach.

CONCLUSIONS

The history of Latino churches within the EFCA reflects the enthusiasm of a young movement. In general, efforts "from below," from the Hispanic common people, have energized the outreach, leading to a healthy contextualization and wide acceptance of Jesus' message. Ministry to Latinos has proved more effective when the leadership is close to the members in terms of work, socioeconomic level, and "legal" status. Many new believers point to the love, hospitality, and care demonstrated by Latino brothers and sisters as the most persuasive evangelistic factor. For many, their new church has stepped into the role of an extended family, with the responsibilities and privileges generally reserved for family and close friends (for example, advice, monetary loans, job recommendations, etc.). Pastoral leadership reinforces these practices with sermons about the church being "the family of God." Latino members view this familial companionship as an expression of divine love.

Educational support has served some churches well. Tutoring services for children, parenting classes, and/or English classes prepare Latino church members for the competitive and discriminatory atmosphere in the United States. Many of the churches studied here prefer to use Spanish in their ministries though they also realize that English is necessary for functioning in society. Contact with members of English-speaking congregations furthers this "bilingualism." However, not everything in the EFCA Latino churches severs the immigrants from their past. Pastoral leadership has encouraged many traditions important to Latino identity. Regional foods, "Mexican nights," and Latin American Christian music played with the appropriate Latino instruments all contribute to the intentional efforts to retain much of Latino cultures.

---

11. This situation has been remedied somewhat with the addition of professor Robert Priest to Trinity's faculty in 1999. He brings to Trinity a wealth of experience in Latin America and has provided strong leadership and encouragement regarding ministry among Latinos in the United States.

Gigantic challenges remain. How will Latino pastoral leadership receive sufficient training to face new difficulties that will arise? How will pastors lead future congregations that become more and more complex with the combination of first-, second-, and third-generation Latinos? Who will develop (and how?) a theology robust enough to tackle practical issues like immigration, fair employment, and discrimination? How will the EFCA open its denominational structures to create more space for Latino churches? With our eyes fixed on Jesus, let us put our hands to the plow!

Appendix

A Stranger at Our Gates:
A Christian Perspective on Immigration

RESOLUTION ADOPTED AT THE 1996 GENERAL CONFERENCE OF THE
EVANGELICAL FREE CHURCH OF AMERICA

During periods of rapid change and economic uncertainty, it is often the vulnerable and marginalized people who are blamed for the misfortune that everyone else experiences or expects to experience. Today a significant amount of attention and blame for a perceived threat to the American way of life is being directed at immigrants. As Christians, we must ensure that our response to the issue of immigration is directed by a world view that is shaped by biblical principles rather than secular rhetoric.

A number of themes relevant to immigration run through the Bible. The first theme is that we ourselves, as Christians, are aliens on this earth. "And they admitted that they were aliens and strangers on earth" (Heb 11:13). Our status as aliens and strangers forms the basis for our attitudes and responses towards those people who live outside our society. A second theme is that our material possessions do not really belong to us. The Promised Land belonged to the Israelites only in the sense that as host, God allowed the Israelites to dwell in the Promised Land as his guests (Lev 25:23). Similarly, as aliens and strangers in the world, the material resources of the world do not belong to us. We have what we have because God, as host, has distributed material resources to us, his guests. As recipients of God's graciousness and generosity, we need to guard against selfishness and possessiveness which would cloud our attitude toward immigrants.

A third theme is protection for the alien. As non-citizens working in their country of residence, aliens exist outside the social and political network of the society they are residing in; thus, they are rendered powerless. Aliens are very vulnerable to exploitation. As Christians, we should recall our roots as aliens and, thus, identify with their plight (Exod 23:9).

A fourth theme is that, for Christians, no one is ever to really be considered an outsider. "The alien living with you must be treated as one of your native-born. Love him as yourself" (Lev 19:34). The Great Commandment is to apply to the alien, because he or she is our neighbor.

A fifth theme is that, in serving the outsiders of society, we encounter Jesus. Because Christ identified with the stranger, we are to extend the same treatment to the alien and stranger that we would extend toward Jesus (Matt 25:35).

Historically, immigration policies of the United States appear to be directed more by racism and economic self-interest than compassion. Immigration quotas favored people groups already established in the United States (western and northern Europe) while limiting immigrants from Asia and Africa.[12] Sometimes certain people groups were allowed to immigrate only when they were needed as menial labor for a specific task, e.g., Chinese railroad builders. Today immigration policy favors those who bring technical expertise or financial resources with them.[13] The present debate over immigration policy and immigrants is often based on stereotypical falsehoods. Immigrants do not displace American workers. They usually fill a shortage of skilled labor or do the menial tasks that citizens refuse to do.[14] Immigrants' rate of employment is higher than the general population, and they work longer hours.[15] They receive less general assistance than the general population.[16] Immigrants pay more in taxes than the social services they receive.[17] The reason state governments are financially burdened by immigrants is that only one-third of the federal income tax paid by immigrants is returned to the state governments who provide public services such as education and emergency medical care.[18]

As we engage in our society's debate on immigration through forums such as the voting booth, community discussion groups, political parties, and church in light of the preceding discussion, we need to raise the following issues:

A. To what extent are our attitudes towards immigration shaped by racism? To what extent do we assume that American culture is

---

12. Stafford, "Here Comes the World," 20.

13. Drachman, "Immigration Statuses," 190.

14. Stafford, "Here Comes the World," 21.

15. Sharry, "Myths," 23.

16. Ibid.

17. Ibid, 24.

18. Ibid.

identified with northern and western European culture; and are we attempting to protect those cultural roots of America from corruption by "foreign" cultures? Are we afraid that this existing cultural dominance will be overcome by the "strangeness" of strangers? Are we denying that other cultures bring gifts that add to rather than detract from our society's culture? Does our cultural identity take precedence over our Christian identity so that we fail to recognize that we are fellow aliens with these immigrants?

B. To what extent are our attitudes towards immigrants shaped by materialism? As aliens and strangers in this world, what is the theological basis for acting as though America were our property and we can hence deny access to it? Are we being overly possessive of our lifestyle or standard of living?

C. Is the fear of running out of limited resources justifiable? How can we say that there is not enough to go around in America? Are we more concerned with the pursuit of affluence than meeting the basic human needs of all human beings?

D. What are the implications of Proposition 187-type legislation (as in the state of California)? Does denying or reducing "safety net" and other public benefits to illegal immigrants and their American-born children imply that in our society some groups of people are not regarded as being equally human as others even though they participate in the economic functioning of our society? Are some groups of people not deemed worthy to receive the minimal goods and services we consider essential for a very basic level of human existence?

E. What about immigration policy? To what extent are we responsible for the living conditions in other countries that motivate people to emigrate? Do the policies of the US government and the US transnational companies contribute to pressures on people to emigrate to the United States? Does an immigration policy that favors the immigration of highly skilled people drain other countries of the skills necessary to improve their standard of living and hence reduce the pressure to emigrate to America?

As evangelicals, we are called by God to aid the vulnerable. Therefore, we must see the alien and the stranger as individuals made in the image of God, the object of Christ's love, and as people of intrinsic worth who are in need of our affirmation and support.

6

Last Call Ministries

Tony Solórzano

BEGINNINGS

MINISTERIOS LLAMADA FINAL (LAST Call Ministries) traces its roots to the Central American country of Guatemala. The leader God designated to carry out this visionary work was the firstborn son of a Christian family in Totonicapán, in western Guatemala. His father worked in a Guatemalan bank, and his mother taught school. They directed their son, Otto René Azurdia, in the way of Christ, a path which would lead Otto to become a great servant of God. On this path he received the vision and mission of what is now known as the *Iglesia de Cristo Ministerios Llamada Final* (Church of Christ Last Call Ministries).

Otto René, after a personal encounter with God, woke up one night in 1976 in a supernatural way. That night had an unforgettable impact on him, definitively rearranging his hopes, dreams, and destiny. The voices Otto René Azurdia heard that night spoke clearly into his ears and heart. He listened attentively to the desire and vision God imparted, according to Joel 2:1, "Blow the trumpet in Zion; sound the alarm on my holy hill. Let all who live in the land tremble, for the day of the LORD is coming. It is close at hand." Through this vision of angels, God planted in the mind and heart of the apostle Dr. Otto René Azurdia a now internationally-recognized ministry. In faith and obedience to the vision, Otto René launched Llamada Final on the basis of this verse in Joel. Llamada Final was officially established in Huntington Park, California, in 1988. The movement continues sounding the trumpet today, alerting the people of God and the lost world about the Second Coming of Jesus Christ to the world.

God has touched many men and women with this contagious vision, and they now join Apostle Azurdia in the task of making this last call public to thousands of people in different places and through different means. Through radio and television programs, newspapers, magazines, massive campaigns throughout Latin America, and the Internet (see www.llamadafinal.com), they reach the entire world.

The Biblical Basis for Llamada Final

Llamada Final responds directly to the vision Dr. Otto René Azurdia received. The ministry's message and vision revolve around the call of Joel 2:1: sounding the trumpet and raising the alarm. God's calendar has not stopped; his plan keeps going. Jesus said, "My Father is always at his work to this very day, and I, too, am working" (John 5:17). All heaven is working arduously because the biggest event, the most beautiful thing humanity can experience, is about to happen: the Second Coming of our Lord Jesus Christ. No other event in God's mind, in God's heart, is as important as the Advent of Jesus. But how many will be preaching or sounding the *shofar* (a Jewish horn) to alert the people to lift their eyes to the Lord?

"Sounding the trumpet" is a key phrase in the Bible. It precedes a manifestation of God. Exodus 19:16–17 says, "On the morning of the third day there was thunder and lightning, with a thick cloud over the mountain, and a *very loud trumpet blast*. Everyone in the camp trembled. Then Moses led the people out of the camp to meet with God" (emphasis added). This sounding of the trumpet is the proclamation of the Word of God, the message that must be preached.

Trumpets played an important role for God's people in the Old Testament. According to Numbers 10:3, trumpets were used to call the people to the door of the tabernacle. The trumpet sound summoned the people and called them to draw close to the presence of God. Many Christians in our world today have distanced themselves from the presence of God; they have lost themselves in a religion, busied themselves with religious service—perhaps very close to religious things but far from God's presence. Today we need to "sound the horn" so that God's people draw near to him. This trumpet sounding focuses on the following calls:

- An intimacy God wants to have with his people
- A personal relationship with God
- A challenge to not live distanced from God's presence
- A challenge to not live "religiously"
- A challenge to live out the reality of God in our midst

The trumpet must ring out to remind people that God is Spirit and that he wants a spiritual relationship with humans. How many in the world need to hear the trumpet blowing? How many need an alarm that summons them once again into God's presence? There is nothing sadder than seeing someone who has grown distant from God, who no longer feels God's companionship, who no longer hears the Lord's voice. Thus the alarm is raised among the people of God to tell them that God remains the same and that he is interested in a personal relationship. Summoning the people to the door of the tabernacle, or calling them into the presence of God, is the trumpet sound's first function.

The trumpet's alarm also served to call the people of Israel to pack up camp and move (Num 10:2). When the alarm sounded, the people started marching. These days, the preaching of the revealed and anointed Word of God revives each person who hears it to do the will of God. Jesus said, "The Spirit gives life; the flesh counts for nothing. The words I have spoken to you are spirit and they are life" (John 6:63). When the trumpet "sounds" today, people start marching; people are eager to follow the orders of the Lord. Today, more than ever, we need God to speak to and guide us. We need that trumpet sound to give us his orders and motivate us to action.

Thirdly, trumpets in the Old Testament announced an impending battle (Num 10:4). Today we experience many battles, some of which can be quite brutal. We have to remember that Satan attacks those who are working for the Kingdom of God. The trumpet alarm not only calls us into God's presence but also summons us to spiritual confrontations. It reminds us that just as we preach about the living Christ, there is a living devil; just as we preach about an all-powerful God, there is a powerful enemy. Yet the trumpet consoles us that "You, dear children, are from God and have overcome them, because the one who is in you is greater than the one who is in the world" (1 John 4:4). No one escapes unscathed from a battle, and no one who dares to tread in enemy territory returns without wounds. However,

God uses Llamada Final within his plan to raise the alarm and to sound the trumpet. "But if the watchman sees the sword coming and does not blow the trumpet to warn the people and the sword comes and takes the life of one of them, that man will be taken away because of his sin, but I will hold the watchman accountable for his blood" (Ezek 33:6).

The biblical concept of Zion is another important component of Llamada Final's vision. The Old Testament describes Zion as "the joy of the whole earth" (Ps 48:2). David experienced this place and did not want to leave; he preferred to spend one day in Zion than a thousand anywhere else. Zion is the seat of God's presence, the place where God pours out blessing and eternal life. "Sounding the trumpet in Zion" calls us to the reality of God's blessing in which we will delight and under which God will grant us the desires of our hearts (Ps 37:4).

Zion is also a place of being covered, of security. "Then the LORD will create over all of Mount Zion and over those who assemble there a cloud of smoke by day and a glow of flaming fire by night; over all the glory will be a canopy" (Isa 4:5). God covers something when it holds glory within, because he wants to guard and protect what is valuable, the glory of his blessing. Thus, we have to sound the horn in Zion to spread the message of joy, the message of blessing, the message of the presence of God, and also the message that the Day of the Lord is near. The apostle Otto René Azurdia and Llamada Final have been charged with this message; this message is the tremendous responsibility given to a sentinel: to sound the trumpet in Zion, alerting the people of God. Joel 2:1 lays out this commission.

ORGANIZATION AND STRUCTURE

The *Iglesia de Cristo Ministerios Llamada Final* is organized under the direct supervision of the apostle Otto René Azurdia and his wife Martha Julia Azurdia. The main church is located in Inglewood, California. The movement holds to the concept of apostolic supervision, meaning that each pastor and each church functions according to the direction and guidance of the movement's ministerial manual, under the leadership of Apostle Azurdia. Llamada Final's internal structure is theocratic since every move depends on the total direction of the Holy Spirit.

The main church supports a wide variety of ministries: children, youth, women (directed by Martha Azurdia), evangelism, etc. The department of evangelism focuses exclusively on evangelism and community service, spreading the gospel in jails, in parks, on the streets of Los Angeles, and to businesswomen and men through a series of activities prepared for each demographic group. Christian brothers and sisters in the department of intercession dedicate their lives to intercessory prayer for all the general ministries of the local church and also for all the areas in which Apostle Azurdia ministers. The department of praise and worship works both within and outside of the church. Its musical group, *Inspiración*, has blessed churches all over the world. The teaching ministry directs the department of prophecy which teaches prophetic vision and instruction, training brothers and sisters to be God's spokespeople. Another group of brothers and sisters makes up the department of service assistants which sensitively maintains order in church services and prays for the needs of God's people. The discipleship department organizes the teachings that are presented in home groups.

The department of Christian workers carries out leadership training for Llamada Final. This department trains those called by the Holy Spirit to serve in ministerial capacities. The department of church supervision oversees the extension of Llamada Final. A group of ministerial assistants in this department collaborates with Apostle Azurdia to supervise and guide congregations and churches. They periodically send worship and preaching volunteers to each church within the movement to update and to refresh the spiritual flow of doctrine, praise, and ministry focus. The apostle Azurdia himself names and supervises these workers.

THE GROWTH OF THE MOVEMENT

Since its beginnings in 1988, Llamada Final has spread throughout the United States and Mexico. The central church in Inglewood, California reports around 2,500 adult members. From California the trumpet has sounded to several states in the United States, including Alabama, Arizona, North Carolina, Colorado, Florida, Georgia, Illinois, Indiana, Michigan, Minnesota, Nevada, New York, New Mexico, Oregon, Pennsylvania, Rhode Island, Tennessee, Texas, Utah, and Washington. The movement currently has seventy churches in the United States with congregations varying between an average of fifty and 300 members.

Llamada Final has also spread throughout Mexico. The main church in Mexico City has some 3,500 adult members. There are fifty congregations in different regions of the Mexican republic, and additional congregations thrive in Retalhuleu, Guatemala; Ahuachapán, El Salvador; Ipiales, Columbia; and Ambato, Ecuador.

The movement grows through two primary ways: planting new churches and incorporating already existing churches into Llamada Final. When Christians receive a personal call from the Holy Spirit, Llamada Final commissions them to minister in a specific place. They begin working as a church layperson, not as a pastor. After a while, and given the growth of the project and God's testimony there, the new congregation establishes itself as an authorized church, and the layperson becomes the new church's official pastor. Already existing churches that decide to associate with Llamada Final undergo a six-month waiting period of seeking God's direction about joining the supervision and mission of Llamada Final. After that six-month period, the church can establish itself as a Llamada Final church.

Llamada Final believes that it is God who gives each individual his or her ministerial call. The main church in Inglewood for a time sponsors any Christians whom God has called to plant a church in a specific place but later allows them to develop on their own according to their particular style of growth. The main church also supervises the new churches in terms of doctrine and other important aspects. The department of Christian workers and the general pastor periodically visit new projects. Furthermore, all Llamada Final pastors meet together in a yearly retreat.

THE FUTURE

> Enlarge the place of your tent, stretch your tent curtains wide, do not hold back; lengthen your cords, strengthen your stakes. For you will spread out to the right and to the left; your descendants will dispossess nations and settle in their desolate cities. (Isaiah 54:2–3)

Leaning on God's promises, the apostle Dr. Otto René Azurdia and Llamada Final broke ground at the beginning of 2003 for new central offices and a new worship center. They are confident that this place will be what God promised, the center of a great revival. The sanctuary, scheduled to open in 2009, will have the capacity to comfortably seat 4,600 people for general services. The most sophisticated sound and video technology will facilitate ministry inside the sanctuary. The property is designed for three buildings: the sanctuary; a building with offices for the ministry departments, a bookstore, and a smaller chapel seating 500 people; and a building with all the necessary accommodations for children's ministry. The administrative building has already been completed. A professional recording studio and a television studio will allow Llamada Final to broadcast central church services around the world via satellite.

Llamada Final also has plans for a private elementary school and a printing company. The latter would print magazines, newspapers, and other written resources both for Llamada Final in particular and for God's people in general. All of these goals are efforts to make good on the responsibility with which God commissioned the apostle Dr. Otto René Azurdia and Llamada Final, generation after generation until the Lord returns . . .

> Blow the trumpet in Zion; sound the alarm on my holy hill. Let all who live in the land tremble, for the day of the LORD is coming. It is close at hand. (Joel 2:1)

SECTION TWO

Characteristics and Challenges of Latin American Protestantism in the United States

A CCULTURATION, THE ROLE AND participation of women in church, politics, church music, mass media, and missiology—these themes are the practical issues on which Latino church life and practice in the United States hinge. The authors in this section in no way attempt to pronounce the final word on these themes; instead, they hope to describe what has happened in our churches and to suggest how we can climb onto the shoulders of those who came before us, survey the land, and wisely apply the gospel in this sometimes rocky but always rewarding terrain of church life.

Juan Martínez begins this section by analyzing acculturation processes of Latinos in the United States. An analysis of acculturation trends among Latinos in general helps us understand the different options specific churches have chosen within these processes.

Nora Lozano sheds much-needed light on the role of women in Latino churches. Being both women and Latina makes this group of female Protestant Christians "doubly invisible" in church history. The author explores not only how women have worked in "spiritual" church spheres but also how they have confronted sexism, classism, and racism in society at large.

Reies López Tijerina stands out as a fascinating figure in the Chicano movement of the 1960s and 70s. Nevertheless, relatively few have studied his life and, in particular, his Protestant Christian roots. In his chapter, Lindy Scott investigates these roots of Tijerina's life and action. This study also sadly uncovers a Protestant community either unwilling to or at a loss as to how to accompany Tijerina and other similar prophetic voices during these decades.

Throughout Christian history, music has played a significant role in the life and witness of believers. In his chapter about Latino hymnology, Daniel Ramírez explores the culture and perspectives that our music expresses. Wise suggestions for future development pepper Ramírez's analysis of the changes and emphases in our Latino hymnology.

Next, professor Carlos Cardoza-Orlandi concentrates on churches along the Atlantic coast, investigating Latino/Caribbean missiology and the contributions these Latinos have made to the worldwide discussion of the church's mission. The author charts the transition from a "border missiology" to a "coastal missiology."

Janet Treviño de Elizarraraz closes this section with a description of how Latino Christians have taken advantage of mass media and mass communication to advance their ministries. She pays special attention to the role radio has played in evangelization.

May the lessons offered in these chapters facilitate a more informed, a more grateful, and therefore a more intimate walk with God!

7

Acculturation[1] and the Latino Protestant Church in the United States

Juan Francisco Martínez Guerra

MANY TIMES, SOCIAL OR political messages drive the various descriptions of the Latino community's acculturation processes in the United States. Those who want to emphasize the importance of the Latino community as a distinct entity speak of the United States as the country with the fourth (or fifth)[2] largest population of Spanish speakers in the world. They emphasize the growth of Spanish-language mass media within the country, the US Census reports about the numbers of Latinos, and the growing Latino influence at all levels in the country.

Those who want to demonstrate that the Latino community is an immigrant community similar to so many other previous immigrant groups in the United States talk about the number of Latinos who marry non-Latinos, the significant percentage of Latinos who prefer to speak English, and the fact that the majority of "successful" Latinos in the United States are those who speak very little Spanish.

---

1. This chapter employs the terms "acculturation" and "assimilation." Acculturation refers to the cultural adaptation that Latinos in the United States undertake in order to function in their new context. Instead of necessarily leaving behind their former customs, they create a new subculture. Assimilation describes the adopting of customs common to the United States in substitution for Latino or Latin American customs. An assimilated Latino would be a person with a Latin American background but whose lifestyle completely reflects US ways. This adaptation process takes place in many cultural, social, and linguistic areas.

2. The United States might have more Latinos than the total population of Argentina or Spain, but not all Latinos speak Spanish. Thus, it is probably not higher than fifth among the Spanish speaking countries of the world.

Without trying to clarify the contradiction between these two positions, and recognizing that they represent different social and political perspectives, this study proposes to recognize the diversity within the Latino community in the United States in relation to the themes of acculturation and assimilation. Forces of assimilation strongly mold the community, yet Latinos continue developing their own distinctive identity.

Speaking about acculturation and its impact on the Latino Protestant church in the United States implies the difficult task of describing an extremely diverse community. "Latinos" are actually very different groups of people whose experience in the United States, while similar in some ways, does not necessary imply a common future.

The US Latino Protestant church's challenge lies in understanding the diversity of its community and the effects acculturation has on this community in order to minister more appropriately in the community's actual context. This chapter will not attempt a description of the complex phenomenon of acculturation within the US Latino community since many excellent studies have already done so. Instead, this essay hopes to trace the Latino Protestant church's role within the reality of a community impacted by US society's assimilating pressure.

Different Latino Experiences

Previous chapters in this collection have pointed out that a "Latino community" as such does not really exist. Instead, a collection of communities has been brought together in the United States under the term "Hispanic"[3] or "Latino." Thus, it is difficult to describe one single Latino experience in the United States. Instead, it is more appropriate to distinguish between the different experiences without neglecting those things that the majority of Latinos in the United States have in common.

Generally, national background is used to distinguish US Latino experiences from each other, something which has a certain logical sense. However, not every person from a certain national background has undergone similar experiences as his or her compatriots. Therefore, it makes more sense to use a typology of the variety of Latino experiences within the United States.

---

3. The Census Department of the United States has unified all communities that have a connection with Latin America, Spain, or the Spanish language under the term "Hispanic" without taking into consideration national, racial, historical, linguistic, and ethnic differences that exist among these communities.

The conquered people. The first Latinos became part of the United States not by immigration but by conquest. When the United States conquered the Mexican territory of the Southwest (Texas, New Mexico, Arizona, California, and Colorado; in 1848, completing a process begun in Texas in 1836) some 100,000 Latino people (Mexican citizens) became an instantaneous part of the United States. Those who chose to remain in the conquered territory (some, especially from southern Texas, decided to move to Mexico) received US American citizenship though, practically speaking, they did not receive the legal rights of their fellow countrymen. The overwhelming majority lost their land due to legal and illegal maneuvers throughout the nineteenth century.

Over the years, many in this community have assimilated into US American society. In northern New Mexico and southern Texas, however, the descendants of this first group of Latinos maintain tight knit communities. The *conquered* people tend to be an invisible community since the distinctions of the US Census[4] do not recognize them and many in Latin America hardly know of their existence.

The first immigrants. The first sizeable wave of Latin American immigration rolled into the United States as a result of the Mexican Revolution (1910–1920). When the United States entered World War I, the country took advantage of the recently arrived Mexicans to fill in for a shortage of manual labor. Though Mexican immigration has gone through different stages, including periods of forced repatriation, it has more or less continued unabated since the revolution. The majority of US Latinos are of Mexican descent. Due to the historical relationship between the Southwest and Mexico, many immigrants feel a certain affinity with this region and with the *conquered people*.[5]

The "citizens." Puerto Ricans that move into the United States distinguish themselves from immigrants from other parts of Latin America due to the special relationship between Puerto Rico and the United States. After the Spanish American War (1898), the United States annexed the island, making Puerto Rico neither a complete colony nor a full state. As members of a US commonwealth, Puerto Ricans are *citizens* of the United States and can travel and establish themselves freely in whatever part of the country

---

4. The United States Census does not include a category for those Latinos who trace their history to the United States instead of to some part of what today is Latin America.

5. For a discussion of this perspective, see Chávez, *Lost Land*.

they wish. Migratory patterns from Puerto Rico have led to large Puerto Rican neighborhoods in such cities as New York and Chicago.

Exiles. The United States has always received *exiles* resulting from the multiple coup d'états in Latin America. The success of the socialist revolution in Cuba in 1959, however, fundamentally altered this phenomenon. For the first time, the United States, with arms wide open, received massive immigration from a Latin American country. These immigrants arrived with their legal paperwork in order, many with full intention of returning to Cuba once Fidel Castro fell (at least that was the perspective of the first generation of exiled Cuban leaders). Over the years new waves of Cuban immigrants have continued arriving on the US shore.

When the Sandinista revolution triumphed in 1979, scores of Nicaraguan refugees flocked to the United States. Many of them have returned to Nicaragua since the Sandinistas left power. The United States has also received small groups of political refugees from other Latin American countries, but these groups have been few and far between, and fewer of them tend to return to their countries of origin once the problem that caused them to flee is resolved.

"Interventionist" immigrants. The United States has a long history of intervening directly in Latin American countries, particularly in those from which the majority of immigrants come (Mexico, Puerto Rico, and Cuba).[6] The last forty years, though, have witnessed an increase in the number of immigrants from other countries in which the United States has directly intervened. In particular, there have been large migratory waves from the Dominican Republic and Central America. The United State's active participation in these countries' internal matters has forcefully altered the countries' political lives. In the case of the Dominican Republic, the United States agreed to accept refugees as part of a political "solution" after a military intervention in 1965. With Central American countries, fear of possible communist governments was behind the United States' toppling of democratic governments and support for bloody military dictatorships in the midst of civil wars. These civil wars created a strong migration push towards the United States.

These migrations have led to unique relationships between the immigrants and their countries of origin. For example, candidates for the Dominican Republic's presidency run a campaign circuit among their

---

6. In his book *Harvest of Empire,* author Juan González analyzes the history of Latinos in the United States in light of US interventions in Latin America.

fellow citizens in New York. And various Central American governments depend on the income of their citizens residing in the United States in order to maintain their national economies.

"Traditional" immigrants. *"Traditional" immigrants* are those Latinos who move to the United States assuming that their future in the new country depends on assimilating to US culture and society as soon as possible. They take it for granted that they or their children will lose their current cultural identity and will become part of the new US reality. There are traditional immigrants in all the groups previously described. This perspective shows up especially among immigrants from South America and Spain who move primarily for economic opportunities within the United States.

"Temporary" immigrants. The phenomenon of *temporary* immigration owes to Latin America's proximity to the United States. *Temporary immigrants* enter the country, many times undocumented, with the goal of earning a certain amount of money and then returning to their country of origin. Many times these immigrants stay for a long period of time, but a growing number, especially from Mexico and Central America, spend only a short amount of time in the United States before returning with enough money to start a business, build a house, pay off a debt, or simply try their luck in a new context. Also, a growing number of people work in the United States and then return to their country of origin for retirement.

The differences between the various Latino experiences multiply when considering generational changes that occur within the communities. Each of these groups demonstrates an acculturation tendency in the "second" generation. They also tend to change perspectives on where they belong. Children of "exiles" no longer view their country of origin as the focal point for their future. "Temporary" immigrants become permanent. Many merely seek to become part of the societies in which they find themselves currently living. All these factors create more distinctions within the communities.

ACCULTURATION TENDENCIES

Many detailed studies describe the phenomenon of acculturation and assimilation of Latino communities in the United States. Some are descriptive while others are prescriptive, reflecting the different perspectives on the place of the Latino community within US society.

When discussing these themes, it is essential to remember that US society has always presented itself as one that assimilates its immigrants, making them part of the country's rich heritage. According to this perspective, it goes without saying that to achieve success in the United States, immigrants need to fully assimilate, maintaining only a marginal (if any) ethnic identity. "Official" US history tells of immigrant communities who struggled upon arrival but, as they culturally and linguistically assimilated, ended up enriching the country.[7] Those who do not assimilate remain isolated from the opportunities the United States offers its people.

From this perspective, the immigrating generation struggles and makes great personal sacrifices, the second generation begins to live in two worlds, and the third generation successfully assimilates within US society. The only piece of the past that remains is a national identity (for census purposes) and a few superficial folkloric preferences that show up in food, celebrations, and music.

In this context, the idea of being bilingual or bicultural carries little importance. The goal is to learn English and to leave behind the "old" language and culture. Even today's current emphasis on multiculturalism focuses not on maintaining linguistic and cultural differences but on sharing distinctions that can enrich the United States' social context.[8]

However, the process of acculturation has never been as simple and clear-cut as the US myth makes it out to be.[9] Latinos obviously acculturate within US society, learning to speak English and to function in this country. And many Latinos have completely assimilated within US society. The

---

7. The myth of the Melting Pot has never adequately explained why people of color, African-Americans, Native Americans, Latinos, Mestizos, and Asians have never fully assimilated. Assimilation has "worked" for people of European background but not for those from other latitudes.

8. The public education system has served as a primary socializing agent in this process. The system sees no reason for a person who speaks a language at home other than English to maintain, much less to improve, that language. Being bilingual has only been counted worthy if a person's first language is English and then, after childhood, he or she learns a second language. Furthermore, studies keep "showing" how being bilingual creates an academic deficiency, as if the brain could not handle two languages at a time.

9. For example, German culture and language played a key role throughout the nineteenth century. Many children studied German as their first language in parochial schools. Voluntary assimilation on the part of communities of German background did not change this trend; the two World Wars against Germany in the twentieth century brought about the changes. Communities that spoke German were obligated to quit using German in order to avoid accusations of betraying the United States.

majority of Latinos, however, maintain their primary relationships with people from their own ethnicity, and the impact of Latino culture and the Spanish language grows stronger every day in the United States.

Researchers have presented countless models to describe the processes of acculturation and assimilation. Perhaps one of the simplest comes from Andrew Greeley. In an article about ethnicity in the United States, Greeley declares that ethnic identity is something optional in this country. People can opt for the level of identification they want to maintain with their background. Greeley suggests that four types of people make up each minority group in the United States. By slightly adapting his typology, we can identify five large groups within the general Latino community as they relate to acculturation and assimilation into US culture and society.[10]

The *nuclear* or *monocultural* Latino makes up the first group. This person lives almost completely within a Latino community. Many times they are recent immigrants or elderly, and the majority speak Spanish as their primary language.

In general, recent immigrants from Latin America are considered *monocultural.* Yet another significant group of Latinos that fits within this category, despite speaking little Spanish or speaking only English, is the group of people who live in areas of concentrated Latino populations (for example, in southern Texas, northern New Mexico, East Los Angeles, or parts of New York, Miami, and Chicago). Having grown up and lived their whole lives within Latino communities, these people have developed a culture that is neither Latin American nor Caucasian US American but is instead a subcultural adaptation to US society. The subculture defines itself with distinct characteristics. Many people live wholly within this new reality created in dynamic reaction to the US context.

The second type of Latino is *bicultural.* The *bicultural* person has adopted many of the US society's customs but at the same time has chosen to maintain his or her roots within the Latino community in some form or fashion. The majority of this type were born and/or raised in the United States. Nearly all are bilingual and live in two worlds. They

10. Greeley suggests four types of ethnic identities: nuclear, fellow traveler, marginal, and alienated (Greely, "Is Ethnicity Unamerican?"). He also says that people can choose to identify themselves with an ethnic group that is not their own, although at a superficial level.

function as well in Latino culture as in US society though occasionally they do not feel fully at home in either.

Marginal Latinos are the third type. The *marginal Latino* has not distanced himself fully from Latino culture but only occasionally identifies with it. He likes Latino things (food, music, etc.) and enjoys spending time inside the Latino community, but he lives his life primarily within the majority culture. Because of the United State's cultural diversity, *marginal Latinos* often join together with other ethnic minorities in the country, especially through marriage.

The fourth type is the *fleeing Latino* who attempts to escape from her culture. She actively seeks to become part of the mainstream culture. Though she may not deny her Latino roots, she desires and aims to slip into US culture as quickly as possible.

Finally, the *assimilated Latino* is the fifth type. These people identify themselves as Latino in US Census reports but culturally live as mainstream US citizens. A vague historical awareness that their ancestors came from Latin America is the only characteristic of Latino culture that they retain. These Latinos reflect the "success" of the assimilating forces of US society.[11]

The assimilating pressure from US society and the reality of the social acculturation and assimilation of so many Latinos beg the question about how a clearly defined entity called "the Latino community" continues to exist within the country. Its continuation owes to four important factors: 1) the historical relationship between the United States and Latin America; 2) the proximity of the United States to Mexico and Latin America; 3) the constant immigration from Spanish-speaking countries; 4) the existence of large Latino communities (cultural hinterlands) in the United States. Because of these factors, the Latino culture and the Spanish language keep growing stronger in the United States despite the strong assimilating influence of mainstream US culture.

A broad generational tendency at the level of ethnic identification shows up in studies, and many speak of "first-generation" and "second-generation" (and subsequent generations) Latinos when describing changes in acculturation and assimilation. While a certain reality backs

---

11. In general there is a direct relationship between a person's level of assimilation and his or her socioeconomic status. The person more assimilated within the United States tends to have a higher level of education and to belong to a higher socioeconomic class than do those who maintain closer ties to their Latino culture. The Cuban community does not demonstrate this trend as much as do other Latino groups in the United States.

up these observations, this perspective fails to explicitly treat the complexity of the Latino experience. In areas densely populated by Latinos, sometimes fifth- and sixth-generation Latinos continue using Spanish. Furthermore, marriage between second- or third-generation Latinos and first-generation Latinos has become more common, thus altering the "process" of assimilation. Due to the constant movement of people between Latin America and the United States, the Latin American influence remains an active daily force in the United States and keeps both Latino culture and the Spanish language alive. While many individuals assimilate, Latino culture and the Spanish language occupy a constantly growing place and importance in general throughout the country.

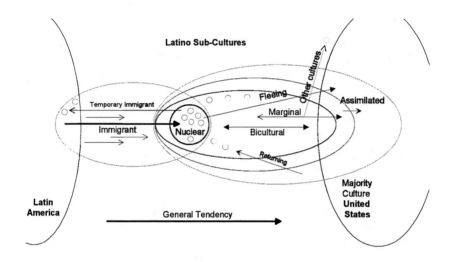

Latinos and their Relationship with Latino Culture in the United States

THE PLACE OF THE LATINO PROTESTANT CHURCH
IN THE UNITED STATES

Ministering within the Latino community inside the United States demands that Christians face the reality of acculturation and assimilation. The Latino community is dynamic and changing. Every ministry within this community ought to be so as well.

Many who minister among Latinos never think about acculturation in a conscientious manner. Yet they still reflect a perspective about the church in relation to acculturation. For some, the Latino Protestant church serves as a type of bridge or translator, a transition place for recent immigrants. This perspective quietly assumes that the "second" generation will assimilate into mainstream culture. The church assists in this process by teaching children's classes in English and by connecting Latinos to the corresponding English-speaking church.

People working in this frame of mind often develop Hispanic ministries or departments within mainstream English-speaking churches. These projects, "under" the primary church's leadership, hope that the second-generation Latinos will gradually become incorporated into the larger English-speaking congregation.

Churches that see themselves as transmitters of Latino values and of the Spanish language fall on the opposite extreme. Scattered churches within many denominations seek to preserve Latino culture. Furthermore, the past few years have brought a new trend of churches "imported" directly from their countries of origin. Using methods similar to the mother churches', these churches minister primarily among immigrants from their particular country. Though they are inside the United States, these imported churches are clear extensions of the mother churches' work in Latin America.

As the Latino community in the United States grows, it establishes new churches in areas that have never before sustained Latino congregations. Many keep believing that the Latino community is headed straight for assimilation, but they recognize that assimilation does not happen overnight or even within one generation; thus they found Latino congregations for those who will not fully assimilate.

The dynamic immigration situation has also stimulated the development of new models of church which have sprouted up in areas full of not only Latinos but also of people from diverse ethnic backgrounds. One new style of church encourages several sister congregations to use the same building. Each congregation focuses on a certain ethnic group though they all form one church. The different congregations then meet together periodically for activities that attempt to celebrate the unity within their diversity.

Intentionally multicultural or multiethnic churches are another new response to the dynamic immigrant communities in the United States. This congregational model openly celebrates its members' ethnic diversity yet also calls them to form one unified church. In general this ministry style attracts bicultural people or those who are ethnically marginal within their own communities.

Ministering within the US Latino Community

To continue ministering within this community, the Latino Protestant church has to keep in mind several points relating to acculturation. It must recognize that the Latino community in the United States includes real people from very different backgrounds whose relationship to the mainstream culture varies widely. A large part of the community is bilingual and bicultural at least to a certain degree, but each individual can demonstrate different attitudes in relation to Latino culture depending on the specific situation.

This knowledge pushes the Latino church to recognize the following: 1) not every Latino can be reached by the same type of church; 2) many Latinos will not respond to any Latino church at all; and 3) many young Latinos will be like young people in non-Latino churches in that they will choose to participate in a different church when they become adults.

An exact connection between an individual's relationship with the Latino community and the type of church that will be most likely to reach the individual with the gospel remains elusive. However, a certain level of probability does exist. The following graph may be helpful in considering what type of ministry will most successfully reach the different types of Latinos in the country.

Types of Latino Identification

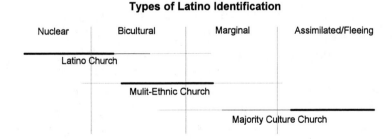

Latino Identity and Types of Churches

Given such diversity, the church must absolutely remember its role and mission. Being church means being a community of believers that fosters health and unity, meaning that the church needs to minister to the whole Latino community and to the Latino family in its entirety, despite cultural differences between individuals. In a changing world the church needs to be a community of support for the whole family. This community will obviously include clear differences between various members of the Latino church in terms of the topics described above.

This situation gives the church a generational responsibility. The United States' education system clearly will not transmit our Latino values and culture. The church, though, can play a role in this process. On the one hand, churches can encourage younger generations to study and understand their background and language. They can also show children and youth that other options than complete assimilation do exist; the church can present educational opportunities beyond the mainstream system. More importantly, the church has the opportunity to teach kingdom values that transcend culture and society. It can help its children navigate the tensions of language and culture and demonstrate that the Kingdom of God is superior to any human system. The church can form young people to be Christians with a worldwide vision, not just with a Latino or a US mindset.

These challenges confront the Latino church with another key issue: the church's role as an agent of social change in terms of acculturation. Many times congregations have reflected the acculturation tendencies within the Latino community but rarely have they taken the active role of protagonists. Latino churches need to seriously consider if they ought to be proponents of Latino culture or agents of the process of cultural adaptation, or both, according to the specific situation at hand.

Throughout the nineteenth century and the first part of the twentieth century, the Catholic church in the United States sought to "Americanize" its Latino members while the Latino Protestant churches kept the use of Spanish alive. Yet Latino Protestant congregations have also pushed the Americanization of their members, even to the point of closing their doors in order to integrate with the corresponding English-speaking congregation. As the number and influence of Latino churches grows, the issue of the social impact they want to have becomes more crucial.

Language is a specific area of social impact. The church must take language into account, whether in relation to a target ministry population or to the church's role as a social agent, because every linguistic option transmits social messages.

The 2000 US Census pointed to very important linguistic practices among the US Latino community. On the one hand, a growing number of people speak Spanish at home and identify English as a language they either do not speak or do not speak well. On the other hand, the population of Latinos who speak English well, even as a first language, continues to grow. Many Latinos are monolingual, only speaking either Spanish or English. At the same time, an increasing number of bilingual Latinos are bilingual not in the sense of transitioning from Spanish to English but instead are actively seeking to maintain and improve both languages.

These results alert the church to cautiously consider language matters while ministering. A large number of Latinos that the church could reach prefer Spanish. Yet Spanish is a complex, varied language with regional differences that can confuse people or even cause a sense of exclusion.

Considering the children and youth in Latino churches complicates the situation even more. The United States educates these children and youth in English as part of its assimilating emphasis. Some parents want their children to assimilate; they speak to their children in English and want the church to do the same. Others want their children to maintain Spanish in church. The children and youth often feel pulled between their parents' vision and the perspective of schools that discourage the use of Spanish. Since the majority of these young people have never studied in Spanish, their Spanish is domestic, often an informal version of Spanglish.[12] Within Latino communities there are also people who feel much more comfortable in English despite living surrounded by a Latino subculture. Others speak English fluently but prefer to worship God in Spanish as a way to stay connected to their ethnic and cultural background.[13]

---

12. Many Latino youth born in the United States want to speak Spanish but become discouraged when adults in their lives (parents, teachers, church members, etc.) make fun of their limited Spanish. The adults want the young people to use Spanish, but they crush their spirits instead of helping and positively instructing them in how to improve their language skills.

13. This phenomenon raises the questions of formality/informality in the use of language. To the degree that Latinos identify church as part of their informal, familiar relationships, they will be more attracted to a Latino congregation. If they see religion as part of the world of formal relationships, they will be more likely to seek an English-speaking congregation.

These complexities create a formidable challenge for the Latino Protestant church in the United States. Latinos who are more assimilated, many of whom do not speak Spanish, are generally much less receptive to Latino churches. Yet the church still has a responsibility toward those that live within its community and toward their children.

This responsibility translates practically into a need for each ministry within the Latino community to have certain bilingual characteristics. Churches that carry out all their programs in Spanish will minister more effectively to the degree that they have the freedom to use English in some parts of their ministry.

Other congregations choose to be conscientiously bilingual. This choice reflects a social position as well. Some churches use English to strengthen their Spanish with the hopes that those in the congregation who speak more English will not get lost and can, in the meanwhile, be improving their Spanish. Others utilize English with the perspective that, since the new generation will inevitably speak English, the church should contribute to their formation in English.

More and more Latino churches are employing English or some form of Spanglish as their primary language. In general this type of congregation functions successfully when located in an area densely populated by Latinos, such as in southern Texas, northern New Mexico, or the large Latino neighborhoods in the country's big cities. When this type of congregation is in an area where Latinos are not the overwhelming majority, it has a greater propensity to assimilate since "justifying" the existence of such a congregation proves difficult when no language difference distinguishes between the area's Latino and the non-Latino churches.[14]

---

14. Language is key in relation to Latino ministries and the impact of acculturation. Acculturation also raises other important points for the Latino church. For example, what perspectives does the church have toward new immigrants? What type of ministries will it develop? The relationship between the Latino church and its mother denomination also factors into the situation. How does acculturation affect the relationship between Latino churches and "Anglo" or English-speaking churches within the same denomination? How do classist and racist tendencies in certain segments of US society affect the relationship between Latinos and "Anglos," English speakers, especially in terms of acculturation?

CONCLUSION

The historical relationship between the United States and Latin America, the long border between Mexico and the United States,[15] the unique position of Puerto Rico, the United States' need for imported manual labor, and Latin America's economic situation are all factors that clearly indicate that the Latino community will continue to play an extremely important role in the United States. Latino migration will remain one of the most obvious impacts of globalization in this country.

Results of the 2000 US Census demonstrate that the Latino community is growing rapidly. It has already become the biggest "minority" within the United States, and the community will keep growing at a faster rate than the population in general. As the Latino community increases numerically, so does the diversity within it.

The Latino Protestant church in the United States plays a crucial role within this diverse Latino community. In the midst of all the community's changes and cultural struggles, the church has the privilege of proclaiming a gospel that both transcends and is relevant within every culture. The church invites people to be followers of Jesus Christ, to form communities of faith and mutual support in the midst of diversity, and to recognize that we are citizens of a kingdom beyond any particular country or culture.

---

15. This is the largest border in the world between a "first world" country and a "third world" country. It is also the meeting place for the world's two most international languages, English and Spanish, and for the world's two largest countries, the United States and Mexico, respectively, that use these languages as their primary languages.

8

Faithful in the Struggle:
A Historical Perspective on Hispanic
Protestant Women in the United States

Nora O. Lozano

THE TASK OF FORMULATING and writing a historical perspective on
Hispanic Protestant women in the United States of America turns
out to be quite complicated due to the lack of available information on
the Hispanic church in general and specifically on women within the
church. This lack of information in no way implies that the history of this
demographic is unimportant; it simply denotes that, viewed from a more
critical perspective, the study, research, and publication of history bow to
such forces as sexism, racism, and classism.[1] In the present investigation,
then, it is both interesting and painful to note the double invisibility of
Hispanic Protestant women in the annals of history due to their condi-
tion both as women and as Hispanics.[2]

---

1. Historian Daisy Machado affirms that, due to issues of racism and marginalization,
very few Protestant denominations in the United States have supported the writing of
the history of the Latino church within their denomination. See Machado, "Latinos in the
Protestant Establishment," 103. Gastón Espinosa supports Machado's idea that the lack
of literature regarding Hispanic Protestant women owes to cultural issues, but he adds
that it also has to do with the false myth that all Latinos are immigrants belonging to the
Roman Catholic Church. See Espinosa, "Your Daughters Shall Prophesy," 25–26.

2. Clotilde Falcón Náñez, in her study of Hispanic Methodist women, provides a clear
example of this invisibility. Falcón Náñez refers to the wife of a pioneer Methodist pastor
in Laredo, Texas: "The following year, he [Alejo Hernández] married a young lady in
Monterrey, Mexico. This first Hispanic Methodist clergy wife remains anonymous, however, because her name is not mentioned in any of the church records." Náñez, "Hispanic
Clergy Wives," 164.

The forces of sexism, classism, and racism have affected the lives of Protestant Hispanic women not only in the world of research and publications but in all spheres, from the private world of the home to the public world of the church and secular political, social, and economic structures. Yet, who are the Hispanic Protestant women in this country? What are their stories? These questions are the basic inquiries of this chapter. The first question requires studying the group composition of Hispanic Protestant women. The second requires placing the Hispanic Protestant woman in her historical context, both general and ecclesial.

HISTORICAL FACTORS THAT HAVE FORMED HISPANIC WOMEN

Hispanic Protestant women in the United States form part of a very heterogeneous group of women. In terms of nationality, 5.7 million Hispanic women in the United States are of Mexican origin, 1.1 million are of Puerto Rican descent, 485,000 have Cuban roots, and 2.3 million trace their origin to other Spanish-speaking countries in South and Central America and the Caribbean.[3] Normally, these women refer to themselves not as Hispanics but instead as members of their respective nationalities: "Mexicans," "Puerto Ricans," "Cubans," "Dominicans," etc.[4]

Economically speaking, many of these women live in poverty due to US society's prevalent sexism under which women generally make less money than men when working the very same jobs. Furthermore, many of these women have received little formal education; thus they find themselves in situations in which the only work available to them is low-paying labor in which they are often exploited and there is little opportunity for advancement. The fact that many of these women are the only sources of economic income for their homes (1.5 million homes report a Hispanic woman as the head of the household)[5] is also a contributing factor in their poverty. These facts do not negate the reality that a small group of middle class and/or highly educated Hispanic women exists. There is a small group of them, and though these women may suffer less in economic terms, they still face issues of racism and sexism.[6]

---

3. Aquino, "Latina Feminist Theology," 144–45.

4. Isasi-Díaz and Tarango, *Hispanic Women*, x.

5. Aquino, "Latina Feminist Theology," 144–45.

6. Isasi-Díaz, *En la lucha*, 27–28.

While it is true that Hispanic women differ in terms of nationalities, economics, and level of education, it is just as true that they share certain traits that unify them as a group. Historically speaking, they branch off from the same root race. The sixteenth century witnessed the clash of Spanish and indigenous cultures in North, Central, and South America. This clash produced miscegenation and, subsequently, a new race that in large part was a product of the physical, sexual, and religious violence of the conquistadors.[7] The clash was violent for all indigenous people but even more so for indigenous women. Indigenous women had to witness the deaths of their fathers, husbands, and sons as the men unsuccessfully defended their territory. They also had to stand by helplessly at the brutal mistreatment of their children. Compounding the suffering, Spanish conquistadors raped many indigenous women.[8] These women then experienced the racism with which their new masters treated the children of these rapes. The offspring of the rapes became a new race called "mestizo" which, on account of being a mixed race, was despised as inferior to the pure Spanish race.[9]

This *mestizaje*, or miscegenational mixing, happened not only on a racial/biological level but also in the religious and social environments. While both Spaniards and indigenous people contributed to the mixture of New Spain's colonial society, it is imperative to remember that Spanish customs, since the Spaniards were the conquerors, dominated.[10] The notion of what it meant to be a woman factored among all the concepts swimming around and mixing in New Spain. Indigenous women were the predominant female group in the first decades of colonization since Spanish women arrived later, after the conquistadors had established themselves in these lands.[11] Thus, it is difficult to determine when and how the two perspectives on womanhood merged. However, despite the confusion, studying a few characteristics common to both groups makes it feasible to reconstruct what it meant to be a woman in New Spain.

Unique characteristics distinguished each pre-Columbian tribe, but, in general, indigenous women before the Conquest received a similar,

---

7. Elizondo, *Galilean Journey*, 9–10.

8. León-Portilla, *Visión de los vencidos*, 151–59, 183–85.

9. Fuentes, *Buried Mirror*, 234.

10. Elizondo, *Galilean Journey*, 10–11; Rodríguez, *Our Lady of Guadalupe*, 9.

11. Stols, "México en la época colonial," 84. Stols states that in 1600 only 25 percent of the women in New Spain were Spanish.

traditional education. They were taught skills and tasks "appropriate" to women such as cleaning, cooking, and sewing. Women were expected to maintain their virginity until marriage and, as wives, to be faithful spouses and good mothers.[12] Although most marriages were monogamous, men, especially men in higher circles within the social hierarchy, were allowed to have extramarital sexual relations. Since slave women were considered objects, sexual relations with them were acceptable. By and large, women depended on the authority of men in the home, whether it be the father or the husband.[13] And at least in the religion of the Nahuatl tribe, women could serve as priestesses to the vast pantheon of gods and goddesses though only male priests carried out certain tasks, such as sacrifices.[14]

Spanish characteristics also influenced what the new mestizo woman would be. Spain itself had experienced extensive racial and cultural mixing throughout eight centuries of Arab occupation (AD 711–1492). Muslims and Spaniards fought for the peninsula in the name of religion, and in the process they exchanged cultures, languages, possessions,[15] and women.[16] The Spanish concept of womanhood included female subordination to males owing to the order of Creation and the woman's role in the Fall. Women were seen as fragile objects, dependent human beings. The Spanish perspective also included the Mary/Eve (Madonna/Sodom) dichotomy, which deprived society of a healthy model of womanhood.[17] On the one hand, the interpretation of Mary as patient, submissive, obedient, pure, passive, and maternally devoted became the ideal model of womanhood. On the other hand, the traditional interpretation of Eve as a sensual and perverted temptress offered the only other option for how to be female. These oppressive and limiting stereotypes allowed men to treat some women as reproductive machines and others as sexual commodities.[18]

The Spanish concept of womanhood merged with the Muslim position which also supported the superiority of men. In Muslim culture, men

---

12. León-Portilla, *Antiguos mexicanos*, 148–54.

13. Cypess, *La Malinche*, 24–25; Melgarejo, *Antigua historia*, 3:38.

14. Clavijero, *Historia antigua*, 168–69; León-Portilla, *Filosofía Náhuatl*, 149–78.

15. Fuentes, *Buried Mirror*, 52.

16. Glick, *Islamic and Christian Spain*, 188.

17. Schipani, "La Iglesia," 5–7.

18. Carmody, *Christian Feminist Theology*, 51–53.

had more privileges and liberties than women in social, religious, sexual, and family matters. The attempts to limit and control the lives of women furthered the conception and treatment of women as objects.[19]

Regarding religion, Spanish men and women were zealously devout in their Christian faith. The Inquisition persecuted all Protestants, Moors, and Jews, including the ones who converted to Catholicism, leaving the Catholic faith as Spain's only and official religion. In Catholicism, only the Christian God, Jesus, the Virgin Mary, and the other saints merited veneration.[20]

All these cultural frameworks (indigenous, Spanish, and Muslim) of what it meant to be a woman converged to form the new identity of the mestizo woman. The common elements in the three perspectives present a mestizo woman who learned from her ancestral cultures that virginity and fidelity were paramount values for a woman to uphold. She also learned that for her, marriage was monogamous while for her husband, it could be polygamous since he could use slave women, concubines, or prostitutes for his sexual pleasure.

Thus, a woman could either be perceived as a reproductive object or a sexual object. A woman also learned to be dependent on the men in her family: father, husband, or sons. In religious matters, the force of Spanish zeal obligated the native tribes to convert to Catholicism. Consequently, the Roman Catholic faith became New Spain's dominant religion. Implicit in Catholicism was the Virgin Mary/Eve dichotomy which, in New Spain, eventually evolved into the Virgin of Guadalupe/Malinche dichotomy. This dichotomy continues to affect Christian Hispanic women because it offers no healthy or realistic model of what it means to be a woman. Since Hispanic culture is predominantly Catholic, the image of the Virgin of Guadalupe has become both a religious symbol for active Catholics and a cultural symbol for the rest of the population. The symbol has profoundly influenced what it means to be a woman in Hispanic culture.[21] Women are expected to be like the Virgin: submissive, docile, passive, sacrificial, patient, and pure. These characteristics, while frequently positive, in many cases turn oppressive when they are abused. If a woman does not manage to fulfill this ideal, she is quickly identified with the Malinche paradigm:

---

19. Ferguson, *Women and Religion*, 92–93, 112–13; Díaz-Paja, *History of Spain*, 14.

20. Fuentes, *Buried Mirror*, 162.

21. For a detailed study of this theme, see my article "Ignored Virgin or Unaware Women."

the traitorous, evil, and sinful temptress. Seen from a critical perspective, neither model is a good option for the Hispanic woman since neither presents her as a real human being, with virtues and defects,[22] struggling to be the whole woman that God calls her to be.

Racial classification also affected the concept of what it meant to be a woman in New Spain. The basic races were indigenous peoples, Africans, and Spaniards. The combinations among these three races determined a person's classification: either as a subject or a vassal, either someone who received tribute or someone who gave it.[23] Sometimes, however, racial classification in New Spain was altered by the delineation of class in terms of wealth or political power. For example, some peninsular Spaniards were so poor they had to work side by side with the indigenous people and the Africans[24] while some indigenous leaders maintained privileged lifestyles under the stipulation that they support Spanish rule.[25] In the same way, these elements of class and race gave rise to different levels of womanhood in New Spain. Indigenous women were considered rationally limited beings[26] and were often treated as beasts of burden; white women, whether Spaniards or Creoles, lived a more privileged life due to their race and economic class.[27] The concept of womanhood forged in New Spain, framed by gender, race, and class issues, has accompanied Hispanic women, in one way or another, up to the present day.

The nineteenth and twentieth centuries witnessed independence movements in many Latin American countries, along with a host of other formative events that shaped the history of Hispanic women in the United

---

22. Alluding to women of Mexican descent, sociologist Roger Bartra suggests that they are part Guadalupe and part Malinche. Both ways of being can exist internally in each woman, and a woman will reflect them depending on her relationships with the men around her. Each woman has the potential to be pure and erotic, trustworthy or traitorous, and she will tend toward one behavior or the other depending on the circumstances and her need to survive. On the other hand, due to the possibility that women can behave in either way, men view women with suspicion and attempt to dominate them. This male domination can at times be so extreme that it requires a woman's complete self-sacrifice. See Bartra, *La jaula de la melancolía*, 171–85.

23. Fuentes, *Buried Mirror*, 234.

24. Villegas, *Historia general*, 1: 444–45, 451.

25. Ibid., 348–49; Gibson, *Los aztecas*, 157–67.

26. Aquino, *Nuestro clamor*, 38.

27. Cánovanas, *Historia social*, 538–39; Villegas, 1:448; Elliot, *Imperial Spain*, 309; de Terreros and Manuel, *Bocetos de la vida social*, 28–29.

States. These movements and events led to the Hispanic community as it is presently known. Regarding the history of people of Mexican descent, many Mexicans lived in the Southwest of the United States long before these lands were taken over by the United States of America. Therefore, a sizeable number of Mexicans in this country did not "immigrate" to the United States; instead, the border crossed over their property in the 1848 Treaty of Guadalupe Hidalgo which robbed Mexico of approximately half its territory. This treaty meant that suddenly many Mexicans found themselves living in a new country, culture, and society.[28] Virgilio Elizondo calls this new reality that the Mexican people faced "the second *mestizaje*." Once again, the mestizo Mexican people with indigenous, African, and Spanish ancestors would undergo the process of mixing, this time with English-speaking US culture. From the beginning, the English speakers perceived Mexicans as the inferior "other."[29] These new relations generated a racism and discrimination against Mexicans that continue to the present day in the United States.[30] The current group of Mexican-Americans in the United States is made up not only of those native Mexicans whose property was subject to border changes but also of all the Mexicans who have subsequently entered the United States whether with or without legal papers.

The people of Puerto Rico entered the United States of America through different means. In 1898, the United States interrupted four centuries of Spanish domination by invading and acquiring sovereignty over Puerto Rico. Since then Puerto Rico has lived as a colony under US power. The US Congress, looking for a way to send Puerto Rican men to World War I, ratified the Jones Act in 1917, giving the islanders US citizenship. Puerto Ricans, then, could freely go back and forth between their country and the continental United States.[31] In 1952 Puerto Rico received commonwealth status. Though Puerto Ricans originally hoped that this status would lead to greater independence and wellbeing for them, the island continues to function more or less as a colony since it does not have autonomy over its international politics. The Puerto Rican population has suffered the same racism and discrimination that the Mexican-American community has experienced. Though Puerto Ricans can enter the United

---

28. Ortiz, *Hispanic Challenge*, 43–46.

29. Machado, "Latinos in the Protestant Establishment," 87–92.

30. Elizondo, *Galilean Journey*, 13–18.

31. Isasi-Díaz, *En la lucha*, 13.

States legally, this legal status does not protect them from being viewed and treated as the inferior other.[32]

Cubans make up the third largest group of Hispanics in the United States. They have been immigrating to the United States since the beginning of the nineteenth century. The flow of migration was relatively slow until Fidel Castro took control of the island in January of 1959. After that historic takeover, the Cuban population in the United States exploded from 40,000 people to just over a million. Many of them left Cuba anticipating a brief stay in the United States just until Castro would be overthrown. The situation turned out differently, though, and now these Cubans live with the pain of exile, unable to return to the country of their familial and cultural roots.[33]

Turning to Central American countries, the immigration of many of their citizens is due to US foreign policy and the fear of communism spreading throughout the continent. Revolutions and violent conflicts compelled 500,000 Salvadorans and 200,000 Nicaraguans to immigrate to the United States in the 1980s. Many of these immigrants entered the country legally, but a large number came without legal papers and at great risk to their lives. People from South America have often opted to immigrate to the United States for reasons of economic advancement. As their countries suffer grave economic crises, men and women look for ways to go north in hopes of providing a better life for their families.[34]

The women from all these groups form the community of Hispanic women in the United States. They share the same mestizo roots and the fact that for different historical reasons they have come to live in the United States of America. In this country they have been victims of a racism that perceives them as the inferior other, victims of a classism that oppresses all poor people in general and especially poor females, and victims of a sexism that undermines all women in general. The combination of these three types of oppressions has been nearly fatal for Hispanic women who keep struggling to develop and grow. Thus Ada María Isasi-Díaz affirms that Hispanic women in the United States face an anthropological poverty that threatens their lives materially, culturally, and ontologically. Survival

---

32. Ortiz, *Hispanic Challenge*, 48–51.

33. Ibid., 51–55.

34. Ibid., 56–57.

is the Hispanic woman's daily bread. In this survival mode, she fights to become the whole human being that God wants her to be.[35]

A Perspective on Hispanic Protestant Women in Church History

Despite the history and context of suffering and oppression that Hispanic women in the United States have endured, Hispanic Protestant women have found hope in their churches' biblical principles. Though it is true that many denominations have developed oppressive practices due to cultural influences, it is just as certain that the gospel is the power of salvation and hope for women. These women's ecclesial history is proof of God's faithfulness in their lives, of the salvation that Jesus offers, and of the Holy Spirit's power. God has called these women to diverse ministries, and, though many times sexist practices in their denominations have limited them, they have been faithful to the call to extend God's reign here on earth. Some women have been called to lay ministries and others to fulltime ministries. Due to space constraints and the diversity of denominations in the Protestant world, this article focuses on women in both lay and fulltime ministries in only three movements: Baptist, Methodist, and Pentecostal. These three groups were chosen because they adequately illustrate the diverse attitudes toward women in Hispanic Protestant traditions. Baptist groups, though not all of them, have been the least open toward women in ministry while the Methodist denomination is on the opposite end of the spectrum. Finally, the Pentecostal tradition poses an interesting study because it both supports women in ministry while at the same time promotes traditional stances toward women in general.

Hispanic Baptist Women

Hispanic Baptist women in Texas provide an excellent case study for appreciating the history of more traditional Hispanic Baptist women in general for two reasons. On the one hand, the Women's Missionary Union of the Southern Baptist Convention began its work among Hispanics precisely in Texas; on the other hand, Hispanic women in Texas, like those in New Mexico and Arizona, have developed their own Spanish-speaking missionary organizations over time at the state level.[36]

35. Isasi-Díaz, *En la lucha*, 29–30.
36. Allen, *Century to Celebrate*, 79–80.

The first Baptist missionary effort among the Hispanic community began in 1888 with Mina S. Everett's work. By that date several significant events between Baptist groups in the country had already transpired. In 1814, the General Baptist Convention reorganized under the name of the Triennial Convention. Immediately, women's societies that had existed since 1800 joined this group to promote their missionary projects. The missionary zeal was so contagious that by the following meeting of the Triennial Convention, 110 women's societies were cooperating with the Convention. Baptists continued to work united until 1845 when, due to conflicts related to the impending Civil War, a group of Baptists from the South decided to separate from the Triennial Convention to form their own Southern Baptist Convention (SBC).[37] The Baptists who remained in the Triennial Convention continued as a foreign mission society until they reorganized again in 1907 as the Northern Baptist Convention, now known as the American Baptist Churches.[38]

The Mexican Baptist Convention of Texas was founded in 1910, and, seven years later, the *Unión Femenil Misionera de Texas* (UFM, Hispanic Women's Missionary Union of Texas) was officially organized. María A. Hernández served as the first president. From the beginning, this group decided to involve itself in missions following the style of English-speaking women's missionary leagues.[39] Groups in the UFM have developed a wide variety of missionary projects. In the area of prayer support, the women pray throughout the year for missionaries and their work. They also promote special weeks of prayer at different times of the year both for state, national, and foreign missions and for the convention's work. During these weeks of intentional prayer, the Hispanic Baptist women try to involve the entire church, and raise awareness of missionary work and the need to pray for it.

Regarding financial support, these Hispanic women collect money all year long, and especially during the special weeks of prayer, to support such diverse missionary projects as theological education in Mexico and Texas or outreaches among Mexico's indigenous population. They minister to the spiritual life and practical necessities of missionaries through

---

37. Ibid., 15–18.

38. Hill and Torbet, *Baptists North and South*, 18–19.

39. Estrada, Vargas, and Bishop, *Fieles al Maestro*, 31–33.

constant prayer and faithful economic donations. The UFM has had the privilege of sending and supporting its own female missionaries.

In terms of education, the UFM women have done excellent work by providing Christian education with a missionary focus and organizing rigorous age-appropriate study groups along the lines of English-speaking women's missionary unions. Women like Adelina V. García, Francisca Chapoy, and Esperanza Ramírez worked arduously in the English-to-Spanish translation of study manuals and materials for special weeks of prayer. In February of 1955, a long-held dream of Texas' Hispanic Baptist women came true when they published the first issue of *Nuestra tarea* (Our Task), a missionary magazine in Spanish for UFM groups throughout the state. Eventually the magazine's circulation extended far beyond Texas when *Nuestra tarea* became the official magazine for all Hispanic women's missionary unions nationwide.[40]

UMF women have also been involved in benevolence ministries and social services such as literacy training, hospital visitation, disaster relief aid, and Habitat for Humanity. Another important ministry for both Texas Hispanic women and Texan Baptists in general centers around the Río Grande. On both sides of the Texas-Mexico border, Baptists serve people who live along the river in great poverty and who have no access to basic services.[41]

In 1964, the Mexican Baptist Convention of Texas merged with the Baptist General Convention of Texas, and the following year the *Unión Femenil Misionera* merged with the Women's Missionary Union of Texas.[42] In the 1970s, both the Mexican Baptist Convention and the Texas UFM began using the term "Hispanic" instead of "Mexican" to acknowledge and include all the different Spanish-speaking demographics in Texas.[43]

The work of Hispanic Baptist women in Texas has been such a significant part of Baptist outreach in Texas due to the great number of Hispanic people living in the state. Other Hispanic Baptist women who live in heavily populated Hispanic areas, such as New Mexico and Arizona, have also formed their own *Unión Femenil Misionera* at the state level. Hispanic women who live in communities with a sparse Hispanic

---

40. Ibid., 63–64.

41. Grijalva, *History of Mexican Baptists*, 131–33.

42. Estrada, Vargas, and Bishop, *Fieles al Maestro*, 77.

43. Grijalva, *History of Mexican Baptists*, 170–71.

population have tended to unite their efforts with their English-speaking Christian sisters.[44]

On a general level, and on top of the work of *Uniones Femeniles Misioneras*, Hispanic Baptist women (within the SBC) have contributed to church life through Christian education, principally children's education. However, lately a new option related to theological education is beginning to open for Hispanic women. Dr. Esther Díaz-Bolet, for example, belongs to the growing number of women committed to training new male and female ministers within the Southern Baptist Convention.

Another way in which Hispanic Baptist women further God's reign is through fulltime ministry. The fulltime ministry options open to women inside the Southern Baptist denomination have historically been limited to being pastors' wives or missionaries. As pastors' wives, Hispanic women have worked side by side with their husbands to support the church's work. They have been models for countless women and have faithfully served with their gifts of prayer, leadership, education, counseling, and hospitality in the church. On the mission field Hispanic women like Leah Garza and Olga Nava have shared God's Word in countries all over the world.

At this point it is important to note that not all Baptist groups share the same position on women in the ministry. The American Baptist Churches (ABC) have historically been more open to women serving and leading within the church. ABC and SBC women share denominational roots up through the 1845 split between Southern and Northern (ABC) Baptists. After the division, women who remained in the Triennial Baptist Convention (now the ABC) continued working through women's missionary unions with the same zeal that characterized them from the beginning.[45]

ABC ministry among the Hispanic community in the United States began in 1901 when the First Baptist Church of Santa Barbara, California started a mission among the Hispanic community there. Today this mission is the *Primera Iglesia Bautista* of Santa Barbara. Missionary work among Hispanics in Los Angeles, California began in 1910 and spread to Fresno, California in 1917.[46] From California, ministry among the Hispanic community expanded east along the railroad tracks. Since constructing and maintaining the railroads provided employment for many

44. Allen, *Century to Celebrate*, 79–80.

45. Hull, *Women Who Carried*, 5.

46. Luna, "Patterns of Faith," 393.

Mexicans, churches sprouted up along the train lines in places like Topeka, Kansas; Fort Madison, Iowa; Winslow, Arizona; and Scottsbluff, Nebraska. Many of these churches were started by Mexican men and women who had developed a fervent faith while living in California.[47]

On the East Coast, the first Hispanic ABC church was organized in New York in 1921. The congregation of this church, just like most others planted in this area of the country, was made up mostly of Puerto Ricans. Many of the founders of that first congregation had participated in ABC work in Puerto Rico before migrating from the island. Hispanic women in these new churches actively participated in women's unions, Christian education, and Bible distribution—activities they used as evangelistic tools.[48]

Today ABC Hispanic Baptist women continue contributing to church and denominational life by supporting national and foreign missions through their work in women's unions. They are church pillars in the areas of children's education, literacy, and support groups for parents.[49] In terms of theological education within the church, women like Elizabeth Conde-Frazier and Loida Martell-Otero are making important contributions by training a future generation of ministers.

The ABC also benefits from the service of Hispanic women in full-time ministry. Among them are pastors' wives who faithfully support the work of their husbands and their churches with their numerous talents. Fulltime ministers also include Hispanic women missionaries like Adalia Gutiérrez-Lee and Mayra Bonilla who work abroad spreading the gospel and women like Miriam Chacón-Peralta who serve in leadership positions inside the denominational structure.

ABC churches have made great strides for Baptist women in general regarding the issue of women in the ministry. While traditionally women could only be missionaries or pastors' wives, the ABC opened up the options for service by ordaining women. ABC churches have supported women in the pulpit and in ordination since the 1880s.[50] Though no Hispanic women were ordained until much later, currently many, like Miriam Baez, Liliana Da Valle, Frances Rivera, and Lydia Velez, are ordained in the ABC and serve as pastors or co-pastors. Other ordained

47. Morales, *American Baptists*, 4.
48. Russell, "From Ocean to Ocean," 161–62.
49. Gutiérrez-Lee and Gutiérrez, *Dios también me llama*, 15–18.
50. See Miller, "Retreat to Tokenism," 1 and Lynch, "Baptist Women in Ministry," 309.

Hispanic women serve as chaplains or are part of pastoral teams with specialized ministries like youth and Christian education. However, while the ABC has welcomed and supported women in ordained ministries on the denominational level, the environment within the local church often leaves Hispanic women in the ministry struggling for acceptance, recognition, and employment.[51]

Hispanic Methodist Women

Methodism began with John Wesley's preaching in England during the eighteenth century. From England, the new denomination spread to the United States, and in 1784, the Methodist Episcopal Church came into being. Unfortunately, the church also fell victim to the raging divisions surrounding the Civil War and, in 1845, divided into Northern and Southern factions. Nearly a century later, in 1939, the groups resolved their differences and, together with the Protestant Methodist Church, came together as the Methodist Church.[52] The Methodist denomination currently known as the United Methodist Church was created in 1968 through the merger of the Methodist Church with the Evangelical United Brethren Church.

From its beginnings, the Methodist church has witnessed the zeal of women serving God. By the latter part of the nineteenth century, different organizations were established to coordinate women's various outreaches and make them more effective. The Women's Foreign Mission Society of the Methodist Episcopal Church, established in 1869, was the first of different missionary societies organized within the diverse traditions that preceded the United Methodist Church. This particular society worked at both the local church and at the national levels.[53]

Hispanic Methodist history began with a few sporadic outreach attempts and then jumped into full swing with Benigno Cárdenas' ministry in New Mexico in 1853. Next, Alejo Hernández in Texas put Hispanic Methodist ministry on the map in 1871.[54] Throughout the 1870s, Hispanic Methodist projects sprouted up in Arizona, California,[55] and Florida.[56]

---

51. Jenks, "Elizabeth Conde-Frazier," 5.
52. Baker, *Compendio*, 287, 351–52.
53. Schmidt, *Grace Sufficient*, 152, 156–58, 160.
54. González, *En nuestra propia lengua*, 44–49.
55. Ibid., 71–73.
56. Ibid., 103.

Two decades later, the work spread to New York in 1892[57] and to Puerto Rico in 1898.[58] Not until 1926 was there a Hispanic Methodist ministry in Chicago.[59]

From the beginning of Methodist work among Hispanics, Hispanic women have made invaluable contributions to the expansion of God's reign. According to Minerva N. Garza, Hispanic Methodist women were working together in *sociedades femeniles* (women's societies) long before they were formally organized as such. Their passion for missions and evangelism led them to recognize the needs of those they served and to try to meet those needs. For example, in 1939, women from the Southwest Mexican Conference (now the Rio Grande Conference) opened a fund for educating young Hispanic ministers.[60] Nearby, women from the Western Conference supported missionary work among impoverished people in Mexico.[61] Another need quickly arose: the lack of study materials in Spanish. Hispanic Methodist women resolved this problem by naming Elida G. Falcón as translator of program books and by appointing Falcón's daughter, Cleotilde F. Náñez, as her assistant. Eventually they realized that regardless of the high quality of the translated materials, Hispanic Methodist women needed their own materials in Spanish, written by Hispanic authors. Thus they launched the production of a program book written originally in Spanish.[62]

Women like Felicidad Méndez, who worked in children's educa-tion in Pharr, a border town on the Mexico-Texas frontier, symbolize the significant contributions of Hispanic Methodist women to the church's work overall.[63] Rosa and Emelina Valdés, serving in Tampa, Florida, also worked in educational ministry.[64] Hispanic Methodist women's interest in secular education has continued throughout the history of the United Methodist Church. For example, in 1959, Luisa García Acosta González, together with her husband Justo González and Eulalia Cook, founded a literacy program called "Alfalit." In 1988, this program was adapted to

57. Ibid., 116.
58. Ibid., 143.
59. Ibid., 134.
60. Náñez, "Hispanic Clergy Wives," 161–77.
61. González, *En nuestra propia lengua*, 83.
62. Garza, "Influence of Methodism," 78–89.
63. Schmidt, *Grace Sufficient*, 250.
64. González, *En nuestra propia lengua*, 105.

meet the specific needs of women.[65] In terms of Christian education, Hispanic Methodist women have been involved in all the different areas of denominational work, teaching new generations about loving God and about the need to preach the gospel. Regarding benevolence and social services, Hispanic Methodist women serve in the areas of childcare, help to political refugees, and assistance to abused women and children.[66]

Hispanic women in fulltime ministry have also made significant contributions to the United Methodist Church's work. According to Cleotilde Falcón Náñez, Hispanic clergy wives have been integral in the expansion of God's reign. Beyond merely supporting their husbands' ministries, they have developed their own ministries in Christian or secular education, evangelism, music, leadership, and missions. Hispanic pastors' wives in the Rio Grande Conference organized and led the *sociedades femeniles*. Furthermore, they had the vision for encouraging the women's societies to establish the fund for Hispanic ministers' education.[67]

Methodist women have a long history of struggling to obtain full clergy rights in the church, and this right was granted in 1956. That same year Julia Torres Fernández became the first Methodist woman ordained in Puerto Rico.[68] In 1965 Noemí Díaz became the first Hispanic Methodist woman ordained in New York.[69] Since then, many other Hispanic women have followed their footsteps. However, there is still a great need for more ordained women to serve in Hispanic churches.

Hispanic Methodist women have also developed a type of prophetic ministry. In the role of prophets, they have challenged denominational structures to include them on all levels within the Methodist groups that hold the power and make decisions. These actions have provided Hispanic women more visibility, voice, and power. For example, women like Hilda Foster, May Alvírez, and Noemí Janes are some of the first Hispanic women to have been elected to the General Conference. In 1985, Minerva Carcaño became the first Hispanic woman to be named superintendent

---

65. Ibid., 113; Garza, "Influence of Methodism," 78–89; Gutiérrez-Lee and Gutiérrez, *Dios también me llama*, 49–51.

66. González, *En nuestra propia lengua*, 117.

67. Náñez, "Hispanic Clergy Wives," 161–77.

68. Garza, "Influence of Methodism," 78–89.

69. González, *En nuestra propia lengua*, 120.

over a district in the continental United States while Myriam Visot became the first to serve in the same position in Puerto Rico.[70]

Though these achievements merit great celebration, Minerva N. Garza's words still challenge the United Methodist Church to become more open to Hispanic women in ministry: "It's time for the Jurisdictions of the United Methodist Church to consider Hispanic women for bishops.[71] Why not? These distinctions are acquired, not merely because they are women, or because they are Hispanic, or to give them an opportunity, but because of their training and experience."[72]

Hispanic Pentecostal Women

The Pentecostal movement traces its beginnings back to the Azusa Street revival in Los Angeles, California in 1906. William J. Seymour, an African-American pastor, led the revival. Hispanics, including Luis López, Juan Navarro,[73] and Abundio and Rosa López, participated in the movement from the very beginning. Originally from Mexico, the Lópezes started the Hispanic Pentecostal ministry in the district of the Mexican Plaza in Los Angeles. Rosa López and Susie Villa Valdez became the first female evangelists within the Pentecostal movement in the United States. These two women developed a holistic ministry that combined evangelistic preaching with social and pastoral work.[74] From Azusa Street, the Hispanic Pentecostal movement spread across the United States and Puerto Rico thanks to the ministries of Henry C. Ball, Alice Luce, Francisco Olazábal, Francisco Ortiz, Juan L. Lugo, and Thomas Álvarez.[75]

Though emphasis on the Person, work, and gifts of the Holy Spirit forms a common denominator among Pentecostal groups, the groups differ on doctrines about God, healing, and sanctification.[76] Another difference among the diverse Pentecostal groups is in the place and role of

70. Ibid., 68–69.

71. At the time of the original Spanish writing of this essay, there were no Hispanic women bishops. Today, however, there is one: the Reverend Minerva Carcaño, Resident Bishop of the Phoenix area of the United Methodist Church.

72. Garza, "Influence of Methodism," 78–89.

73. Villafañe, *Liberating Spirit*, 85, 89.

74. Espinosa, "Your Daughters Shall Prophesy," 27–28.

75. Villafañe, *Liberating Spirit*, 90–94.

76. Ibid., 86.

women. According to Gastón Espinosa,[77] the difference in the recognized roles of women is evident in the two largest Pentecostal denominations: the Apostolic Assembly of the Faith in Christ Jesus and the Hispanic Districts of the General Council of the Assemblies of God.[78] Both groups trace their roots back to the Azusa Street revival and share the basic idea that the Holy Spirit gives gifts freely to both men and women. Thus, they encourage women to exercise the gifts they have received but, of course, to do so within denominationally-imposed limits. The relationship of ecclesial authority and authority within the home—the combination of freedom that the Holy Spirit gives and the limits imposed on women— becomes paradoxical for groups that ordain women. On the one hand, women have authority in the church; on the other hand, at home they must submit to their husbands who are perceived as the heads of the household.[79]

The Apostolic Assembly of the Faith in Christ Jesus began with R. E. McAlister's affirmation that God had revealed to him that baptism was to be administered only in the name of Jesus and not in the name of the Trinity. This denomination insists that women must wear skirts and cover their heads when praying, and it forbids them to cut their hair or wear jewelry or makeup. The movement has maintained a very conservative position regarding women's roles in the church. However, Gastón Espinosa points out that at the beginning of the movement, women served as deaconesses, evangelists, and church planters. For example, Romanita Carbajal de Valenzuela was a preacher in Los Angeles, California and in Chihuahua, Mexico in the second decade of the twentieth century; Nicolasa de García, Delores de González, and María Apolinar Zapata were involved in the deacon ministry. Espinosa explains that theological and cultural changes within the denomination's leadership, along with conservative readings of Scripture, led the group to prohibit women from ordained ministry (deacon and pastor). Yet progressive sectors within the denomination have, in the last few years, challenged this restrictive position that dates back to 1929. Despite the limitations imposed on them because of their gender, women within the Apostolic Assembly have carved out spaces for exercising their talents. Like Baptist and Methodist women, they have

---

77. This section about women in the ministry in Pentecostal churches is based largely on the excellent research by Gastón Espinosa, "Your Daughters Shall Prophesy."

78. Ibid., 28.

79. Ibid., 26.

organized their work into women's societies that promote Christian education, spiritual growth, and missionary work. These Apostolic women have excelled with their distinguished ability to raise funds for foreign missions. Despite being a conservative group, the denomination allows women to carry out evangelistic work and also to teach men in such settings as Sunday school, missions, and marriage seminars.[80] Pastors' wives have also made a relevant contribution with their ministries.[81]

The Hispanic Districts of the General Council of the Assemblies of God (AG), in contrast to the Apostolic Assembly, affirm a Trinitarian theology. This Pentecostal group also differs from the Apostolic Assembly in their stance on women in the ministry. Based on Joel 2's prophecy that in the last days both men and women will prophesy, they ordain women. The Hispanic AG do not require women to cover their heads while praying nor do they forbid them to cut their hair. They only ask that women use modesty with their dress, makeup, and jewelry. Gastón Espinosa attributes this more open attitude toward women to the close ties the Hispanic denomination maintains with the English-speaking denomination of the Assemblies of God.[82]

The first AG women to minister within the Hispanic community were Anglo-Saxons: Aimee Semple McPherson, Kathryn Kuhlman, and Alice E. Luce, who worked in Los Angeles, California and in Texas. Espinosa points out that these women modeled female ministerial leadership for many Hispanic women who later accepted the call to ministry. The first Hispanic woman to be ordained was Dionisia Feliciano who was ordained together with her husband Solomon. The Felicianos worked in California, Puerto Rico, and the Dominican Republic. Nellie Treviño Bazán (1895–1995), also ordained together with her husband in 1920, was the first Mexican-American Pentecostal woman ordained to minister in the United States. She and her husband planted churches in Texas, Colorado, and New Mexico. Concepción Morgan Howard (1898–1983) preached evangelistic messages throughout Arizona, California, and northern Mexico. She served alongside her husband as co-pastor and was ordained to the ministry in 1928.

---

80. Ibid., 28–33.

81. Adams, "Perception Matters," 103.

82. Espinosa, "Your Daughters Shall Prophesy," 33–34.

Espinosa underscores the fact that the majority of women ordained in the denomination's first forty years were ordained alongside their husbands. This pattern greatly limited single women who ended up receiving a license instead of ordination and could serve only as assistants. The situation began to change in the 1960s with women like Aimee García Cortese who, after challenging the sexism of her denomination's Hispanic leaders and appealing to Anglo-Saxon leaders, was ordained in 1962. However, no church would call her to minister. With much trepidation, García Cortese decided to organize her own congregation. Today her church is one of the largest churches in New York. Female pastors Julie Ramírez and Julia Hernández are also examples of successful women who have developed fruitful ministries with congregations of over 500 members.[83] Samuel Solivan asserts that female Pentecostal pastors are much more respected today, to such a degree that some have been named bishops in their denomination.[84]

Gastón Espinosa also explains that for some Hispanic Pentecostal women, the pre-1960s relative freedom to minister was not sufficient; therefore, they opted to form their own denominations. Such is the case of Rev. Leoncia Rosada Rosseau (Mamá Leo) who, in New York in 1939, helped found the Pentecostal denomination the Damascus Christian Church.[85] On top of being an excellent preacher, Mamá Leo, together with her husband, developed outreach ministries to the most marginalized sectors of society such as drug addicts. Mamá Leo's church became a seedbed for future male and female ministers who followed her example of faithfulness and service to God.[86]

CONCLUSION

The life of Hispanic Protestant women has been one of struggle. Since the time of the Conquest through the political and economic movements of the nineteenth and twentieth centuries, the struggle to survive has been the daily bread of Hispanic women. Unfortunately, church life has not been an exception. While it is true that Hispanic Protestant women have found great solace in their faith, and that they are valuable as complete

---

83. Ibid., 34–39.

84. Solivan, "Sources," 145–46.

85. Espinosa, "Your Daughters Shall Prophesy," 37–38.

86. Villafañe, *Liberating Spirit*, 94–96.

human beings made in the image of God, it is also true that they have often had to struggle just to survive within the church. Hispanic Protestant women have wrestled to find spaces in which they can faithfully serve God despite the limitations imposed on them by their denominations. Some have worked in women's missionary unions which afford them the opportunities to lead their own ministries and to collaborate with the larger missionary movement. Others have been faithful in their ministries as pastors' wives. Still others have engaged the struggle to carve out a place for themselves within domestic or foreign missions in order to obey God's call in their lives. And some others have fought to open doors in ordained ministries and have turned into models of determination and faithfulness for future generations of Hispanic Protestant women.

Who is the Hispanic Protestant woman? She is the married woman, the single woman, the mother, grandmother, daughter, child, missionary, pastor, pastor's wife, treasurer of the women's society, Sunday school teacher, secretary, nurse, doctor, maid, student, Cuban, Puerto Rican, Mexican, and Salvadoran who has accepted Jesus into her heart and who strives courageously to follow God's call within the churches of the Lutherans, Methodists, Pentecostals, Baptists, Presbyterians, Disciples of Christ, or any other Protestant denomination. All of these women, in one form or another, have struggled to survive in the face of sexism, racism, and classism in their secular and religious lives, and they remain faithful because they recognize the call they have received and the God who has called them. They are confident that the One who began the excellent work in their lives will be faithful to the end and will one day greet them with, "Well done, good and faithful servants! Enter the joy of your Lord." Amen!

9

Reies López Tijerina:
The Visions and Obedience of a Pentecostal Activist

Lindy Scott

JUNE 5, 1967, SEEMED like a typical a day in the little town of Tierra Amarilla, New Mexico. The extreme heat had practically vacated the plaza of any passersby. Suddenly, twenty men in four cars and one truck pulled up and parked in front of the courthouse. Bearing arms, they entered the building. They fired a few shots when they met resistance. Two hours later, the twenty men drove out of the town with two hostages, leaving behind several wounded. The National Guard promptly showed up looking for the "criminals." The surprise behind the attack lies in the fact that its leader was Reies López Tijerina, a man who had been a Pentecostal preacher and who believed that God and the Bible approved of his actions.

The storming of the courthouse in Tierra Amarilla and the following events catapulted Reies Tijerina into national prominence. He became one of the most visible leaders of the Chicano movement in the United States in the 1960s and 1970s. Together with César Chávez, José Ángel Gutiérrez, and Rodolfo "Corky" González, Reies Tijerina provided strong leadership for advancing the Chicano movement. The attack in Tierra Amarilla was part of Tijerina's quest to recover lands that had been taken from Mexican-Americans in the nineteenth century.

What motivated Pastor Tijerina to take such drastic actions? How did he harmonize his Christian beliefs with his violent actions? Was his cause consistent with the Christian faith? His personal history helps answer these questions.

Reies López Tijerina was born on September 21, 1926, in Fall City, Texas. The story goes that when he was four, Reies had a special dream in which Jesus took him by the hand. His mother Herlinda, a devout Catholic who prayed and read her Bible consistently, encouraged Reies to explore the dream's meaning and to fulfill it. When Reies was eight, his mother died. Growing up with his father from then on, the young boy soon personally experienced a forced displacement from home. Some white US Americans, as was typical in the day, abused the legal system and took over the land that belonged to Reies' father near Laredo, Texas. In 1939, Reies' father moved the family to Michigan to work in the fields cultivating beets. A Baptist preacher gave Reies a Bible one day in 1942, and Reies said, "I didn't put the book down that night until I'd read the whole thing. Later, I gathered my brothers and sisters and read it to them a second time."[1] The Beatitudes and the message of the prophets touched his heart especially deeply: " . . . in the prophets I saw the satisfaction of the heart's cry for justice and peace. I found that the word 'justice' is used with the same frequency as the word 'love.'"[2]

In 1946 Reies began attending the Assemblies of God Bible Institute located in Isleta, Texas. There he met his future wife, María Escobar. Brother Kenzy Savage, the school's superintendent, found Reies Tijerina to be a very good student. Savage invited Reies to accompany him in a pastoral ministry in Santa Fe. The superintendent recalls, "He was a good speaker, with a lot of courage and spirit. I really appreciated his ministry back then . . . . When he attended the school, he was a very sincere student. I don't know, though; when he left the school, he began having these strange ideas about how people ought to live."[3]

This chapter will analyze four of these "strange ideas" that Reies practiced during his life. First, Reies directed the creation of a radical Christian community. Next, Reies received visions and revelations that, according to him, came directly from God. Obedience to these revelations pushed him to leave the radical community behind in order to implement a new strategy for changing the status quo. Third, his popular style of communicating his teachings sharpened the effectiveness of his calling. Finally, his denouncing of sins in the style of Biblical prophets, especially

---

1. Quoted in Gardner, ¡Grito!, 37.
2. Ibid.
3. Ibid., 39.

his denunciation of the structural sins of the rich and powerful in the United States, provoked a violent reaction to him and to his ministry.

THE VALLEY OF PEACE ("VALLE DE PAZ") COMMUNITY

By 1956, Reies Tijerina had already grown disillusioned with institutional churches, both Catholic and Protestant. He turned away from churches in general because they no longer followed the teachings of the "Man from the Holy Lands." He explained his decision in the following way:

> I had fought with the church (with all religions) during ten long years, trying to get it to take the side of the poor in the struggle against the rich, but I had failed. They told me and I convinced myself that my struggle was futile. I began looking for an alternative. Saving my family and whomever else wanted to separate themselves from the system of the church and corrupt society was my alternative.[4]

He wanted to break with his ecclesiastical past and begin a new style of obedience by forming a radical Christian community. Working in 1955 in California's Betabel Ranch, Reies and several of his followers had saved up $1,400. They decided to abandon city life with "all its vanity and corruption" in preference for the Arizona desert. They bought 160 acres of virgin land that would be "far from the danger, the temptation, and the influence of the monopolies." They especially wanted to educate their children freely, without the harmful influence of the church and public schools.

Due to limited funds, Reies and his friends began building "underground houses." They dug deep pits and later covered them with car hoods scavenged from the city dumps of Casa Grande and Eloy, Arizona. During the day they worked in the fields, harvesting cotton to make a living. Daily life was very simple. Women made their own dresses and the clothing for the whole family. They cooked over stoves fashioned from gas tanks, also scavenged from the garbage dumps. The food pantry was held in common, and in the early days, each family educated its children with full freedom. Later, Tijerina went to the capital, Phoenix, and obtained the necessary permits for the community to build and direct its own school for their children.

Within a short period of time, the community began to earn a reputation throughout the entire state. Many "Mexicans, Indians, and Blacks

---

4. Tijerina, *"King Tiger,"* 1.

from the surrounding areas began to visit"[5] the community, first out of curiosity about the community's dream and convictions. Later, they visited to talk about their problems and grievances to see if Tijerina and his group could give them assistance. Many asked Tijerina to help them free beloved relatives from jails where they had been incarcerated, frequently under false accusations.

The Valley of Peace Community lived out its faith very simply. The people's relationship with God determined everything and dominated both their public and private lives. For example, a daughter was born into the Tijerina family on April 18, 1956, and Tijerina named her "Ira de Alá," or "Anger of God." He explained his daughter's name in the following way:

> Some ten years earlier, the United States had begun to make atomic bombs day and night without pause. And they continued. I was convinced that the church harmed humanity more than any other organization on earth. I knew that if there was a just God, he had to be angry and unhappy with those that managed our government and religion here on earth, and that is the reason that I gave my daughter the name of Ire of Allah. I also was very unhappy with the form in which men are managed.[6]

The community began having problems with government authorities when representatives of the county's board of education insisted that the community's children attend public schools in Casa Grande or Eloy, even though under this requirement the children would have to walk three miles through the desert to even catch the school bus. Tijerina and the community refused to obey, basing their actions on their previously authorized legal permits. Later, the judges and the attorney allied with the board of education against the community and tried to invalidate the permits. Various attacks and acts of vandalism against the community followed, including the destruction of some houses and roofs. The government authorities did nothing to protect the community.

As this discussion of the community indicates, Tijerina had adopted early on a worldview in which true Christians ought to live in a counter-culture position; that is, they ought to be a pure community separated from contaminated society.[7] At the same time, Tijerina and his follow-

---

5. Ibid., 2.

6. Ibid., 2–3.

7. In Richard Niebuhr's terms, the community falls in the "Christ against culture" paradigm. See Niebuhr, *Christ and Culture*, 45–82.

ers tried to live in accordance with the government's laws. However, not much time passed before Tijerina received a vision which, in the long run, would change the trajectory of the community and his own worldview.

Revelations from God

Throughout his life, Tijerina talked about several visions which, according to him, came from God. He based important decisions on these visions as answers to his constant search to know and live out God's will. Tijerina and other men from the community left the Valley of Peace to work on ranches in California. They sent the money earned back to their families who remained in Arizona. On one occasion Tijerina dedicated himself to fasting and praying in search of God's will. That night he received a vision:

> A man landed near my subterranean home. Behind him another landed to his right and surveyed the surroundings. Then a third, dressed similarly to the other two, landed nearby. The three sat over something that appeared to be a cloud. They spoke to me. My wife followed me. They told me they came from far away, that they were coming for me, and they would take me to an old ancient regime. My wife said, "Why my husband? Aren't there others?" The three responded, "There is no other in the world that can do this job. We have searched the earth and only he can do this." At that moment, I interrupted and I asked, "What job?" They responded, "Secretary." And without saying more, they lifted themselves, and I saw them leave high up above the ground.[8]

The dream went on to include flying horses, lightning, ancient kings, elders with shining faces, and many other symbols similar to the biblical visions of the apostle John. Tijerina opened his eyes and was convinced that he had received a message from God. He immediately ran to recount the vision to his brothers Rodolfo and Manuel. His life began to take a new direction. Little by little, he arrived at the conviction that he had to dedicate his life to recovering the lands stolen from Mexican-Americans. He was going to be their "secretary," that is, their representative in legal matters. Tijerina dedicated the rest of his life to this task. He began learning the rights of the Mexican-Americans by studying historical documents, going back to the Treaty of Guadalupe Hidalgo (1848) and even farther back to the laws of New Spain. Later, Tijerina utilized his knowledge of

---

8. Tijerina, *"King Tiger,"* 4–5.

the laws to promote justice. The vision mentioned above began a new process of "conversion" in his life. He gradually abandoned the project of constructing a pure, separated community in favor of a project of national relevance: the struggle to recover the lands that had been taken illegally from the Mexican-Americans.[9]

For more than a century, white US American authorities had disregarded the validity of Mexican-Americans' property titles. They used their power in courts to unjustly acquire these citizens' lands. Finally, Tijerina shouted, "Enough!" and began his fight to recover the lands. He decided to strategically unite the Chicanos[10] into an organization, the Alliance of the Free Peoples (*"Alianza de Pueblos Libres"*), to carry out the fight. He summoned Chicanos to different events with the purpose of obligating the authorities to grant justice and thus respect the Mexican-Americans' land rights. In the summer of 1966, Reies gathered 330 people to march on foot from the city of Phoenix to Santa Fe, the capital of New Mexico, a total of sixty-seven miles. The Associated Press publicized the event well and *Newsweek* nicknamed Tijerina "Don Quixote." Since the hearing with the governor in Santa Fe did not produce the desired results, Tijerina proposed the seizure by force of the land of San Joaquín del Río de Chama. This land had belonged to more than 350 Mexican-American families for centuries. On October 22, 1966, hundreds of Hispanics in more than 150 cars and trucks initiated the official takeover. Tijerina and his collaborators seized the land and occupied it for five days before turning themselves over to Judge Bratton. After the Alliance paid his bail, Tijerina walked away free and more determined than ever to continue his struggle for justice.

Tijerina utilized the radio to attract more supporters for the cause. He announced a Great Convention of the Alliance in Coyote to be held in the first days of June 1967. However, the state police blocked all roads leading to Coyote on June 2, 3, and 4. In this context the previously described "attack" on Tierra Amarilla's courthouse took place. Reies evaded the police for several days. Later, he decided to turn himself in to the authorities. He had to appear in court to face sixty-four charges. After the legal prosecution, Tijerina received an absolution for these activities.

---

9. In Niebuhr's terms, Tijerina's worldview changed from being "Christ against culture" to "Christ transforming culture." See Niebuhr, *Christ and Culture*, 197–236.

10. The word "Chicano" became the most common term to refer to Mexican-Americans who fought in favor of human rights in the 1960s.

Later, he was condemned (under false accusations) to three years in jail for a minor offense.

Tijerina's Style of Communication

Tijerina's preferred method of communication was the parable. One of his favorite parables was the cricket and the lion.

> Once upon a time there was an insect, a cricket. One day this cricket ran into a lion. The lion, of course, is the king of the tigers, is the king of the elephants, is the king of the giraffes, is the king of all the big animals, and the lion says to the cricket, "Why are you making such a racket with 'cricket, cricket, cricket'? Aren't you ashamed of yourself? If I were you I wouldn't make any sound at all because you are such a tiny king, you don't matter one bit."
>
> The cricket tells him, "Yeah, but why are you shaming me? Why are you mistreating me? What do you see in me that makes you mistreat and humiliate me? If you want to test out your strength, I'm ready to fight you whenever you want."
>
> And the lion says, "What? Fight with me?" That's what the establishment, the government, the rich people, the bankers often say. You? Fight with me? That's what the lion said to the cricket. But when they began to fight, the cricket jumped up into the lion's ear, buried himself inside, and began tickling the lion from deep within. The lion, since he had a lot of sharp teeth, a lot of claws, a lot of strength, said, "Now I'll get you out!" He started digging and scratching to get the cricket. Pretty soon the lion felt himself growing weak. It's because he was bleeding, and he was getting weak. And the cricket stayed inside, just sitting with his legs crossed.
>
> The lion got even angrier. He gathered his strength all the more. He sharpened his claws and dug in again. He didn't feel the pain caused by his own claws because he was angry; he was so irate that he no longer knew what he was doing. He grew so weak he had no more strength left. He couldn't scratch any more.
>
> My brothers and sisters, that's what happened in Tierra Amarilla. And that's what happened in New Mexico.[11]

Tijerina used parables, anecdotes, popular sayings, allegories, and other methods of folk pedagogy to communicate his ideas with the common people. In this sense, he followed the teaching example of the "Man from the Holy Lands." However, just like Jesus with the Pharisees,

---

11. *Yo soy chicano.*

Tijerina also knew how to utilize the precise legal terminology of case law when necessary.

In 1968, Tijerina had to appear in court for his part in the events in Tierra Amarilla. He decided to be his own lawyer and to represent himself. Recalling the biblical story, Tijerina declared, "Here I am like David before Goliath."[12] He employed an uncommon strategy. The United States has a rarely-applied law, called a "citizen's arrest," in which one citizen can arrest another if he or she finds the other violating the law. In the trial, Tijerina demonstrated his skill as a lawyer as the following description demonstrates.

> I questioned all these witnesses on civil rights and the right of citizens to arrest a person that commits a crime. The jury and the public in attendance were surprised to learn, as I was, that they did not know civil rights law. I asked the witnesses, "You carry guns with which to kill people without knowing the law? Does Joe Black allow you to carry a gun without informing you about the rights of people?" They all had to answer me in the affirmative, including Nick Sais, who had been wounded in Tierra Amarilla. I asked him, "Don't you think that being armed, without knowing the rights of people, that you are a danger to the society?" He admitted he was. I went further and asked him, "Who do you think is at greater fault, you or your superiors, in arming you without teaching you the rights of people and the law?" He twisted and turned in the witness chair, but finally answered that his superiors were at fault. In a surprise move, I asked that Alfonso Sánchez take the witness stand. I wanted to prove to the jury and court with his expert testimony that these law enforcement officials were ignorant of the law and, therefore, incompetent to enforce the law. That is why things turned out as they did in Tierra Amarilla.[13]

In response to this agile defense, the press gave wide coverage to the trial. The *Albuquerque Journal*, with great admiration, nicknamed Tijerina "a modern day Clarence Darrow." Finally, after five weeks in court, December 13, 1968, the day of the verdict arrived. The judge asked Tijerina and the entire courthouse to stand. Three times the words "Not guilty" rang out. Later, Tijerina confessed that "those words were the most

---

12. Ibid.
13. Tijerina, *"King Tiger,"* 123.

beautiful I had heard in my entire life."[14] The national press recognized Tijerina as a Chicano hero. *The Denver Post* (December 18, 1968) reported "New Mexico in state of shock over the triumph of Reies López Tijerina." *The San Francisco Chronicle* (December 22, 1968) proclaimed it a "bloodless coup d'état," and *The New York Times* (December 19, 1968) affirmed, "Tijerina continues his fight for the land."[15] This legal victory earned Tijerina an important place among national Chicano leadership. From there he continued his struggle to recover the stolen lands.

Denouncing Structural Sin

Many years of arduous struggle sharpened Tijerina's awareness of the reality of structural sin. People not only commit personal sins, they also utilize political, economic, and social structures to execute their sins. Referring to police action in Coyote/Tierra Amarilla, Tijerina denounced white Americans' structural sin. The Anglos had violated

> the United States constitutional amendment that secures the right to free assembly. What they did was to destroy a meeting in which we were going to talk about constitutional rights. This was a crime, but the Anglo-Americans, *accustomed to legalizing all their crimes*, don't see it as such. Their conditioned mentality doesn't let them accept the opinion of those they oppress.[16]

Tijerina personally experienced the effects of this structural sin. He later articulated how the white Americans manipulated the various structures at their disposal in order to crush him. After raising his bail from $2,500 to $50,000, Tijerina protested:

> But in the case of the Tiger King [another nickname given to Tijerina], things got worse because I fight for the justice, property, and culture of my people. *The judges and the press, the politicians, and the bankers joined together to destroy me* and kick me out of New Mexico. This combination of powers surrounded Judge Larrazolo and the jury that they gave me in Albuquerque. These combined powers were and still are protecting the policemen who are covering up the report about Salazar's blood.[17]

---

14. Ibid., 126.
15. Tijerina, *Mi lucha*, 265.
16. Ibid., 147 (emphasis added).
17. Ibid., 254–55 (emphasis added).

Tijerina recognized that, to fight structural sin, it was necessary to join forces with others in order to offer a "structural" resistance. Thus, he founded the Alliance of the Free Peoples to fight to recover the stolen lands. After Martin Luther King, Jr.'s death, Tijerina led the Chicano delegation in the March on Washington to form a stronger and wider alliance with African-American and Native American leaders. With his dominance of the legislation of the Treaty of Guadalupe Hidalgo and his self-representation in court, the "Tiger King" showed that structures can also be used for good to overcome evil. Tijerina's example provides some useful insights for future battles against structural sin.

CONCLUSION

Reies López Tijerina was one of the most important personalities of the Chicano movement due to his arduous struggle to recover lands that had been illegally taken from Mexican-Americans. To a degree, Tijerina's organizations and actions proved successful. Regardless of the long-term effects of his work, Tijerina himself remains one of the Chicano movement's most fascinating characters. In the beginning he expressed his Christian faith through Protestant ministries. He later founded a radical Christian community in order to practice his faith more "purely." Then he expanded his horizons and tried to change society as a whole by using the government's own laws in favor of Chicano rights. In all these developments, however, Tijerina never abandoned his Christian faith. On the contrary, his frequent reading of the Bible nurtured his hunger and thirst for justice.[18] The long fight for Mexican-American lands was his response to the special vision that, according to him, came from God. His pedagogy reflected a creative following of the teacher Jesus, the Lord and Savior who was Tijerina's constant inspiration. Throughout his life, Tijerina demonstrated a faith full of justice and obedience to the Lord.

Sadly, many churches did not know how to accompany Tijerina in his struggles. Suffering from an anemic concept of the gospel of Jesus Christ and denying the ethical and social dimensions of our Christian mission, churches did not heed Reies Tijerina nor other similar prophetic voices. May we learn from our mistakes and follow more faithfully in the footsteps of the "Man from the Holy Lands!"

---

18. Matthew 5:6.

10

Alabaré a mi Señor:
Culture and Ideology in Latino Protestant Hymnody

Daniel Ramírez

I stepped over last evening to a chapel opposite my hotel, where one of these congregations was holding service. . . . It was after nine, and the regular meeting had closed. But there stood a group of twenty or so in the upper corner, "going it," like a corner after a revival meeting, in these same songs of Zion. . . . they all put with all their heart and voice, a few sitting about on the benches enjoying the exercise. It was so perfectly Methodistic that I wished to go forward and tell them it seemed just like home.[1]

METHODIST BISHOP GILBERT HAVEN'S 1875 eyewitness report on liturgy within the proto-Anglican *Iglesia de Jesús* (Church of Jesus), founded by liberal, dissident Roman Catholic priests, surely stirred the hearts and loosened the wallets of potential benefactors in the United States. The hearty anthems sung "lustily" by a Mexico City congregation heralded the dawn of Christian truth after dark centuries of "popery." They also evoked, in their primitive power, painful comparisons with the cooled liturgical passion of Haven's home denomination, the Methodist Episcopal Church, in the postbellum period.

The missionary strategist got it half right. Latin American and Latino converts would indeed learn to sing new versions of the Lord's song in their own and strange lands. But they would also insist, as time passed, on authoring their own version of that song. Such assertions inevitably led to (or reflected) contests over aesthetics, autonomy, and power. In the end, music

---

1. Epigraph from Haven, *Mexico*, 95–96.

would prove essential in the shaping of Latino Protestant identities. Both the historian seeking to understand this process and the musicologist seeking to understand the ethnopoetics of these new songs may benefit from closer study of the life trajectories of the composers and singers.

Early Latino Protestant Hymnody

US Latino Protestantism begins with the half-century of evangelization efforts by mainline US denominations in the southwestern United States, northern Mexico, Florida, and the Caribbean. Also, by the last quarter of the nineteenth century, Protestants in Spain had constituted themselves as the Spanish Reformed and Lutheran Churches. The bulk of hymnody from this period reflected the missionaries' preferences. The repertoire contained few surprises. The hymns of Martin Luther, Isaac Watts, Charles Wesley,[2] Fanny Crosby, and Ira Sankey proved ubiquitous in early Spanish-language compilations.[3] The period of vigorous missionary expansion coincided with the apex of the latter two collaborators' careers. Accordingly, the translated music of Fanny Crosby (1820–1915) and Ira Sankey (1840–1908) occupied a privileged position in the liturgy of the missions.[4]

An important cadre of Protestant leaders from Mexico, Cuba, and Spain proved equally as active in translation work as the missionaries. In Spain these included Anglican bishop Juan Bautista Cabrera (1837–1916), translator of Martin Luther's "A Mighty Fortress is Our God," and Pedro Castro (d. 1887), who collaborated in translation/compilation, under the auspices of New York's Tract Society, with Henry Riley (1835–1904). Among the Mexicans and Mexican-Americans, Methodists Vicente Mendoza (1875–1955), Pedro Grado (1862–1923), Juan N. de los Santos (1876–1944), and Nazarene Honorato Reza (1913–2001) proved prolific

---

2. The Wesleyan revival in England and in the First and Second Great Awakenings in the United States had wrested Reform Protestant liturgy loose from the strictures of lined-Psalms, the only acceptable form of congregational song in Puritan New England. See Dickinson, *Music in the History.*

3. Translations of the top five hymns ("All Hail the Power of Jesus' Name," "Jesus, Lover of My Soul," "Am I a Soldier of the Cross," "Alas! And Did My Savior Bleed," and "Rock of Ages, Cleft for Me") ranked by frequency of publication in 225 historic (English-language) US hymnals are ubiquitous in Spanish-language hymnals. See Marini, "From Classical to Modern," 1–38.

4. For Sankey's collaboration with evangelist Dwight L. Moody and composer Fanny Crosby and his significance as "gospel song's" chief composer/compiler/publisher/promoter/popularizer, see Wilhoit, "'Sing Me a Sankey,'" 13–18.

translators as well. One result of the combined efforts (pre-Reza) was the *Himnario evangélico*, published in 1893 by the American Tract Society, and thoroughly revised as the *Nuevo himnario evangélico* in 1914 for use in Methodist, Baptist, Congregational, and Presbyterian churches. In 1905, Mendoza and Grado each published modest hymnals, *Himnos selectos* and *La pequeña colección de himnos*, respectively, for use in Mexican and Mexican-American churches in the Methodist Episcopal Church (MEC) and Methodist Episcopal Church South (MECS) denominations.[5]

Original compositions also began to appear—albeit rarely—alongside translations. Mendoza's original composition, "*Jesús es mi rey soberano*" ("Jesus is My Sovereign King"), composed during a long sojourn in California, ranks as Latino and Latin American Protestantism's most widely sung hymn.

Harvard-trained and Nashville-based Episcopalian Primitivo Rodríguez (from Mexico's *Iglesia de Jesús*) undertook a significant compilation/redaction project at the behest of Cuban Methodists.[6] The official editor and translator of Spanish-language material for the MECS's Board of Missions and Methodist Publishing House,[7] Rodríguez sifted through twenty-seven preexisting Spanish-language hymnals published between 1869 and 1907 to compile his authoritative *Himnario cristiano* in 1908, one that would "be for the good of Spain and Latin America" and one that contained more of Charles Wesley's hymns than any other extant hymnal. Rodríguez limited his redaction of Iberian hymnody to the previous forty years, because the earlier hymnody of the peninsula, although attractive in some aspects, was hopelessly mixed with "the leaven of Romanist teachings."[8]

---

5. Mendoza, *Himnos selectos*; Grado, *Pequeña colección*.

6. MECS, "Cuba Mission," 193.

7. Rodríguez's official collaboration began in 1888. His translations of a significant part of the John Wesley theological corpus were used extensively in Methodist Spanish-language ministerial training curricula. He also created/redacted the MECS's Sunday school Spanish-language curriculum. Upon his death in 1909, the denominational eulogy boasted that "two-thirds of the Protestant Sunday School children in Mexico are using our literature; in fact, through Mr. Rodríguez's skill and industry our Church has been brought to the front rank in the matter of Spanish literature, and in that respect is steadily widening its influence." MECS, "Rev. P. A. Rodríguez," 122–23. See also Náñez, *History of the Rio Grande*, 56–57.

8. Rodríguez, *Himnario cristiano*, iv–vii. Of the twenty-seven hymnals, sixteen had been compiled/published in Spain, three in Mexico, three in New York, and one each in Nashville, Philadelphia, Buenos Aires, London, and Laredo (Texas). The MECS Board of

The new compilations did not meet with universal acclaim. Spanish classicist Marcelino Menéndez y Pelayo relegated the heretics' latest poetic attempts to a disdainful footnote at the end of his voluminous survey, *Historia de los heterodoxos españoles.* "In general," he sniffed, "the Spanish Protestant muse is one of deplorable and drowsy monotony and insipidity."[9]

Perhaps Menéndez y Pelayo, defender of Spanish Catholic orthodox identity and arbiter of taste in turn-of-the-century Madrid, doubted the muse's authenticity. He may have been on to something. Although the revised *Nuevo himnario evangélico* contained an impressive 348 hymns, only about 4 percent (13–15) were original Spanish-language compositions. The situation was not improved in the more evangelical sectors of the church. As late as 1955, the fourth edition of *Cantos de alabanza, pureza y poder* (Songs of Praise, Purity, and Power), published by the Free Tract Society in Los Angeles, maintained a similar proportion of 4 percent original Latino composition among its 234 hymns. The least inclusive hymnal was produced under the aegis of the emerging Assemblies of God (the flagship denomination in American Pentecostalism), the *Himnos de gloria* (Hymns of Glory), compiled in 1916 by H. C. Ball, the Texas-based longtime superintendent of the Assemblies' Spanish-speaking work and a MECS-trained preacher. Less than 2 percent of *Gloria's* 229 hymns were of original Latino composition. That the most widely disseminated Spanish-language hymnal of the twentieth century bore faint Latino imprint says as much about Anglo-American paternalism as it does about Latino and Latin American dependency.[10] Only J. Paul Cragin's *Melodías evangélicas,* first compiled in 1928 and circulated widely up through the 1960s, contained a significant representation of original Latino composition, 25 out of 165, or 15 percent. (Of these, about one-third were borrowed from the Apostolic hymnals discussed in the following section.)

Missions posthumously characterized Rodríguez's opus as "his last and in his own estimation, his greatest work ... perhaps the very best hymnal in the Spanish language [which] has met with a most favorable reception among Protestants in all Spanish-speaking countries. ... [It] is being used by other denominations ... and was exhausted in a short time after its appearance." "Rev. P. A. Rodríguez," 122.

9. Menéndez y Pelayo, *Historia,* 448n1.

10. At least 115,000 copies of *Himnos de gloria* were reported to have been sold in the first decade of publication. See Luce, "Latin-American Pentecostal Work," 6. For a critical assessment of the "pious paternalism" of H. C. Ball and Alice E. Luce, his Los Angeles-based collaborator, see Espinosa, "Borderlands." For an uncritical chronicle of the tutelage, see de Leon, *Silent Pentecostals.*

The role assumed by English-speaking missionaries in hymnal redaction helps to explain the suppression of indigenous musical culture. More recent critiques of US Latino and Latin American Protestant music have argued that mainline Protestant church music facilitated subordination of popular liturgical development through the introduction of Euro-American ethnocentrism, Greek body-soul dualism, concepts of faith and practice, devaluation of folk culture, and the exclusion of indigenous (Latino) musical styles.[11]

Missionaries conflated aesthetics and morality. The musical sphere seemed especially transgressive to orthodox ears—and alluring to the Anglo libido. "Voluptuous and fascinating as the Mexican women are," recollected one Texan observer in 1845, "they are never more so than when excited by soft music and the rapturous *fandango* of which they are so fond. Love then sparkles in their eyes, and their sensitive hearts then yield irresistibly to the pleasures which it awakes."[12] The establishments of such cities as Austin, San Antonio and Brownsville did not share the pioneer's tender nostalgia. Newspapers and civic leaders in those cities called for the *fandango's* banishment in the 1870s.[13]

Elite censure proved of little avail, at least in the Southwest's *colonias*. Writing half a century later (1925), Vernon McCombs, superintendent of the MEC's Spanish and Portuguese district (southern California conference), lamented the sinful state of affairs in his report on Mexican missions work in the United States:

> Vice is the threshold between play and sin. All too frequently the witchery of music and easy flow of merry words and laughter degenerates into vice. The dancing girl and the wine cup are star attractions in every Mexican colony. The Santa Rosa Club, the Independence Day ball, and the Benavides pool hall form an

---

11. Lockwood, "Recent Developments," 16. United Methodism's 1996 *Mil voces para celebrar* appears to squarely face the Lockwood critique. See Martínez, "*Mil voces*," 25–29. An equally remarkable ecumenical compilation project, with significantly greater Pentecostal content than *Mil voces*, appeared three years earlier under Mennonite auspices. *Alabanzas favoritas, no. 2*, with 232 hymns, represented a scoring and expansion of the original *Alabanzas favoritas*, compiled in 1954 by Mennonites in Chihuahua, Mexico. See Iglesia de Dios en Cristo, *Alabanzas favoritas, no. 2*. For a discussion of hymnody contestation between Brazilian Baptists and missionaries, see Spann, "Tale of Two Hymnals," 15–21.

12. Page, *Prairiedom*, quoted in de León, *They Called Them Greasers*, 37.

13. De León, *Silent Pentecostals*, 45.

altogether disproportionate and unwholesome attraction for the
social and physical welfare of these pleasure-loving Latins.[14]

Small wonder, then, that missionaries and their spiritual progeny
insisted on strict boundaries in the arena of music and liturgy. In a 1928
address to the Baptist State Association of Chihuahua (reprinted in full
in the Methodist *Evangelista mexicano*), a speaker rhapsodized about the
centrality of one privileged instrument:

> Music should never be absent from the church. As far as the in-
> struments to be used, in my thinking, it is the organ that should
> never be absent from the church. Although it may not lend
> itself to the adornment of music, it is the most appropriate to
> accompany religious songs. It is not only songs that the organ
> can accompany; it can also be used to play preludes for the ser-
> vices, which is of utmost importance, as this prepares us better
> to receive the message. During the offering time something can
> be played. If not a classical piece, since the organ or organist may
> not be up to it, then something slow and sweet.[15]

The speaker proceeded to call for a removal of all melancholy and
languidness from hymnody. A missionary need not have been present at
the conclave to affirm the concern for liturgical propriety. Indeed, after a
half-century of tutelage, Latino converts seemed to have thoroughly en-
dorsed the value of a liturgy bleached of folkloric elements.

Small wonder, then, that in his landmark study of Mexican immigrants in the late 1920s, Manuel Gamio downplayed the possibility of any
significant inroads among this population, due to the "cold, intellectual,
moralistic quality of Protestantism, and lack of color and artistic impres-
sion."[16] Clearly, Gamio had mainline Protestantism in mind; he derived
much of his data from Protestant settlement houses and relief agencies. A
survey of the more emotive, folkloric "*aleluya*" barrio and rural churches

---

14. McCombs M., *From Over the Border,* 86.

15. *El evangelista mexicano,* 136–37.

16. Gamio, *Mexican Immigration,* 117. For concern over proselytizing by *aleluyas* (the popular epithet for Apostolics and other Pentecostals) among gullible immigrants, see Gamio, "The Leader and the Intellectual," in *Life Story,* 223. The study, commissioned by the Social Science Research Council, excerpted interviews conducted during 1926–1927 with seventy-six Mexican immigrants (including one Methodist and two Baptist minis-ters) by Mexico's foremost anthropologist. *Life Story* is the companion book to the more analytical *Mexican Immigration.*

then springing up throughout the Southwest and Mexico may have led Mexico's foremost anthropologist to other conclusions.

Historian Russell Richey has characterized early American Methodism as a "movement of the voice—a preaching, singing, testifying, praying, shouting, crying, arguing movement,"[17] a description that carries important explanatory value. However, not all these voices carried over into adolescent Methodism, the Methodism encountered by Mexicans and Chicanos, nor were they all within the hearing range of Latino would-be converts. It was when their voice was stifled that Latino Methodists and other Protestants sought out other vocal and aural spaces, spaces many found in Pentecostalism. The religious musical culture forged in these alternative sonic spaces would crescendo and later find echo in the experience of both popular Catholic and mainline Protestant believers in Mexico and in the United States.

Early Latino Pentecostal Hymnody

In contrast to mainline Protestantism's retreat from folk culture, Pentecostal hymnody recaptured the *fiesta* of Mexican and Latino culture, liberating it from seemingly intractable pathologies of alcoholism and double-standard sexism, and returning it to the sacred place of ritual, performance, and spectacle. Pentecostals forged a new aural universe that incorporated as much sensory corporeality as the earlier popular Catholic visual one of saints, candles, gilded altars, and paintings (which had been erased by earlier mainline Latino Protestantism).[18]

Musical Cultural Practice
among Early Latino Pentecostals

In 1925, one of the fledgling Chicano Pentecostal movements (hereafter referred to interchangeably as Apostolic) had gathered in its inaugural convention in San Bernardino, California as the *Iglesia de la Fe Apostólica Pentecostés*. Its leading ministers, Francisco Llorente and Antonio Nava

---

17. Richey, *Early American Methodism*, 82.

18. Mikhail Bakhtin argues that the medieval festivals and carnivals in the works of Rabelais "always represent[ed] an essential, meaningful content" in uneasy tension with official church-sanctioned feasts. Bakhtin, *Rabelais*, 8–9. Similarly, over and against missionary censure, borderlands Pentecostals reintroduced a measure of the carnivalesque (laughter, weeping, body movement, profane instruments, feasts, etc.) into liturgical space and time.

(the latter a refugee from Mexico's revolutionary upheaval), carried credentials issued by Garfield T. Haywood, the African-American leader of the Indianapolis-based Pentecostal Assemblies of the World (PAW), at that time the biracial (black and white) flagship denomination for the Oneness (non-Trinitarian) wing of US American Pentecostalism. Bernardo Hernández, the convention secretary (and a former Baptist elder from Yuma, Arizona), recorded in his minutes that the first ministers' meetings were opened with the hymns: "*Ama el pastor sus ovejas*" ("As the Shepherd Loves His Sheep," a translation of "Dear to the Heart of the Shepherd"), "*Cerca, más cerca, oh Dios de Ti*" ("Near, Nearer, oh God, to Thee," translation of "Nearer, Still Nearer"), and "*Jesús, yo he prometido*" (translation of "Oh, Jesus, I Have Promised" ["Angel's Song"]). Hernández listed sixteen of the hymns sung by the conventioneers—all but four taken from Spanish-language Protestant hymnals. He also highlighted the debut of several compositions by Marcial de la Cruz, early Apostolicism's most prolific composer (seventy-plus compositions by the time of his death in 1935), and his daughter, Beatriz.[19]

During this time the movement also appropriated African-American musical forms (call and response), theology (radical monotheistic doctrine), and ecclesiology (episcopal polity). Although he remained monolingual in Spanish, de la Cruz proved an avid student of the music he encountered in his fellowship with black congregations and with African-American members of Latino Apostolic churches (e.g., Watts, California). Antonio Nava, who took up the mandolin to form a duet with the guitarist de la Cruz, recalls his colleague's immediate repetition of rhythms and chords he heard in such services.[20]

For at least the first decade and a half of growth, Latino Apostolics, while negotiating their place as newcomers on the half-century-old Latino Protestant block, forged alliances with other marginalized groups on the religious and social periphery, groups similarly cut off from the ecclesiastical structures and institutions at the center. Latino Apostolics found in African-American heterodox hymnody a ready-made "defensive,

---

19. Hernández, *Estatutos acordados*. Marcial de la Cruz also served as an evangelist in southern California, Arizona, and New Mexico. He was said to introduce hymns into his services that he had composed on the spot after fasting in a pup tent carried with him for that purpose. See Ortega, *Mis memorias*, 279–80. See also Lerma, *Marcial de la Cruz*.

20. Antonio C. Nava, interview, September 13, 1994.

Alabaré a mi Señor

counter-ideological, symbolic expression"[21] to employ on behalf of their community's identity, continuity and autonomy.[22] And when strengthened, this autonomy bred creativity.

ELVIRA HERRERA

Such creative agency presents itself in the case of Elvira Herrera, a member of one of the few Mexican Methodist families in the California-Mexico border town of Calexico in the early twentieth century. The immigrant family settled in Calexico in the latter part of the 1910s after three years in the Central Valley town of Fresno. Elvira and her younger brother, Luis, finished high school in the United States. Both were bilingual.[23]

During the same period (1918) the MECS established an outreach to Mexicans and Mexican-Americans in this border region. Northern Methodists had begun a year earlier, with the arrival of Tranquilino Gómez from Los Angeles.

MEC superintendent McCombs saw Calexico as a "center from which to work godless Lower California," especially Mexicali, "where they assemble in troops in the harlots' houses," and where "the devil has certainly sported undisturbed these decades past."[24]

Despite the zone's bleak morality, religious musical culture flourished there, at least for the young Herreras and other borderlanders. With Luis as her accompanist, Elvira translated or adapted several English-language hymns into Spanish. Her most popular one was disseminated widely throughout the hemisphere in Spanish-language Protestant hymnals

21. For a discussion of these Gramscian strategies in a different albeit related context, see Peña, *Texas-Mexican Conjunto*.

22. The reciprocity of black-Latino contacts is indicated by reports in the 1920s and 1930s of African-American enthusiasm for Mexican worship in south Texas: "The brethren worship in a large room in a private house, perhaps some thirty gathering there, and in the back part the colored people gather. These colored people are anxious to hear Pentecost preached in their own language, but a white man could hardly preach to them in this part of the country. Yet, these colored people have learned to sing the Spanish songs with the Mexicans, even though they know very little Spanish. I hope that some colored Pentecostal preacher will go to Edna sometime and hold a meeting among them." Ball, "Work Prospers," 13.

23. Luis Herrera, interview, September 16, 1994.

24. McCombs, "Spanish and Portuguese District." Information on the MEC Latino work in southern California is taken from annual *Journal of the Southern California Annual Conference* reports from 1901–1927.

during the twentieth and twenty-first centuries.[25] *"Es la oración"* ("Prayer Is") represented an extremely loose adaptation of F. M. Lehman's 1909 composition, "The Royal Telephone," or "Central's Never Busy," which was published in more than eighteen Evangelical, Holiness, and Pentecostal hymnals from 1914 to 1949.[26]

"The Royal Telephone" Author: F. M. Lehman (1909)	*"Es la oración"* Tr./Author: Elvira Herrera (c. 1921)	("Prayer Is") (*translation of Herrera lyrics—mine*)
I Central's never busy, always on the line You may hear from heaven almost any time 'Tis a royal service free for one and all When you get in trouble give this royal line a call	I Es la oración un medio que el Señor le dejó a su grey, que anda con temor Viendo Su Palabra, en ella tú verás que la oración te acerca a Cristo más y más	I Prayer is a medium that the Lord left his flock that walks in the fear (of God) Looking at His Word you will see that prayer brings you close to Jesus more and more
C Telephone to glory, O what joy divine! I can feel the current moving on the line Built by God the Father for his loved and own We may talk to Jesus thro' this royal telephone	C ¡Oh! Hablar con Cristo, ¡qué felicidad! Y contarle todo, todo en verdad Exponiéndole tu necesidad Él te escuchará desde su Trono Celestial	C Oh, to speak with Jesus, what happiness! And to tell him everything, everything in truth Laying bare all your need He will hear you from his celestial throne
II There will be no charges, telephone is free It was built for service, just for you and me There will be no waiting on this royal line Telephone to glory always answers just in time	II Si estás tú triste, ponte en oración Habla hacia la gloria con el corazón Es un mandamiento que el Señor dejó Y tendrás respuesta porque así lo prometió	II If you are sad, put yourself in prayer Pray toward Glory with your heart This is a commandment that the Lord left (us) And you'll receive an answer for so he has promised

---

25. del Pilar, *Himnos de "El avivamiento."* J. Paul Cragin, an independent Holiness missionary, correctly attributed the hymn to Herrera in his *Melodías evangélicas*. The hymn continues to circulate throughout the continent, appearing in the latest edition of the hymnal of Mexico's *Iglesia Evangélica Independiente*. See Parra Herrera, Huerta de Parra, and Rodríguez Cámara, *Himnos de victoria*, 338n.

26. Letter from Mary L. VanDyke, The Hymn Society, to Daniel Ramírez, October 28, 1998.

Alabaré a mi Señor

"The Royal Telephone" author: F. M. Lehman (1909)	"Es la oración" tr./author: Elvira Herrera (c. 1921)	("Prayer Is") (translation of Herrera lyrics—mine)
III	III	III
Fail to get the answer, Satan's crossed your wire By some strong delusion or some base desire Take away obstructions, God is on the throne And you'll get the answer thro' this royal telephone	¿Estás en espera del Consolador? Ten fe y paciencia, constancia y amor Y el Señor al ver tu ferviente prez Cumplirá tu gozo dándote un Pentecostés	Are you tarrying for the Comforter? Have faith and patience, constancy and love and the Lord, upon seeing your fervent press(ing) Will fulfill your joy giving you a Pentecost
IV	IV	IV
If your line is "grounded," and connection true has been lost with Jesus, tell you what to do Pray'r and faith and promise mend the broken wire till your soul is burning with the Pentecostal fire	Si no hay respuesta, ora más y más No te desanimes, Cristo no es falaz Siempre a sus promesas, fiel responderá Lo que necesites, esto Él te lo dará	If there is no answer keep praying on and on Do not be disheartened, Jesus never fails To his promises he will always hold Whatever you may need this he will give you
V		
Carnal combinations cannot get control of this line to glory, anchored in the soul Storm and trial cannot disconnect the line held in constant keeping by the Father's hand divine		

What is most striking in this example is Herrera's decision to excise completely any mention of the still-novel appliance, the very title of Lehman's song! Although this omission may disappoint scholars of material religious culture,[27] Herrera seems to have been very purposeful in moving from the material to the symbolic. In an era of economic scarcity and limited communication technology, her coreligionists could scarcely identify a luxury appliance that only *gringos* and wealthy Mexicans owned. So rather than get lost in the metaphors of US American consumerism, better just to have an intimate talk with Jesus instead: Jesus the Shepherd, Jesus the Word-giver, Jesus who sits on the throne—all metaphors readily understandable in popular religious idioms. The spirit of the message, the direct line to the heart of Jesus, remained intact, helped along by Herrera's aggressive translation/adaptation.

27. See McDannell, *Material Christianity*.

We can surmise that Herrera adapted the hymn early in her shift from Methodism to Apostolicism. The Herrera home, which hosted Bible studies with Baptist and Salvation Army evangelists, was the site of the first Apostolic congregation in the Calexico-Mexicali area. Elvira and Luis' prior musical training in the Methodist church equipped them for the tasks of hymn translation and performance—gifts they generously shared with the Apostolic and broader Pentecostal movement.

The case of this early twentieth century gospel hymn distills the essence of my argument. Clearly, the Herreras were more than restive Methodists or prodigal Catholics. Rather, Elvira was a creative agent, busily fashioning an identity in the margins between two societies: Protestant United States and Catholic Mexico. For her, that periphery was a center, a zone in which she moved comfortably, usually oblivious to the hegemonic centers. In the case of such borderlanders, robust agency is especially evident when they are left to their own devices, either by design or neglect from their would-be sponsors. Eventually, for Herrera, Methodism's tentative support system in the Imperial Valley (the MEC reported that the Mexican mission in Calexico and surrounding towns was without pulpit supply in 1918 and 1919), like the telephone metaphor, proved inadequate to her community's needs. She and her family embraced a heterodox Pentecostal movement represented in the charismatic ministry of a young immigrant evangelist, Antonio Nava, who established his transborder base in Calexico in 1921 (the same year that the MEC began building a parsonage for a Mexican pastor).

It is likely that the mobile religious proletariat was voting with its ears as well as its feet, as much enchanted by the cultural musical repertoire as by the charisma of the early tongues-speaking evangelists/healers. The case of Elvira Herrera and her religious community challenges us to reconsider a seemingly inconsequential border region as a central site for the popular religious imagination, for contest over religious identity, and for production of religious musical culture. It invites us to recognize the ability of the subjects of our study to assume agency and to move around in those zones—sometimes enmeshed in webs (structures) of ideology, sometimes inhabiting them as tricksters, and sometimes breaking free of them—as they forge identities and sing songs of their own making.

SCARCITY AND FECUNDITY

The onset of the Great Depression initially wreaked havoc upon young Latino Pentecostal churches. Political scapegoating compounded already dire economic straits. Federal, state, and local authorities combined to push nearly half a million Mexicans and Chicanos south of the border.[28] This persecution tore at the fabric of *barrio* life. Ultimately, however, that fabric proved resilient, and in the case of Pentecostal communities, stretched to encompass a broad swath of territory far beyond the movement's origin in southern California. Solidarity amidst scarcity bred fecundity. Also, the retreat of sponsor denominations under financial duress left wider margins for innovation.

Set against the grim backdrop of economic recession and political persecution, Apostolic hymnody (to take just one Pentecostal variant) expanded into such a large corpus that the first compilation effort in the early 1930s, *Himnos de consolación*,[29] contained more than 200 hymns, the large majority of them original compositions. A concurrent compilation effort in Mexico, *Himnos de suprema alabanza*,[30] gathered more than 160 hymns; again the vast majority were organic to the movement. Even after accounting for a significant number of simultaneously published hymns, by the late 1930s, the overall number of published original Apostolic hymns can be conservatively estimated at 300. This fecundity throws into sharp relief the stark situation in the mainline Protestant churches. Apostolics and other Pentecostals were certainly grateful to inherit the mainline churches' hymns, but they judged them to be inadequate in style and problematic in doctrinal content (e.g., Trinitarian doxologies).

Apostolic hymn writers matched perennial Mexican poetic themes (e.g., pilgrimage) with popular musical genres (e.g., *polka*) to produce a sensory and physical experience that resonated in the community's ears, hearts, and bodies. They composed songs for every ritual occasion: births/child dedications, water and Spirit baptisms, initiations, birthdays, communion services, marriages, partings, welcomings, offerings, and death—thereby reuniting popular music and religious ritual in a stronger bond than even

---

28. Hoffman, *Unwanted Mexican Americans*, 174–75. The number represented at least 35% of the overall "Mexican" population of 1.3 million reported by the US Census in 1930. http://www.census.gov/apsd/wepeople/we-2r.pdf.

29. Nava, *Himnos de consolación*.

30. Gaxiola, *Himnos de suprema alabanza*.

Mexican/Chicano Catholicism enjoyed at the time and in a vein similar to that of Nahuatl and other ancient Mesoamerican cultures. Beginning in the late nineteenth century, Mexican Catholicism had experienced a revival of high art and cathedral choral music that had once again pushed folk music and instruments out of that country's principal sanctuaries and relegated them to village churches and the external performance spaces of pilgrimages and *fiestas*.[31] The situation for Mexican-American Catholics under the tutelage of a Baltimore-based hierarchy bent on "Americanizing" the culturally and theologically recalcitrant southwestern flock seemed even bleaker.[32]

Form mattered as much as content in Apostolic and Pentecostal hymnody. Composers appropriated most of the contemporary popular Mexican musical idioms and instruments: from *polka* to *ranchera* to *corrido* to *vals* to *huapango* to *marcial* to *canción romántica* to *bolero*—all, apparently, except *cha-cha-cha* and *danzón*, which were probably considered too irredeemably wedded to the carnal dance floor. Yet, even the latter's exclusion cannot be maintained strictly, given the *bolero*'s derivation from the *danzón*, *conga*, and *contradanza*, the former two demonstrating clear Afro-Cuban roots and the third Afro-Cuban adaptations.[33] Although introduced into Mexico (Yucatán) and Central America through marimba bands in the nineteenth century, *bolero*'s wider dissemination awaited transmission in the 1930s through Mexico City's powerful XEW radio station and the virtuoso interpretation of the genre by guitar *tríos* such as *Los Panchos*, *Las Calaveras*, and *Los Diamantes*.[34] Almost simultaneously, *bolero*'s slightly syncopated 2/4 rhythm (eight beats with the third left out) crowded out its Andalusian cousin-progenitor and was applied to Mexican regional repertoires and to Pentecostal hymnody.

Apostolic musical poetics, emanating from the fields and orchards where many of the songwriters labored, could not help but reflect the contours of the borderlands. Indeed, their music output captured something of the experience of exhausted bodies dragged in from a day's work, quickly splashed with water and nourished with beans and tortillas before

---

31. Campos, *El folklore*, 191–96.

32. See Dolan and Deck, *Hispanic Catholic Culture* and Dolan and Hinojosa, *Mexican Americans*.

33. Kahl, "Bolero," 870–71.

34. Af Geijerstam, *Popular Music*, 77.

dashing off to the campsite or tent service to embrace other bodies in fervent and ecstatic worship.

The process of inspiration/composition itself often occurred in the workplace, as in the case of Filemón Zaragoza, author of the tender *vals* hymn, "*Mi plegaria*" ("My Plea"). The melancholy melody and lyrics came to him as he toiled in the cotton fields outside of El Paso in 1940. Zaragoza understood the epiphany as an answer to a long-standing prayer he had often breathed in envy of other church members' ease in hymn composition. The Ciudad Juarez resident stooped to trace the lyrics in the dirt rows and returned to the spot throughout the work day to commit the words to memory. Upon returning across the border to Juarez after the day's work, and before going home to wash the dirt off his weary body, he dashed to the church to find paper and pencil.[35] The song proved an instant hit in Pentecostal churches in Juarez, El Paso, Chihuahua City, Las Cruces, New Mexico, and beyond.

Borderlands Pentecostal composers drew liberally from mundane agricultural metaphors, such as "*Vamos todos a la siembra*" ("Let's All Go to the Sowing") and "*El sembrador*" ("The Sower"); bakeries; barren and flowery landscapes such as "*Rosa de Sarón*" ("Rose of Sharon") and "*Como la primavera*" ("As the Springtime"); and even railroads and trains, as in "*El tren del evangelio*" ("The Gospel Train"). The sweet emotive wells of matriarchy and maternity inspired numerous elegies, such as "*Mi madre oraba por mí*" ("My Mother Prayed for Me"). The bitter fruit of poverty, in hymns such as "*Tú eres refugio del pobre*" ("You are the Refuge of the Poor"), fed scathing prophetic and social commentary in hymns such as "*Profecía de Habacuc*" ("Prophecy of Habakkuk"). Composers wrapped entire biblical passages in *corrido* and *décima* forms, a practice essential for the improved general and biblical literacy of a community long denied ready access to the scriptures. Traditional Christian hagiography received similar treatment. For example, a ten-stanza-long, graphic *corrido* about Christian martyrs in the Roman Coliseum opens with the troubadour's obligatory announcement ("*Hermanos, voy a contarles . . . allá en el siglo primero*"—"Brethren, I am going to tell you . . . way back in the first century") and respects metric (e.g., octosyllabic lines), lyric, and other conventions of the *corrido* genre.

---

35. Filemón Zaragoza, interview, September 17, 1994.

During the same period in other locales, similar liturgical reforms were afoot. Juan Lugo, the "Apostle of Pentecost to Puerto Rico" and founder of the *Iglesia de Dios Pentecostal* (now the commonwealth's largest denomination), found a ready musical collaborator in Juan Concepción.[36] Francisco Olazabal's independent *Concilio Latinoamericano de Iglesias Cristianas* spawned an indigenous hymnody as well.[37] Like Nava, both leaders had led breakaway movements spurred by a disenchantment with *gringo* (Assemblies of God) sponsorship, Lugo after a long period of alternating eager and ambivalent collaboration and Olazabal more purposefully and earlier on.[38] Also, the financial straits of white sponsors hampered attempts to contain newly assertive cultural nationalisms. In the case of the Disciples of Christ, the recall of missionaries from Puerto Rico coincided with a successful move for independence by islanders. The ensuing revival and emergence of an indigenous, proto-Pentecostal hymnody so transformed the *Discípulos* religious culture that longtime Mexico-based Disciples missionary Frederic Huegel, upon a trip to the island in 1951, complained that his hosts had carried their liturgy beyond the point of recognition.[39] In these cases, the guitar and kindred instruments emerged as markers of a new liturgical practice and space, a zone replete, as one observer remarked, with transgressive significance: "The (Disciples) revival of '33 redeemed the guitar. This was not well received in devotional circles. Folks thought it too romantic, forgetting that the Gospel itself is a romance."[40]

The contested marker of the guitar and other signifiers prompts an interrogation of traditional historiography, one that will consider insights from ethnomusicology and related disciplines. Early photos of Latino Pentecostal musicians display the ubiquitous guitar (previously disdained as profane—and erotic—by mainline missionaries and their converts), which, according to pioneer Antonio Nava, was often the only instrument available to a working-class church: "*La guitarra . . . p'al pobre . . . la gui-*

---

36. Concepción, *Ecos de vida*.

37. Gutiérrez, *Nuevo himnario*.

38. See Espinosa, "Borderlands."

39. Huegel, *Apostol de la cruz*, 273–74.

40. Florentino Santana, "Address to the Annual Assembly of the Iglesia Discípulos de Cristo en Puerto Rico," February 19, 1983. Quoted in del Pilar, *Himnos de "El avivamiento."*

tarra" ("The guitar . . . for the poor . . . the guitar").[41] The guitar and banjo could combine in ensembles of wind, string and percussive instruments, such as the *bajo sexto* and the *tololoche* (upright bass)—two favorites in *tejano conjunto* style. The Latino mainline-Pentecostal contrast seems similar to the tensions between *tejano orquestra* (the middle class Chicano preference exemplified by Little Joe y la Familia) and *conjunto* music styles (the working class folk preference exemplified by the Conjunto Bernal). As noted by ethnomusicologist Manuel Peña in his study of the two genres, these boil down to a class-informed preference: "*música pa' high society*" versus "*música pa' los pobres*" ("music for high society" versus "music for the poor").[42] The Pentecostal proletariat also democratized liturgy, creating a communitarian performance space for any lay member, singly or in family or auxiliary groups, to express or declaim musical and poetic creations.

Los Hermanos Alvarado: Migrating Faith

The guitar as a controversial symbol suggests other contestations over culture, ideology, and theology.

In a sense, Pentecostals led the way toward a Protestant reencounter with culture. The emergence of a majority Pentecostal movement within Latino and Latin American Protestantism presents an interesting case of the Pentecostalization of the mainline, especially in terms of liturgy and music. The marginal social position of Pentecostals also led to assertions of social solidarity with fellow sojourners. Pilgrims sang Zion's song to other wanderers. The study of borderlands religious musical culture thus reveals interesting continuities between the region's two most popular religiosities: Pentecostal and Catholic. The agents of this transformation remain generally anonymous; such is the nature of social movements. However, several interesting cases present themselves. Among these, the family biography and musical career of the *Hermanos Alvarado*, a guitar-strumming trio whose musical career spanned three decades (1950s through 1970s), could serve as a template for the broader story under discussion as well as for twentieth-century Mexican-American history.

Pascual and Dolores Alvarado emigrated from northern Mexico early in that country's decade-long revolution. Pascual had fought on the

---

41. Antonio C. Nava, interview, September 13, 1994.
42. Peña, *Texas-Mexican Conjunto,* 139. See also Peña, *Mexican American Orquesta.*

side of Francisco Villa and then with Venustiano Carranza. The couple's seven children were born in Texas, Arizona, and California. The parents and maternal grandparents were among the first generation of Apostolic converts in Bakersfield, California (baptized in 1916). Thus, a tight-knit, sectarian Pentecostal community provided the religious formation for the Alvarado children.[43]

In 1932, in spite of her children's US citizenship, Dolores was ordered to repatriate to Mexico. In order to keep the family intact, the parents decided to both return there with their children. After arriving by rail to Torreón, Coahuila, they slowly made their way, following the railway northward, back to the border. Pascual took welding jobs and Dolores sold tortillas to finance the seven-month trek. An infant son, Juan, was kept alive by the milk of a donated goat. Adolescent daughters Luz and Guadalupe died from malnourishment soon after their arrival in Ciudad Juárez, a stone's throw away from the country of their birth. On their arrival in Juárez, the Alvarado parents set about securing housing and a livelihood and reconnecting with the Apostolic church. A small ranch outside the city limits met the first need; an Apostolic congregation pastored by Juan Ramírez met the second. Apparently, the transborder networks set in place through the preceding decade by Apostolic leaders and laity served to keep the Alvarado and many other families connected during a period of persecution and dislocation (the family dedicated the infant Juan in Torreón's *Iglesia Apostólica*). Such solidarity was lacking in other Protestant church movements, even Pentecostal ones, especially those led by *gringos*, as was the case with Aimee Semple McPherson's International Church of the Foursquare Gospel, whose Latino ministerial ranks were decimated by repatriation. That denomination's roster of Mexican-American pastors and congregations completely disappeared in the wake of the political persecution. Repatriated Apostolics, on the other hand, could seek out sister congregations in Mexico or could establish new ones.

As they entered their teen years, the Alvarado sons took up guitar playing, soon becoming proficient. As has been the case with African-American gospel and blues musicians, the venue for performance and the choice of musical genre became sites of struggle for the artists' souls. Elder brother Román decided early on to dedicate his talents "to the Lord," while

---

43. Information on the family biography and trio's career was gathered in a series of oral history interviews with Rosario, Juan, and Román Alvarado in San Jose and Whittier, California, from August 5, 1999 to December 29, 2000.

Rosario and Juan opted to play in *cantinas.* When pressed by Román, the two prodigals would agree to accompany him in performance in religious services. The trio's virtuosity soon won them a following in the Apostolic churches of Juárez. The brothers experienced a presentiment of things to come when they were invited to perform on a local radio station program. Within a few years, Rosario unequivocally joined Román and the church, leaving behind, in classic conversion mode, a womanizing and drinking past (Juan would wait two more decades to convert).

Interestingly, after conversion, Rosario and Román exchanged Rosario's smaller *requinto* guitar for the latter's larger, standard one, reasoning that the move to the simpler strumming instrument would help Rosario resist the tempting *cantina* memories evoked by the *requinto*'s fancy riffs. The Alvarado's repertoire consisted chiefly of music composed by Román and other Apostolic songwriters in the United States and Mexico. Popular Mexican musical genres provided the musical forms adapted—and sacralized—by the Alvarados. The thematic emphases on pilgrimage and endurance represented as much a defiance of majority intolerance as a reworking of ancient Mesoamerican and medieval Catholic motifs. The singers intertwined sweet melancholy with joyful encounter and sheer doggedness in order to articulate a poetic vision similar to Aztec pilgrim hymns or medieval Iberian Catholic ones. A closer ethnomusicological analysis of the Alvarado discography would present, of course, interesting issues of performance, marketing, technology, class, and aesthetics, among others.

After nearly two decades in Juárez, the Alvarado family made their way back to Los Angeles. This locus exposed their musical talents to an ever-widening circle of Latino Protestant churches, a development that discomfited the Apostolic leadership. A fortuitous encounter with Dale Evans and Laura Harper, wives of famous Hollywood musical cowboys, propelled and broadened the Alvarados' artistic trajectory in ways the singers had never imagined. The 1959 episode bears recounting here.

After assisting two Anglo matrons (Evans and Harper) with their shopping bags at the downtown Broadway market, Pascual Alvarado agreed to accompany them home to Hollywood Hills to repeat the favor. While standing in their driveway, he heard music drifting from a rear window (probably the music of the Sons of the Pioneers). The Good Samaritan, Pascual Alvarado, boasted to Harper that his progeny could sing much better. Intrigued, she took him up on his claim. After an audition the trio was invited in to record in a state-of-the-art studio. The resulting five-volume LP project, managed by Harper, ushered in a long period of expanding fame as the hemisphere's most widely heard *evangélico* musical group, a period that lasted until their disbanding in 1973.

While outsider savvy and capital may have provided important initial impetus to the Alvarados' career, *gringa* imagination and gaze also crippled them at home. Harper's decision to photograph the *tejano* singers in *jarocho* costume (from Veracruz) for the LP covers confirmed their coreligionists' suspicions that the group had become "*mundano*" (worldly). Yet, as doors to sectarian Apostolic churches in Los Angeles closed, others opened in the wider Latino *evangélico* community.

The appeal of the Alvarados' music in that era seems to have been matched only by that of Guatemala's Alfredo Colom (1904–1971), whose compositions were broadcast through HCJB, the Voice of the Andes, a powerful missionary radio station in Quito, Ecuador.[44] The broad dissemination of the Alvarados' music occurred by means of the LP project, several tours sponsored by Harper and the Christian Faith organization and widespread pirating (which persists to this day). That the musical influence of these Texas and California-born troubadours extended far has been borne out by recent research in Oaxaca. A veteran Nazarene pastor in that state credits three factors with keeping the first generation of *evangélicos* in southern Mexico "faithful" in the face of great intolerance in the 1950s and 1960s: 1) *la Biblia* (the Bible), 2) *la oración* (prayer), and 3) "*la música de los Hermanos Alvarado*" ("the music of the Alvarado Brothers").[45]

The Hermanos Alvarado never visited Oaxaca, but their music certainly arrived early on, possibly in the luggage of the first returning *braceros* (guest workers), or of immigrants caught up in the *migra* raids of Operation Wetback, or of converted female migrants returning from domestic service jobs in Mexico City. As early converts to Protestantism in southern Mexico set about constructing an alternative aural universe out of new and old cultural elements, they brought home (from Mexico City or the United States or elsewhere) religious remittances of great symbolic value, including, especially, music. The historicization of that process remains a pending task for scholars.

---

44. Colom M., *Música en su alma*.

45. José Hernández, interview, May 20, 2002, Oaxaca de Juárez, Oaxaca.

Alabaré a mi Señor

Migrating Music

Although not the principal focus of this study, the contemporary religious musical culture of Latino Catholics provides intriguing clues about the wandering nature of music. Of the borderlands under study, those of confessional identity seem most porous, as discomfiting as this might prove to ecclesiastical authorities who insist on orthodox practice. Catholics, too, perform their own type of bricolage, combining readily recognizable Marian prayers with borrowings from *aleluya* (this common epithet for Protestants in general hints at the ubiquity of Pentecostal practice) musical culture. Clearly, someone is not minding orthodoxy's store. The sound of Pentecostal *coritos* now reverberates in rural mountain pilgrimages, as well as in urban spaces such as Mexico City's Basilica of the Virgin of Guadalupe. By the time Vatican II opened the doors and windows of the mass to vernacular languages and sounds, the *aleluya* siblings and cousins of Catholics had prepared an engaging repertoire for ready borrowing, probably via the charismatic renewal. Once again, those inhabiting borderlands of religious belief and practice proved themselves adept and creative agents. The difficulty in precisely tracing the origin and dissemination of most Latino Pentecostal hymns and choruses suggests that these ride in the luggage and in the hearts of a very mobile religious proletariat that often does not bother to check in with civil (immigration), ecclesiastical, and academic authorities. How, for example, did "*Alabaré a mi Señor*" ("I Will Praise My Lord"), "*No hay Dios tan grande como Tú*" ("There Is No God Greater than You"), and "*Mas allá del sol*" ("Beyond the Sun") travel from Pentecostal to mainline Protestant and popular Catholic hymnody?[46] In the end, in the US-Mexico borderlands, popular Pentecostalism and popular Catholicism may have more in common than typically assumed. The continuities seem as important as the discontinuities.

---

46. The 1989 Spanish-language Catholic hymnal *Flor y canto* includes, among others, old Pentecostal standards such as "*Una mirada de fe*" ("A Glimpse of Faith"), "*Alabaré*" ("I Will Praise"), and "*La mañana gloriosa*" ("The Glorious Morning"), the latter an anonymous *evangélico* hymn from Colombia. Alstott, *Flor y canto*. Edwin Aponte's discussion of *coritos* as "religious symbols in Hispanic Protestant popular religion" can thus be expanded to include their resonance in popular Latino Catholic religiosity. Aponte, "Coritos as Active Symbol," 57–66.

Los Evangélicos

Suggestions for Further Study

A dialectical approach to Latino Protestant (mainline vs. Pentecostal) hymnody may hold interpretive value, but it also may obscure important features. This examination of Pentecostal musical practice invites a re-interrogation of mainline precursors for similar assertions of agency. Assuming the agency of early Latino Protestants, the work of such prolific translators as Mendoza, Grado, and Reza deserve deeper study. Did they view themselves solely as translators of an imported musical liturgy, as facilitators in an enterprise that would replace features of Mexican and Chicano musical culture with Anglo-American ones? How faithful were their translations? What can we glean from their deviations from the English-language originals and from their redactive decisions? What can we learn from the corpus of their *original* compositions?

Given the ample documentation for both mainline and Pentecostal trans-border movement and networks,[47] the study of American Protestantism must transcend geographical boundaries to include heretofore ignored influences from regions south of the border and at the periphery. The academy's reticence to do so mirrors earlier missionary indifference/bias and is challenged by an inconsistent readiness to include non-US sites, especially England and Canada, in the meta-narrative of modern US Protestantism.

A metaphor of concentric or overlapping circles of religious history and experience may prove useful for a new mapping of the North American religious landscape. Such an enterprise should reflect more hemispheric contours and interdisciplinary methods. The new mappings will require careful soundings as much as careful sightings.

47. Mendoza and fellow Mexican Methodist Gonzalo Báez-Camargo assumed key roles at the 1929 Protestant Congress in Havana, as president and secretary of the gathering, respectively—non-Latino leaders occupied thirteen of the US delegation's twenty-two slots. See Inman, *Evangelicals at Havana*, 163–74.

11

Gospel, History, Border, and Mission: Notes for a Missiology from a Hispanic/Latino Perspective

Carlos F. Cardoza-Orlandi

MISSIOLOGY IS THE INTERDISCIPLINARY science of studying the transmission and reception of the Christian faith. Its intromissive character means that it explores and employs methods and models from a variety of disciplines, thus giving theological institutions difficulty in deciding the appropriate place for missiology within the classical divisions of theology. At times, this "institutional confusion" works in missiology's favor, allowing it to infiltrate many disciplines and offer new perspectives or confront the discourse or practice of whatever discipline with which it is in dialogue. At other times, however, the "institutional confusion" limits missiology's curricular impact and reduces its academic legitimacy with the accusation that it is too general a discipline, that it is five miles wide and two inches deep. Whatever the case may be, missiology is neither monolithic nor homogenous. Its multidimensional and heterogeneous nature equips it for dialoguing with other disciplines and enriching their academic and ecclesial applicability despite the occasional critique against missiology's academic superficiality.

Missiology attempts to study everything related to the transmission and reception of the Christian faith. Unfortunately, the beginnings of the discipline in Protestant circles emphasized primarily the study of the *transmission* of the Christian faith, leaving only a few theologians off in the fringe to study the *reception* of the faith in particular contexts. K. S. Latourette's multi-volume *A History of the Expansion of Christianity* pro-

vides an eloquent example of this focus. The series, save a few descriptions
of complexities in the reception of the Christian faith, concentrates its
efforts on narrating and analyzing the transmission, that is, the activity of
communicating the gospel of Jesus Christ in various contexts, including
missionary practices within Christendom.[1]

Our Protestant missionary heritage—missionary both in practice
and in theology—reinforces this tendency to focus on the transmission of
the Christian faith in missionary work.[2] The "Great Commission" passage
in Matthew 28 resounds in congregations and groups interested in missions, summoning the church to be a community of mission, whether this
mission be of personal evangelization or of communal work to protect
the environment. A focus on transmission, a focus on the communication
and/or strengthening of the Christian faith in a particular context, both
provides a point of departure for and guides the purpose and results of
this missional task.

Obviously, this interest in missional transmission obligates a missionary group to identify affinities and antagonisms between the culture
or cultures of its missionary context and the gospel to be communicated.
However, the task of transmission many times presumes that the gospel
being transmitted is "pure," free of a cultural setting that would affect its
transmission.[3] Though different groups vary in the level of analyzing this
transmission process, the "eschatological urgency" and the "missionary
commitment," missiological criteria that so characterize Protestant missional work, contribute to a limited, hasty analysis that at times lacks the
tools necessary for developing theologies and practices of mission that
are healthy for their particular contexts.[4]

---

1. Monastic movements, in large part, carried out mission activity within and outside
of Christendom before the Protestant Reformation. Many missiologists aptly identify the
Protestant Reformation as another missionary expression within Christendom, an effort
to "correct" deviations in the theology and practice of the Christian faith. See Latourette,
History of the Expansion, volumes over the Middle Ages and the Protestant Reformation.
See also Scherer, *Gospel.*

2. See, for example, Costas, *Theology of the Crossroads* and *Liberating News*; see also
the Protestant Congress reports in Panama 1916, Montevideo 1925, and Havana 1929.
Other recent literature also continues to stress this aspect of missions.

3. This pattern of missions—identifying the cultural context's affinities with and antagonisms toward the gospel while assuming a "pure gospel"—is called the "translation
model." See Bevans, *Models of Contextual Theologies.*

4. Latin America, particularly the *Fraternidad Teológica Latinoamericana* (Latin
American Theological Fellowship), has lived a slow and difficult process that reflects many

The study of World Christianity recognizes the demographic change that the Christian faith is experiencing. It is more and more evident that the vital center of the Christian faith is moving from the northern and western hemispheres to the South and the East.[5] Together with this demographic change, and given the theological vitality in these new contexts, missional work and missiological reflection are recovering a healthy balance between the transmission and the reception of the faith. Furthermore, we can say that missiology is discovering in a clear and evident way that the transmission and reception of the gospel are mutually interdependent. Thus, the creativity of a certain group of Christians in communicating the gospel is implicitly linked to its creativity to contextualize the gospel in its surroundings, and vice versa.

This article proposes a historical-missiological matrix that groups together, relates, contrasts, and illustrates the complexity of the historical-religious events of the Latino/Hispanic Christian community. In physiological terms, the matrix has a creative, mediating, and nourishing function akin to a mother's womb that sustains the life of a baby. The historical-missional matrix creates, mediates, and nourishes interpretations of the Latino/Hispanic community's life in varied and complex contexts. This historical-missional matrix revolves around the reception and transmission of the gospel in the Latino/Hispanic context. In this essay I hope to reflect on this process of contextualization—considering historical, religious, ethnic, cultural, and biographical elements—as a means of discovering our Christian Latino/Hispanic identity. I propose, furthermore, that this reflection on the contextualization of the gospel will help us discover a new conscience—*una nueva consciencia*—regarding the transmission of the gospel, a practice that has heretofore been dominated and enslaved by models exogenous to our idiosyncrasies and spirituality.

profound tensions in the development of missional theologies and practices focused on transmission. Not until very recently, in particularly in CLADE III in 1992, did the shift toward the reception dimension begin, though punctuated with many question marks given the historical force of focusing on transmission. The *Consejo Latinoamericano de Iglesias* (Latin American Council of Churches), near the end of the 1980s, began taking steps toward questioning the receptor agency of the gospel, in particular new agents like women, indigenous groups, groups of African descent, and children.

5. See *World Christianity Encyclopedia*; Jenkins, *The New Christendom?*; Walls, *Missionary Movement* and *Cross-Cultural Process*; and González, *Changing Shape*.

Los Evangélicos

Border and Mestizaje:
Mission from the Hispanic/Latino Perspective

The term "border," which I have used in other studies,[6] is rich, novel, and forceful. The genius of Virgilio Elizondo, particularly in his works *Galilean Journey* and *The Future is Mestizo*, describes the biographical, anthropological, theological, and epistemological character of the borderland. Roberto Goizueta summarizes Elizondo's concept of the border:

> Virgilio Elizondo's Christology [and theology for that matter] is profoundly marked by the reality of the border as a *locus theologicus*, the *mestizo* reality of the borderland as a truly sacramental reality. For him, the border is not only a place *in* which he is located, or *from* which he comes; the border is *who* he is as a *mestizo* person—like all Latino/as whose very identity and reality is "in between."[7]

So central to the theological task, this *mestizo* reality is situated within the historical reality of the Latin American and Hispanic/Latino community, particularly the Mexican-American community. Instead of being abstract and utopian, the concept of the border is historical and eschatological. The mestizo reality of the border, the reality of multiple interpenetrations in an asymmetrical encounter of cultures, is situated in the existential crossing of identities and realities, of complex movements from which a new cosmic creation and reality arises.[8] This new cosmic creation and reality has ecclesiological implications. Elizondo proposes what he calls the Jerusalemite principle:

> In speaking about itself, the church uses such terms as *mystery* and *people of God*. It is incarnated in the world but not swallowed up by it. It expresses itself through the language and symbols of the people, but its message revolutionizes the meaning of both the language and the symbols. The church is the *mestizo par excellence* because it strives to bring about a new synthesis of the earthly and the heavenly (Eph 1:10). It is the "third" or new people, which assumes the good that was there before and gives it new meaning, direction, and life: faith, hope, and charity.[9]

---

6. See my chapter "Mission at the Borders" in *Presbyterian Mission*.

7. Goizueta, "Christology for a Global Church," 150–51.

8. Elizondo, *Galilean Journey*, 81–88; *The Future is Mestizo*; and "Mestizaje as a Locus," 106–23, especially 121.

9. Elizondo, *Galilean Journey*, 107.

174

This theology with both mestizo—a violent encounter of cultures—and border—a space for a new creation and a new cosmos—characteristics uncovers a missiology that is prophetic at the same time as festive/eschatological. The prophetic aspect of this missiology lies in its bicultural nature which allows it to confront structures of oppression from the margin with a degree of legitimacy earned from also belonging to the center. The border character of the life of faith enables this "double-edged" missional practice.[10] The festive and eschatological character arises, as Gustavo Gutiérrez has said, from the historical hope and strength of the poor who, in the midst of their struggles, "can rise above them and experience and radiate authentic joy and hope, peace and serenity."[11] This mutual and mestizo relationship between the prophetic and the festive/eschatological offers a profoundly missional liturgical dimension. Elizondo phrases it beautifully:

> The prophetic without the festive turns into cynicism and bitterness or simply fades away. On the other hand, the festive without the prophetic can easily turn into empty rituals or even degenerate into drunken brawls. It is the prophetic-festive [celebratory] that keeps the spirit alive and nourishes the life of the group as a group . . . . There was a power in those celebrations [prophetic-festive celebrations in the Hebrew Bible, New Testament, and the early church] that human powers could neither grasp nor destroy.[12]

Justo González is even more precise in his missional understanding of the border. He categorically declares that, "mission, like *mestizaje*, takes place at the border, at the place of encounter."[13] He then defines the border:

> A frontier is by definition unidirectional. It can only move ahead. Anything moving back across it is an incursion of the forces of evil and backwardness into the realm of the light and progress. A border, in contrast, is by definition bi-directional . . . . Both the frontier and the border are growing edges. But at the frontier growth takes place by conquest, by pushing the adversary back, while at the bor-

---

10. Ibid., 119.

11. Ibid., 120.

12. Ibid.

13. González, *Santa Biblia*, 84.

der growth takes place by encounter, by mutual enrichment. A true border, a true place of encounter, is by nature permeable.[14]

For González, therefore, mission is an encounter in which the community of faith exercises the aptitude of permeability, discovering the grace of God in the encounter and in the mutual enrichment.

In summary, both González and Elizondo find the following within the border and within mestizaje: 1) a historical-cultural space of encounter that is critical, asymmetrical, and very human; 2) a space for synthesis, new creation, and new cosmos that offers the exploited and oppressed world a new vision of the grace of God despite encounters that are often violent and destructive; 3) a space for developing a missional, open, and celebrative consciousness of prophetic character in which human redemption unites with the redemption of the cosmos in the new creation of which the church is a part; and finally 4) an existential space in which the Holy Spirit renews the people of God through mission and liturgy.

The work of these Hispanic/Latino theologians is thoroughly enriching. The scholars in the Hispanic/Latino camp who have studied or are studying the border concept that Elizondo and González have proposed are numerous. I have frequently used this concept to develop missiological ideas from a Hispanic/Latino perspective. Without the contribution of these two men and other Latino men and women colleagues, and without having reflected a great deal myself on this topic—a work in process—I would never have begun to explore "the shore" as a metaphor for Christian Caribbean identity.[15]

The border is the place of beginning, of birth. I started out with a metaphor that has informed my identity as a Hispanic/Latino in the United States. My identity as a Hispanic/Latino arises in the typical process in which the dominant culture names and identifies minority groups at its discretion. Therefore, in this context, the dominant culture removes my Caribbean identity and imposes the Hispanic/Latino label. Not until I struggle with this new identity am I able to rediscover my Caribbean identity from a fresh perspective. The encounter between my Caribbean identity and my Hispanic/Latino identity, imposed yet real, and the context of the United States creates a dynamic that elevates the suppressed

---

14. Ibid., 86–87.

15. For a discussion on Caribbean Christian identity see my article "Re-discovering Caribbean Christian Identity," 114–44.

culture—Caribbean—in critical moments. The search for my Caribbean identity extends beyond the encounter between two cosmologies, two realities; it is a complex search in a multidimensional and at times chaotic reality.

On the other hand, the border evokes a space of fixed ground, many times quite elusive. In the vast majority of countries, the border is a political construction built and protected by law and police or military force. In the United States, the border marks the difference between prosperity and poverty, the land of dreams and the land of survival, the new world order and the old order. However, occasionally borders are suspended; they are evasive and elusive, particularly when, in the asymmetrical configuration of the encounter, the centers of power need the margins. Borders testify to the movement of communities, observing legal and illegal crossings, watching families that cross for vacation, and grieving the desperation of families that cross for survival. Unfortunately, borders also muffle the secrets of injustice between countries and embrace the dead bodies of the anguished pilgrim community.

TESTIMONY: BIOGRAPHY, HISTORY,
THEOLOGY, AND MISSIOLOGY

Rubem Alves describes the relationship between history, biography, and humanity in the following way:

> Biography and history go together . . . . The fact remains that our personal destiny is rooted deeply in the destiny of civilizations. In one way or another, our biography is always a symptom of the conditions prevailing in the world. That is the reason behind the discovery we all frequently make. Despite the fact that we live in different places, posts, and political contexts, our biographies st[r]ongly [sic] resemble slight variations of one and the same script. They have the same structures. They go through the same sequence of hopes and frustrations.[16]

In the theater, a play has one script yet many storylines. The script is the life story, life's rollercoaster and the struggle to stay seated, focused, and on track. The storylines are the multiple forms in which human beings respond to the highs and lows of the ride and to the changes in angle and velocity. Some respond with fascination and enthusiasm. Others (like

---

16. Alves, "From Paradise to the Desert," 99.

myself) grow pale merely glimpsing the route and the somersaults ahead. The sequences of frustrations and hopes, of assurance and ambiguities, and of faith and doubt are responses that characterize human creation and existence. They illustrate the complex yet common dilemma of living.

For Alves, this dilemma of living links biography and history. Furthermore, he proposes that the commitment to face this common human dilemma with bravery and a sense of direction is the connection between biography and theology. Alves declares:

> [t]heology and biography go together . . . . Religion is the procla-
> mation of the axiological priority of the heart over the raw facts
> of reality. It is a refusal to be gobbled up and digested by the sur-
> rounding world, an appeal to a vision, a passion, a love.[17]

This calling "to a vision, a passion, a love" in the midst of desperation provides the foundation for integrating my biography with the missional task of rediscovering my Christian Caribbean identity.

Biography and theology find their means of integration in *testimony*. In a *testimony*, a community theologizes its biography and draws a picture, a map, of its theology, essentially forming its missiology. At the same time, a *testimony* proclaims and incarnates the eschatological experience of living through and in the grace of God. It is the word and incarnation of what we are, what we are becoming, and what we are called to be in Christ through the Holy Spirit. In my grandparents' Pentecostal tradition, *testimony* played a critical role in defining the character of the believer's and the community's faith. *Testimony* is the word/deed activity that integrates the story of the gospel with the biographies of the believer and the community. Therefore, testimony has levels of maturity. The word/deed matures when 1) the story of the gospel intertwines with the personal and communal story, integrating the personal and communal biographies with the gospel story; and 2) when the activity of word/deed, the testimony, concentrates on the deed, the in-carnation of the gospel, without minimizing the word. Both principles, one attached to the contextualization (reception) of the gospel *with* our story and the other attached to the transmission of the gospel *in* our story, join together to establish the link that makes transmission and reception two sides of the same coin: mission.

---

17. Ibid., 100.

BORDER, MESTIZAJE, AND TESTIMONY:
A HISTORICAL-MISSIONAL HISPANIC/LATINO MATRIX

In review, for González and Elizondo, the border and mestizaje as theological metaphors signal 1) a historical-cultural space of encounter that is critical, asymmetrical, and very human; 2) a space for synthesis, new creation, and new cosmos that offers the exploited and oppressed world a new vision of the grace of God despite encounters that are often violent and destructive; 3) a space for developing a missional, open, and celebrative consciousness of prophetic character in which human redemption unites with the redemption of the cosmos in the new creation of which the church is a part; and finally 4) an existential space in which the Holy Spirit renews the people of God through mission and liturgy.

Testimony is the word/deed expression that communicates, in a contextual and particular form, the activity of God in the world. While the border and mestizaje form the cosmic scenery of human/divine activity, that is, the drama of human/divine interaction, *testimony* is the expression, in word and deed, of this activity. Historical and cultural forces have their office in the borderlands space and are incarnated in the mestizo experience. The force of the Holy Spirit, likewise intertwined with historical and cultural forces, is an equal protagonist in the border and the mestizo experience. The understanding (or lack thereof) and human expression of these forces and their immediate, contextual, and particular impact are the incarnation of the gospel. The human character of the meeting of these forces—historical, cultural, and divine—expresses itself in *testimony*: it is, on the one hand, an eschatological and cosmic expression and, on the other hand, historical and contingent. From a missional perspective, border, mestizaje, and testimony are a matrix that integrates and generates the Latino/Hispanic religious experience. When we discover and analyze the experience of the reception and transmission of the Christian faith or whatever other religious experience in the Hispanic/Latino context, the dynamics of border, mestizaje, and testimony are woven together like a chord of three strands. Every Hispanic/Latino theological and missional reflection ought to discover, then, the border character, the mestizo configuration, and the testimonial incarnation of the contextual experience.

The resources for our Christian identity are the resources of our Hispanic/Latino identity; there can be no rediscovery of our Christian Hispanic/Latino identity without an intersection, a multidimensional crossing, with other social, religious, and cultural realities of our Hispanic/

Latino heritage and reality. My mentor, Charles Ryerson, provides a critical perspective for discerning this complex yet necessary crossing:

> Groups which have been marginal to society often enter into history especially explosively, whatever the ages of the individuals involved, although youth may be the most explosive. These groups and individuals, long invisible to history, have a special problem. They need a useable past—a sense of continuity—if they are to "enter into history" and have an effective psychological base for cultural and political action.[18]

The resources of our Hispanic/Latino identity are varied and, on many occasions, in conflict with each other. In my personal life, Protestant from birth, my family kept me at a safe "distance" from other religious and cultural resources that were considered a threat to my Protestant identity. They kept me on one side of the border, denying my religious and cultural mestizaje under the assumption that this location would safeguard a "pure" faith. Such Protestant "protectionism" only leads to theological and ecclesial isolation: a death recipe for the Christian faith.[19]

If we accept these notes regarding a Hispanic/Latino historical-missional matrix, we ought to consider the following declarations for our historical and missional reflection and action:

1. We need to develop a missional conscience—*una consciencia misional*—that recognizes that our Christian identity and our religious, social, and cultural practices are interdependent. For example, our collective Christian missional identity, my personal practice and transmission of the faith, and our common cultural identity, together with social, economic, and historical forces, both inform and form what it means for me to be a Christian.

2. Consequently, our Christian *testimony* is not monolithic. On the contrary, our *testimony* is a complex of historical, social, economic, and cultural interactions with divine activity, a complex that signals the struggle of human beings with sin—both personal and systemic—and the hope of our new life in God. Hispanic/Latino history and missiology is full of the tensions and the push-and-pull that the community lives out in its context.

---

18. Ryerson, "Meaning and Modernization," 2.

19. Historians and scholars of World Christianity have continually argued that the vitality of the Christian faith lies in its intercultural character and not in the false presumption of dominion and absolutism or exclusivity and cultural isolation.

3. The Hispanic/Latino historical-missional matrix recognizes and demands that our theological action must take seriously *lo coti-diano*—the daily life experience[20] in all levels of life and creation. It is indispensable, then, that in our historical and missional work we use categories that help us identify the agents of our dailiness. Some of these categories include: (a) religious experience and phenomenon; (b) class issues and struggles; (c) gender and sexual orientation issues; (d) generational issues and struggles; (e) issues and struggles of social movements; and, among others, (f) regional and language issues and conflicts. As a result of these categories, the historical and missional task ought to approach such issues as religiosity and popular religions, syncretism, immigration, work, education, health, economy, women, the home, childhood, adolescence, the kitchen and food, recreation, and nature. It is absolutely necessary to write a history and to forge a missiology that takes into consideration the religious, social, and cultural "traffic" and movement that our Latino/Hispanic community experiences every day.

4. Finally, the Hispanic/Latino historical-missional discipline must be linked to global history. For example, how did the Great Depression—early in the twentieth century—shape the arrival and participation of Latino groups in the United States? What effect on the history of Christianity in the United States did the Cuban Revolution and the arrival of Cuban immigrants to different states in the nation have? What effect do Latin American students who study in US seminaries and serve in Latino/Hispanic, African, and Asian communities have?

The gospel, border, mestizaje, and testimony form a historical-missional matrix that provides certain categories for historical and missional reflection on the Hispanic/Latino community. This matrix in no way exhausts the list of possible theological, historical, and cultural categories that can contribute to a missiology/theology of the history of the Christian Latino/Hispanic people. However, this matrix does affirm the complex and fluid movement of the Latino/Hispanic religious experience, recovering the agency of historical forces and conditions intertwined with the activity of God in the world and the protagonism of the community of faith in history.

---

20. *Lo cotidiano* is a very common theological term among Hispanic/Latino theologians, but particularly Hispanic Latina and feminist Latin American theologians.

12

Mass Media and Latino Churches

Janet Lynn Treviño de Elizarraraz

IN THE PRESENT HISTORICAL moment Hispanics are the largest minority group in the United States of America.[1] Recognizing this fact, the Christian church has sought ways to more effectively minister among the changing culture and has utilized the radio as an instrument for spreading the gospel especially among the Spanish-speaking public. This essay explores different radio ministries that have succeeded in reaching the Latino masses in the United States.

Christians called by God to impact the Spanish-speaking population began utilizing the radio for spreading the gospel in the 1940s. Subsequently, huge waves of Latino immigration captured the attention of the whole world and, certainly, of the North American continent. The diaspora of Latinos within the United States has overthrown the idea that "missions" means going to a foreign country beyond one's own borders. Now, every race is at our front door.

> Initially, the concept of missions was based on an individualistic version of the gospel and was defined in geographical terms. To "do missions," one necessarily had to cross borders. Now, the perspective has changed since missions ought to help people cross the border between faith and unbelief. Jesus' style is what we are called to put into practice in evangelization.[2]

---

1. In accordance with the estimate from the Census Department published on June 18, 2003, there are 38.8 million Hispanics in the United States. This figure demonstrates a percentage increase of 9.8 since the April 2000 census (with 35.3 million). http://www .census.gov/Press-Release/www/releases/archives/population/011193.html.

2. ALC, "Dios propone la transformación integral del hombre, dice René Padilla," January 23, 2004. http://www.noticiacristiana.com/news/newDetails.php?idnew=408&country=0.

In response to these social changes, the Christian community in the United States has responded with radio missions in the same format that Christians have used in Latin America, both to reach non-Christians and to build up the entire audience. This study will present the brief histories of several US radio ministries directed toward the Hispanic community and an explanation of their programs and distribution throughout Latin America and the United States.[3] Finally, it will analyze the impact of these radio ministries on their public and conclude with challenges for the future.

Radio ministries have arisen from various fronts. Christian denominations have played a prominent role in opening new missions using mass media to reach their Hispanic neighbors. Some English-speaking parachurch organizations have also decided to focus on Hispanics in the United States through radio. The next front includes a lesser-known but nonetheless important group made up of the network of transmitters dedicated to broadcasting Christian radio programs throughout the country and around the world. Finally, a few well-known individuals promote and contribute to radio ministry.

DEDICATED DENOMINATIONS

Three denominations in particular have worked admirably in radio ministries directed toward the Latino community within the United States: the Lutheran church (Missouri Synod) with *Cristo Para Todas Las Naciones* (Christ for All the Nations), the Church of God (Anderson) with *"La hermandad cristiana"* ("Christian Broadcasting Hope"), and the Christian Reformed church with *"La hora de la reforma"* ("The Reformed Hour").

From the denominational front—and in comparison with all the ministries discussed in this chapter—the Lutheran church has the privilege of being first in the wise decision to begin a radio program directed toward Hispanics in the United States. Having been designed and developed in the same country, the program always keeps in mind the national context in which their audience is immersed. Given their exclusivity for the United States and Puerto Rico, the programs deal with migratory situations and the needs of expatriates. The themes respond to pertinent

---

3. This article in no way pretends to be exhaustive. Rather, fully aware that important ministries may have been left out due to space limits, it hopes to take the first step toward writing this history.

social needs like the separation of families between two countries, long work hours, continuing education, etc.

The Lutheran denomination is a bulwark of ministries all over the world, specializing in mass media in several languages. The general Lutheran radio ministry, "Lutheran Hour Ministries," has a branch called *Cristo Para Todas Las Naciones* that reaches Latinos in Latin America, Canada, and the United States.

The Lutheran church began its mission in Texas in 1926, and the first radio program, "The Lutheran Hour," aired in English on October 2, 1931. Ten years later, in 1941, Dr. Andrés A. Meléndez began hosting the first program in Spanish. For thirty minutes each week his voice broadcast "*La hora luterana*" ("The Lutheran Hour") all over Latin America, Spain, and the United States. Dr. Meléndez's messages encouraged his Latino audience to be sensitive and wise in following God's mission and in responding to God's call.[4] He continued the program until 1972 at which point the Spanish-language program ceased while the English-language counterpart continued. That year the Lutheran church launched a different Hispanic radio ministry.

From 1972 to 1996 the program "*Ayer, hoy, y siempre*" ("Yesterday, Today, and Forever") carried life-affirming messages throughout the United States, Puerto Rico, and Canada. The program continues to be rebroadcast even now. "*Ayer*" airs for fifteen minutes every day with the purpose of "encouraging listener response, achieving a dedicated following, and referring interested listeners to local ministries."[5]

The Lutheran program "*Un momento con Dios*" ("A Moment with God") is produced in Venezuela. This location lends the sixty-second program an expatriate flavor as the program encourages Latinos living outside their home countries that even in their most difficult moments there is someone who loves them and is always with them.

"Instead of knocking on doors, through the radio we get inside homes,"[6] summarizes what the radio ministry *Cristo Para Todas Las Naciones* (CPTLN) actually accomplishes. In the last few decades CPTLN has expanded its ministry focus by branching out into other mass means of communication. The general CPTLN ministry of the Lutheran church

---

4. http://www.lutheranhour.org/speakers/melendez.htm.

5. www.caminoajesus.org.

6. Susan González, interview, October 21, 2003.

began broadcasting television programs in 1972. Since the initial airing of realistic, effective commercials, television has become CPTLN's preferred method of media outreach. This transition has not diminished the impact of CPTLN's radio programs, however.

Program distribution in the United States, as compared to within Latin America, is impressive. The Lutheran church focuses exclusively on North America and speaks directly to specific local situations unique to the United States or to its neighbor, Canada. In 1994, "*Ayer*" aired on more than 165 radio stations in the United States, but due to the 1996 cessation of the program, the numbers have since decreased. The program's webpage lists eighty-three stations that still rebroadcast "*Ayer*" and an additional thirty that air "*Un momento con Dios.*"[7]

Christian Broadcasting Hope (CBH), formerly known as Christian Brotherhood Hour, is a ministry of the Church of God with central offices in Anderson, Indiana. Two decades after producing its first radio program in English, CBH contracted three radio stations to start broadcasting "*La hora de la hermandad cristiana*" ("Christian Brotherhood Hour") in Spanish on July 4, 1965.[8] CBH wisely combined the talents of Rev. Guillermo Angulo and Fidel Samorano who faithfully ministered together for thirty years through this radio program. After Angulo's death in 1995, Dr. Gilberto Dávila replaced the broadcasting pair and continues the program which is today known merely as "*La hermandad cristiana.*"

For thirty minutes every Sunday, "*La hermandad cristiana*" airs from Texas and California and broadcasts throughout Spain, Latin America, the Caribbean, including Cuba, as well as throughout the United States. Dr. Gilberto Dávila dispatches to his listeners messages of love, hope, and salvation through a combination of music, prayer, preaching, and reading letters from listeners in Latin America and North America. Some common program themes include prayer, service to God, resentment, and self-control. Even though Dr. Dávila broadcasts from the southwestern United States, the majority of the program's listeners reside outside the United States.

The Christian Reformed church formed its denominational communications ministry in 1965. That same year, under Rev. Juan S. Boonstra's direction, the denomination formally began its Spanish-language radio program "*La hora de la reforma.*" The first radio stations used short wave

---

7. www.caminoajesus.org.

8. http://www.elsitiocristiano.com/ministries/La_Hermandad_Cristiana/.

radio to transmit the program with electromagnetic waves to the most remote areas. In the 1980s, the Christian Reformed church incorporated a new Spanish-language program, "*Reflexión*" ("Reflection"). The denomination invited Rev. Guillermo Serrano to join Boonstra in the 1990s. Since Boonstra's retirement in 1991, Serrano continues hosting the programs up to the present. The programs are also available now in digital format.[9]

"*La hora de la reforma*," airing weekly for fourteen minutes and thirty seconds, presents a sermon and concludes with songs by well-known Christian artists. The sermons offer a contemporary challenge based on historic Christian faith; for example, a sermon might teach how problems faced by the first-century church can help today's church resolve issues of immorality, greed, and division among local churches. The program "*Reflexión*" lasts four and a half minutes and airs five days a week. It reminds listeners to pause, to reflect on their lives, to think about where they want to go, and to pursue a closer walk with God. The Spanish-language programs of the Christian Reformed church hardly reach the Latino population within the United States at all. Of the 487 stations that daily broadcast the programs, only forty transmit within the United States; that is, only slightly over 8 percent of the Christian Reformed church's Spanish radio ministry reaches Latinos in the USA.[10]

Dedicated Parachurch Organizations

A parachurch organization exists outside of well-defined ecclesial structures and thus often enjoys greater flexibility and freedom for innovation. Throughout the twentieth century, the majority of religious broadcasting stations were run as parachurch organizations which, instead of promoting a certain denomination, emphasized the general spiritual growth of the listener.[11] The parachurch organizations presented below aim to both build up and educate their listeners.

Focus on the Family (Focus) and Radio Bible Class Ministries (RBC) have developed extensive, multifaceted ministries that, in their mission to

---

9. Reformed Radio, http://www.radioreforma.com/index.php?option=com_content &view=article&id=44&Itemid=53.

10. http://www.radioreforma.com/index.php.

11. Jeffrey K. Hadden, "Parachurch Organizations," Religious Broadcasting, http://etext .lib.virginia.edu/relbroad/parachurch.html.

spread the gospel of Christ to the nations, utilize printed material, videos, and the radio.

Focus on the Family exists to preserve traditional conservative values and the institution of the family, including the Hispanic family. Compared to Focus' other ministries, the radio projects have a rather short history; nonetheless, Focus has managed in a very short time to enter the Latino community in the United States and win their respect through radio. On February 1, 1988, Focus aired its first Spanish-language program, a direct translation of the corresponding English-language program. It lasted for five minutes and, based on the book *Dr. Dobson Answers Your Questions* (Tyndale, 1982), discussed the question, "Is marriage worth it?" Two and a half years later, in August of 1990, a new fifteen-minute program aired and examined themes of "tough love and self-respect." Roberto Cruz (acting as Dr. James Dobson) and one of two speakers (either Isidro Olace or Alejandro Alba) adapted books by Dr. Dobson into question-answer formats for these two programs.

In December of 1992, Focus produced its first program written originally in Spanish. The program, *"Conversando con Luis Palau"* ("Talking with Luis Palau"), was centered around a visit from the Argentine evangelist Luis Palau. Subsequent programs in this format have continued inviting Hispanic leaders and professionals from the United States and Latin America to discuss themes relevant to the family. In 1995, Focus launched a series of 90-second commentaries in Spanish based on the content of the corresponding 90-second commentaries in English. Two types of programs have developed over the years: those translated directly from English and those produced in Spanish that address particular Hispanic needs.[12] Translated programs offer advice regarding needs common to every culture, such as marriage, infidelity, corruption, etc. The original Spanish-language programs respond to specific needs within the Hispanic community like machismo, poverty, immigration, discrimination within the larger English-speaking society, etc.

The translations into Spanish are acceptable but not universally accessible. For example, one broadcast uses the word *cantina*, common to Mexico and to lower social classes, instead of the word "bar," an Americanism used by middle- and upper-class Spanish speakers.

---

12. Darrel Eash of Focus on the Family, interview, October 2003.

The main Spanish-language program takes its name from the name of the ministry itself, "*Enfoque a la familia*." Some titles of the different episodes include "Problems with In-Laws," "Healing from Emotional Wounds," "How to Overcome Anxiety," "My Unbelieving Loved One," and "Successful Marriages." In general, programs begin with a short introduction to the problem to be discussed and its relation to the family, followed by an interview with a specialist (whether it be an author of a pertinent book, a doctor, a psychologist, etc.) in the day's theme.

An average of 160 stations distribute Focus' programs within the United States.[13] Since many of the productions revolve around US public policy or family-related societal events within the country, US radio stations have a significant advantage over Latin American radio stations that distribute the programs. Focus places great importance on the speed with which radio stations receive the productions, wanting the broadcasts to offer relevant answers to current news topics. On average, there is no more than a three-week delay between the time Focus records a production in English and a US radio station airs the production in Spanish; yet this process stretches to nearly ten weeks for Latin American stations. With the use of the Internet, this situation has improved somewhat. Stations have begun offering their programs (live or recorded) not only within the United States but also around the world. Many recorded programs are available in MP3, allowing other stations to hear and rebroadcast them easily. Focus takes advantage of this technology to stay current regarding what affects the family and what the Christian community needs to know.

Faithfully living out its purpose for over sixty years, RBC Ministries (Radio Bible Class since 1994; formerly called Detroit Bible Class) continues to carry the gospel to many nations and in particular to the Hispanic community in the United States. Begun as Detroit Bible Class in 1938 by a doctor-turned-pastor, M. R. De Haan, the ministry's goal was to feed those who hungered spiritually. The goal evolved into a commitment, through teaching the Word of God on the radio, to bring people of all nations into a personal relationship with Christ, to encourage their growth in Christ's image, and to urge their participation in local churches.[14] Richard De Haan, the next president, oversaw the development of programs in Spanish beginning in 1977. The strength and uniqueness of RBC

13. Focus on the Family, http://enfoque.family.org/radio/A000000101.cfm.
14. RBC Ministries Hispanic website, http://www.rbclatino.org/acerca.htm.

Ministries also lie in the publications and literature that work in conjunction with the radio ministry.

RBC Ministries, following the vision of its founder, produces four Spanish-language radio programs.[15] "*La clase bíblica radial*" ("Radio Bible Class") offers biblical teaching for the Christian life in a format of fifteen-minute segments; "*Tesoros escondidos*" ("Hidden Treasures") is a one-minute inspirational thought; "*Nuestro pan diario*" ("Our Daily Bread") is a reading of the famous devotional of the same name; "*Descubramos la Palabra*" ("Let's Discover the Word") is a fifteen-minute dynamic biblical conversation about themes of current interest.

DEDICATED NETWORKS OF TRANSMITTERS

Today there are organizations that are known neither for the programs they produce nor for the popular names that surround them but instead for the commitment they have with all the other ministries discussed in this chapter. A few important transmitters have dedicated themselves to providing airspace for Christian programs and seeking ways to open new Christian stations throughout the United States and the entire world. A transmitter is a station that broadcasts a message using electronic signals. HCJB World Radio (HCJB for "Heralding Christ Jesus' Blessings")[16] is a network of transmitters that spreads the gospel in a unique missionary method: where there are no "preaching" radio stations, HCJB acquires or builds one. HCJB World Radio began its ministry in 1931, using short wave radio to transmit programs in Ecuador since the majority of the audience lived in remote rural areas. As most listeners moved to the cities, HCJB began using local AM and FM stations; later, the technology developed to use satellites to broadcast programs over large regions of Asia and Africa. These opportunities to experiment with new and developing technology strengthened HCJB's mission and effectiveness. HCJB has developed cooperative agreements and partnerships with other transmitters. In general HCJB will enter a region in order to build a metaphorical road for future Christian programming, offering its experience in communications as well as essential aid in acquiring licenses (in the midst of a bureaucratic sea) to broadcast using whatever technology fits each particular station.

---

15. http://www.rbclatino.org/.
16. http://www.hcjb.org/.

In 1976 HCJB World Radio established the World Radio Network in Texas. Dr. Abe Van Der Puy, who had served for twenty years as president of HCJB World Radio, was the first director of World Radio Network which was a network of FM broadcasting stations that served and/or still serve the Hispanic community along the US-Mexican border from Texas to Arizona. In 1994, World Radio Network launched its satellite broadcasting system which makes Spanish-language programs available twenty-four hours a day to all affiliate stations. The ministry hopes to continue expanding throughout the entire United States. With more than twenty commercial-free stations, World Radio Network's mission is to communicate the gospel of Jesus Christ to the Hispanic border community, to encourage all Christians in that region, and to assist the Christian community with informative programs.[17] The organization carries out its mission by providing the knowledge and technological experience sufficient for starting short wave, local (AM and FM), and satellite radio stations that will carry Spanish-language Christian programs twenty-four hours a day, seven days a week. Some of the programs aired through the network along the US-Mexican border include, among others, "*Enfoque a la familia*," "*Un momento con Alberto Mottesi*" ("A Moment with Alberto Mottesi"), and Hermano Pablo's "*Un mensaje a la conciencia*" ("A Message to the Conscience").

Dedicated Individuals

Finally, a few individuals in the Protestant world have had such a large impact on Spanish-language radio that it is essential to study their influence on the Hispanic community in the United States. The first, Paul Finkenbinder, or popularly known as *Hermano Pablo* (Brother Paul), grew up in an English-speaking missionary home. The next two men, Luis Palau and Alberto Mottesi, are Argentines who have made history throughout the Americas with their massive open-air campaigns and the radio follow-up to these events.

Hermano Pablo, as his Latino audience knows him, moved his ministry to Costa Mesa, California in 1964. The Association of Hermano Pablo aims to be the voice of God to the conscience of every Spanish speaker. After forty years on the radio, Hermano Pablo celebrates that his program "*Un mensaje a la conciencia*" is heard all over Latin America and the United States. His impact in Latin America has been undeniable;

---

17. http://www.hcjb.org/worldwide/worldwide/world_radio_network.html.

nevertheless, Hermano Pablo has a long way to go toward reaching out to Hispanics in the United States. Of the 1366 known stations that broadcast his program, only 170 serve the United States—a mere 12 percent. Hermano Pablo has not taken advantage of marketing techniques to publicize his program to a greater number of committed stations. Instead, individual broadcasters who depend on donations to finance the program approach the Association of Hermano Pablo on their own initiative.

The 170 stations that broadcast Hermano Pablo in the United States transmit his program an average of 2365 times per week throughout the country. Keeping in mind the target audience of Hispanics who do not have a personal relationship with Jesus, Hermano Pablo treats such diverse themes as a relationship with God, vices, marriage, and family. He offers practical, biblical advice for daily life in order to spread the gospel among non-Christians. After getting his listeners' attention with an introductory story, Hermano Pablo sows seeds that, over the years, grow within the listener into a vivid recognition of his or her need for Jesus Christ. Hermano Pablo follows three goals in his program format: 1. Make it enjoyable so that listeners will tune in every day; 2. Make it educational to appeal to the culture and to raise listeners' moral standards; 3. Make it evangelistic to confront listeners with their need of Christ and to help them understand Christ as the only answer.[18]

The next dynamic radio personality, Luis Palau, has gained widespread airtime as a result of his mass evangelistic campaigns. His two programs, *"Luis Palau responde"* ("Luis Palau Responds") and *"Cruzada con Luis Palau"* ("The Luis Palau Crusade"), distinguish themselves from each other in audience and content. *"Responde,"* a five-minute program directed toward non-Christians, presents Jesus Christ as the answer to the world's griefs and woes. The program moves from the known (questions from listeners) to the unknown (the Bible's answers to these questions). *"Cruzada,"* on the other hand, contains fifteen minutes of systematic biblical teaching more accessible to people who are already Christians. After Palau preached to the largest crowd that had ever gathered for an evangelistic crusade in Latin America, the renowned psychologist, widely published author, and host of the radio program *"Enfoque a la familia,"* Dr. James Dobson, interviewed Palau on the radio. The interview resulted in the publication of a pocket-sized book in which Dr. Dobson asks ques-

---

18. Hermano Pablo's website, http://www.hermanopablo.org/.

tions of vital importance to the family and Palau responds with how we ought to behave in our homes.

Palau's radio distribution in the United States is weak but growing. Of the 930 stations that transmit his programs in the Americas, only 10 percent broadcast within the United States, and these are all religious stations.[19] Interested radio stations can obtain Palau's programs in four ways: through the mail on compact disc, through the *Manantial* satellite radio chain, through *Cadena Voz Cristiana* from Miami, Florida, and through the website www.luispalau.net.

Speaking at some of the largest mass evangelistic campaigns in the history of the Hispanic community brought the third dedicated individual, Alberto Mottesi, into the spotlight as one of Latin America's most well-known preachers. In 1976 he moved from Argentina to the United States and in 1977 founded the Alberto Mottesi International Evangelistic Association, which then began the radio program "*Un momento con Alberto Mottesi.*" The Association bought a new administrative building in 2002 in Huntington Beach, California, with plans to construct a mobile radio and television studio.

Though Hermano Pablo and Palau address the family and society, Mottesi focuses specifically on healing within families. "*Un momento*" airs for five minutes six days a week, in which time Mottesi uses specific family and societal situations as a springboard to discuss Jesus as the heart of the gospel.[20] The Mottesi Association explains its lower rate of distribution in the United States as compared to in Latin America as a result of the lack of recent revival in the United States. Though only 20 percent of the program's broadcasts air in the United States, the Mottesi Association is proud that every state in the Union receives the transmission.[21]

FINAL ANALYSIS

Statistics forecast that by the year 2050, one in every four people in the United States will be Hispanic, with a total Hispanic population in the USA of over 100 million people. In light of this prediction, have the ministries studied in this essay considered that since Hispanics are the largest minority group in the United States—with more than 40 million people,

19. Luis Palau's website, http://www.palau.org/media/radio.
20. Alberto Mottesi's website, www.albertomottesi.org.
21. Assistant to Alberto Mottesi, interview, October 2003.

counting Puerto Ricans[22] and undocumented immigrants—the United States becomes, day by day, the third largest Spanish-speaking country after Spain and Mexico? This fact, combined with everything explored in this chapter, points to very high and growing expectations for the church and, in particular, for Christian Hispanic radio. The majority of the ministries discussed above focus around 10 percent of their efforts on Latinos within the United States. A mere 10 percent is insufficient for a nation with the third largest Latino population. Radio ministries obviously need to reconsider their distribution levels within the United States; their future goals should also include strategizing how to branch out from Christian radio stations into secular stations and bettering their program quality in order to appeal to a wider Hispanic audience.

As the population grows, so does the percentage of Hispanics who listen to the radio. A July 2001 statement from *Radio Business Report* summarizes the situation in the following way:

> There are now 480 stations using foreign language programming in the Arbitron-rated markets.[23] Of this group, the vast majority are using one of several Hispanic formats. [Of those 480], 294 of them had measurable listening in the Fall 2000 Arbitron survey. The format's total listenership places it sixth among 14 format groups, following New-Talk, AC, CHR, Country and Urban. It is more listened to than Classic Rock, Alternative, Standards, Religion, Smooth Jazz and Classicals.[24]

The above quote indicates that Hispanic radio formats, for example, regional Mexican music, have superseded rock or alternative English-music formats in popularity in the United States. This chapter has studied Christian programs, but if these programs converted to a format that did not present itself with the name "Christian," they might more easily reach the millions of Hispanics in the United States.

---

22. Puerto Rico has a population of 3,884,400, according the SEC Form 10K filings by Spanish Broadcasting System and Radio Única, http://www.nrb.org/partner/Article_Display_Page/0,,PTID308776%7CCHID568024%7CCIID1585402,00.html.

23. This number continues to increase. See Arbitron, "Hispanic Radio Today: How America Listens to Radio, 2004 Edition," http://www.arbitron.com/downloads/hispanic radiotoday04.pdf, which indicates that of 13,800 radio stations, around 650 utilize a Latino format.

24. *Radio Business Report*, July 2, 2001, quoted in Miguel Escobar and Manuel Cortés, "The Rainbow's End," http://www.nrb.org/partner/Article_Display_Page /0,,PTID308776%7CCHID568024%7CCIID1585402,00.html.

However, radio ministries in the United States function with very real economic limitations that all but prohibit their accessing the secular radio market and thus becoming the conscience to a generally non-Christian audience. Most religious broadcasting in the United States depends on donations, which makes it impossible to consider paying extremely high prices for very little air time—paying the equivalent of a commercial's airtime on popular, highly rated stations.

One Florida radio station rises to the challenge of using a secular format to reach the masses of Hispanics. This Hispanic Christian station has become the "fiercest" competition for the most popular secular station as the two jockey for first place in popularity ratings in Orlando. According to an article in ChritianityToday.com, the station WRLZ, Radio Luz, has struck the perfect balance between offering a complete service of news, sports, and advice for a non-Christian audience, including, for example, "how to buy a house, how to finance a car, how to stay healthy," according to Luis Hernández, Radio Luz's general director.[25] That is, the station takes a keen interest in the fundamental, practical aspects of its listeners' lives. In this sense, the station heeds the implications of the following quote: "Each human need is a missionary field. Priorities among these fields are fighting hunger, unemployment, disenfranchisement, drugs, prostitution, and marriage problems."[26]

In this historical moment, Hispanics in the United States have many practical needs: public health, learning a new language, seeking what they lost by leaving their homes, and ignored labor rights, to name a few.[27] The Lutheran church, with its concentration on Hispanics within the United States and commitment to all aspects of Hispanic life, also merits special recognition for providing a holistic radio ministry.

Returning to Orlando's popular Hispanic Christian radio station, Spanish-language Christian music makes up 75 percent of Radio Luz's programming, as opposed to most religious broadcast stations that depend largely on preaching and teaching.[28] Radio Luz's format challenges educational programs and questions the future of such programming for

---

25. Kenneth D. MacHarg, "Broadcasting: Hispanic Christian Radio Grows by Blocks and Blends," Christianity Today, http://www.ctlibrary.com/ct/1998/may18/8t6019.html.

26. ALC, "Dios propone."

27. Ibid. God has purposed to reestablish all things in Christ. Just as the Fall of Man affected every dimension of life, so reconciliation encompasses the totality of life: God, neighbor, creation.

28. MacHarg, "Broadcasting."

future generations of listeners. Radio Luz's success offers food for thought in the quest to minister to Hispanics in the plenitude of their lives within the United States without selling out in faithfulness to the gospel while acquiring popularity.

Turning on the radio is no longer the only way to listen to the programs of the ministries studied above; now, Internet connections provide listeners with access to the messages. At least 50 percent of Hispanics in the United States over 18 years of age have used the Internet. In general, 11 million Hispanic adults have access to this technology and are more than enthusiastic to use it since on any given day 61 percent go online.[29] A joint strategy between radio and Internet mediums could involve a wider audience. For example, a program could promote or direct listeners to a website and on the corresponding webpage offer further information to help foster disciples of Jesus Christ. People could listen to the station live or on recorded programs through the Internet. Ministries could also consider broadcasting solely over the Internet since virtual "frequency" costs are so much lower compared to radio air time.[30]

The website www.oneplace.com offers a directory of radio stations, including a section of Spanish-language stations, with radio ministries accessible through the Internet. Though this site does not represent every Christian station for Hispanics that can be found online, it at least indicates the potential presence Hispanic Christian stations could maintain on the World Wide Web.

Nevertheless, Hispanic radio stations face potential risks and abuses. George Walker Bush took advantage of Hispanic radio stations for political purposes. His weekly reports to the nation called "*Iniciativa de fe y comunidad*" ("Faith and Community Initiative"), a direct translation from the corresponding English program,[31] air on Christian Hispanic stations. One station of HCJB's World Radio Network claims on its webpage to be apolitical, uninvolved in local or national politics. Nevertheless, the station took the initiative not only to broadcast Bush's programs but also to give airspace to Vicente Fox, president of Mexico (2000 to 2006).[32]

---

29. Tom Spooner and Lee Rainie, "Hispanics and the Internet," Pew Internet and American Life Project, http://www.pewinternet.org/PPF/r/38/report_display.asp.

30. "A Chat with Hermano Pablo," NRB Trade talk, September 2001, www.nrb.org.

31. The program is in the voice of an interpreter.

32. World Radio Network's webpage, http://www.hcjb.org/worldwide/worldwide /world_radio_network.html.

Furthermore, at one time the Hispanic National Religious Broadcasters (HNRB) saw Bush's presidency as an opportunity to form an alliance with the White House. The HNRB based this decision on how Bush had expressed his "faith in Christ," openly talked about his beliefs, encouraged the country to pray, and directed the country to Scripture in times of national tragedy. In its visit to Washington, the HNRB described to Bush its vision and mission, its availability to serve the government in whatever way possible, and its openness to communicating the president's future projects.[33] Given such a disposition by one influential element of the Hispanic Christian radio contingency, what influence could Hispanic Christian radio have in the country's political life? Will it merely preserve the status quo or will it challenge the norm with Jesus Christ's lordship? Radio ministry has the opportunity not only to spread the gospel of salvation but also to apply the gospel to communications between the United States and Latin American governments and their Hispanic audience.

In conclusion, gratitude surfaces as the primary response to studying how God has opened and sustained these diverse "fronts" unique in the evangelizing work among Hispanics in the United States. The history of the denominations, parachurch organizations, transmitter networks, and individuals involved in radio ministry demonstrate varying levels of impact within the US Latino community. In some aspects, these ministries challenge listeners and inspire further opportunities to share the gospel and holistically build up the Latino population. In other aspects, these ministries and others leave much to be desired in terms of considering and addressing the needs of the US Hispanic community. Fortunately, the histories do not end here. Today and tomorrow are further opportunities to reflect on and to act in the best interest of US Latinos; at the same time, the future will bring other people and organizations within the Christian church that will dream and work under a renewed vision of using the radio to serve Latinos with Christ's practical, hopeful love.

---

33. Hispanic National Religious Broadcasters, http://www.hnrb.org (site now discontinued).

Conclusion

Visions of the Future

LOS EVANGÉLICOS: PORTRAITS OF Latino Protestantism in the United States is a small contribution to a much larger project. In the first place, this book arises from the vision born at the formation of the Comisión de Estudios de Historia de la Iglesia en América Latina y el Caribe, Commission for the Study of the History of the Church in Latin America and the Caribbean (CEHILA), in 1973. It is part of the effort to write church history from the perspective of those who have had no voice, those who have not been allowed to reflect on their own history. Yet it is also a volume specific to CEHILA's Protestant Area that came into being in 1984. We Protestants are a minority in Latin America and among Latinos in the United States. However, our histories have been an indispensable part of the history of Christianity both in Latin America and among US Latinos.

Los Evangélicos: Portraits of Latino Protestantism in the United States aligns itself with previous efforts to open up a space for the histories of the Latino Protestant community. More than twenty years ago, CEHILA United States published Fronteras: A History of the Latin American Church in the USA Since 1513 (San Antonio: MACC, 1983), a book focusing on Latino Catholicism that nonetheless includes a section on Protestants. One decade later APHILA (Academy for the History of the Latino Church), a short-lived entity that sought to recover Protestant Latino history and open spaces for the development of Latino historians, published Hidden Stories: Unveiling the History of the Latino Church (Decatur, Georgia: AETH, 1994). Sporadic regional efforts have at times resulted in studies like Hacia una historia de la iglesia evangélica hispana de California del sur (Towards a History of the Hispanic Protestant Church of Southern California; Montebello, California: AHET, 1994). Besides these multi-denominational efforts, many Latino women and men have published books, articles, and chapters about Latino presence in specific Protestant denominations.

In the prologue, Justo González says that this book ought to serve as a call to gather more "photos" of Latino Protestantism, to organize these photos according to different interpretive schemes, to analyze the photos with their historical contexts in mind, and to utilize these results to challenge the traditional ways in which the history of Christianity in the United States is generally told. We thank God that the Latino Protestant church in the United States can now point to capable people to carry out these tasks.

There are many histories left to be told. We need to listen to other denominational experiences and see how they compare with the experiences already recounted. Many congregations without denominational affiliation could enrich the global history of Latino Protestantism if they shared their stories. On the other hand, there is a great lack of people ready to analyze the many aspects of Latino Protestant history, people to study the same stories from many different perspectives.

A global history of Latino Protestantism in the United States is also missing. The Latino Protestant community needs people to rise up and interpret within wider contexts the stories told in this volume and elsewhere. We need historians to collect our stories within a historiographic framework, to help us understand how our history fits within Protestant history and the larger history of Christianity. For example, the place of Protestant history within a mostly Catholic Latino community is still unclear. Also, no one has richly articulated Latino Protestantism's impact on US Protestantism or how to define and maintain both a Latino and a Protestant identity in the context of the United States. Though this book is part of CEHILA's collection, defining how it is that we, within the United States, are part of the history of today's Latin American church—CEHILA's focus—still eludes us.

Latino Protestants live as a minority in the midst of many majorities. Historically, this minority status has pushed many of us into isolation. Yet we can have an impact on our world as Christians. Telling our stories is both a testimony that God has been present in our pilgrimage and a confession regarding the future. The same God who accompanied us this far will remain among us. Thus, we will keep collecting "photos" and preparing to take new pictures of whatever God may do in the future.

Our photo "album" closes at a dynamic moment for Latino Protestant churches in the United States. From many different perspectives, the authors of this book have presented a growing, enthusiastic church ready to serve the Lord. The portraits show how much has been done and yet how much remains to do. There are many more stories to tell.

Bibliography

Adams, Anna. "Perception Matters: Pentecostal Latinas in Allentown, Pennsylvania." In *A Reader in Latina Feminist Theology: Religion and Justice*, edited by María Pilar Aquino, Daisy L. Machado, and Jeanette Rodríguez. Austin: University of Texas Press, 2002.

af Geijerstam, Claes. *Popular Music in Mexico*. Albuquerque: University of New Mexico Press, 1976.

Allen, Catherine B. *A Century to Celebrate: History of Woman's Missionary Union*. Birmingham: Woman's Missionary Union, Southern Baptist Convention, 1987.

Alves, Rubem. "From Paradise to the Desert: Autobiographical Musings." In *Frontiers of Theology in Latin America*, edited by Rosino Gibellini, translated by John Drury. Maryknoll, NY: Orbis, 1979.

Alstott, Owen, ed., *Flor y canto*. Portland: Oregon Catholic Press, 1989.

Aponte, Edwin. "Coritos as Active Symbol in Latino Protestant Popular Religion." *Journal of Hispanic/Latino Theology* 2, no. 3 (1995): 57–66.

Aquino, María Pilar. "Latina Feminist Theology: Central Features." In *A Reader in Latina Feminist Theology: Religion and Justice*, edited by María Pilar Aquino, Daisy L. Machado, and Jeanette Rodríguez. Austin: University of Texas Press, 2002.

———. *Nuestro clamor por la vida: Teología latinoamericana desde la perspectiva de la mujer*. San José, Costa Rica: Departamento Ecuménico de Investigaciones, 1992.

———. Daisy L. Machado, and Jeanette Rodríguez, eds. *A Reader in Latina Feminist Theology: Religion and Justice*. Austin: University of Texas Press, 2002.

Asamblea Apostólica de la Fe en Cristo Jesús. *Constitución de la Asamblea Apostólica*. Rancho Cucamonga, CA: AAFCJ, 2004.

Baker, Robert A. *Compendio de la historia cristiana*. El Paso: Casa Bautista de Publicaciones, 1981.

Bakhtin, Mikhail. *Rabelais and His World*. Translated by Hélène Iswolsky. Bloomington: Indiana UP, 1984.

Ball, H. C. "The Work Prospers on the Mexican Border." *The Pentecostal Evangel* (July 8, 1922).

Bartleman, Frank. *Another Wave Rolls In!* Monroeville, PA: Whitaker Books, 1962.

———. *Azusa Street*. South Plainfield, NJ: Bridbe Publishing, Inc, 1980.

Bartra, Roger. *La jaula de la melancolía: Identidad y metamorfosis del mexicano*. Mexico: Grijalbo, 1987.

Bazán, Nellie. "Reseña histórica." *La luz apostólica* (June 1964): 10.

Bevans, Stephen. *Models of Contextual Theologies*. Maryknoll, NY: Orbis, 2002.

Brackenridge, R. Douglas and Francisco O. García-Treto. *Iglesia presbiteriana*. San Antonio: Trinity UP, 1974.

Burgess, Stanley M. and Gary B. McGee, eds. *Dictionary of Pentecostal and Charismatic Movements*. Grand Rapids: Zondervan, 1988.

Bibliography

Campos, Rubén. *El folklore y la música mexicana: Investigación acerca de la cultura musical en México, 1525–1925.* Mexico, DF: Secretaría de Educación Pública, 1928.

Cánovanas, Agustín Cue. *Historia social y económica de México, 1521–1854.* Mexico: Trillas, 1970.

Cardoza-Orlandi, Carlos F. "Mission at the Borders." In *Presbyterian Mission for a New Millennium*, edited by Patricia Loyde-Siddle and Bonnie Sue Lewis. Louisville: Geneva Press, 2001.

———. "Re-discovering Caribbean Christian Identity: Biography and Missiology at the Shore." *Voices: New Challenges to EATWOT Theology* 27, no. 1 (June 2004): 114–44.

Carmody, Denise L. *Christian Feminist Theology.* Cambridge: Blackwell, 1995.

Chávez, John R. *The Lost Land.* Albuquerque: University of New Mexico Press, 1984.

Clavijero, Francisco Javier. *Historia antigua de México.* Mexico: Porrúa, 1974.

Colom M., Alfredo. *Música en su alma: Autobiografía de Alfredo Colom M.* Guatemala: SABER, 1985.

Concepción, Juan, ed. *Ecos de vida: Selección especial de himnos y canciones espirituales por compositores hispanos.* Brooklyn: Ebenezer, n.d.

Corum, Fred T., ed. *Like as of Fire: The Azusa Street Papers.* Los Angeles: Manna Apostolic Publications, 1986.

Costas, Orlando. *Liberating News.* Grand Rapids: Eerdmans, 1989.

———. *Theology of the Crossroads in Latin America.* Amsterdam: Rodopi, 1976.

Cox, Harvey. *Fire from Heaven.* Reading, MA: Perseus Books, 1995.

Cypess, Sandra Messinger. *La Malinche in Mexican Literature: From History to Myth.* Austin: University of Texas Press, 1991.

de León, Arnoldo. *They Called Them Greasers: Anglo Attitudes Toward Mexicans in Texas, 1821–1900.* Austin: University of Texas Press, 1983.

de León, Victor. *The Silent Pentecostals: A Biographical History of the Pentecostal Movement among the Hispanics in the Twentieth Century.* Taylors, SC: Faith Printing Company, 1979.

de Terreros, Romero and Vincent Manuel. *Bocetos de la vida social en la Nueva España.* Mexico: Porrúa, 1944.

del Pilar, Luis F. *Himnos de "El avivamiento."* 2nd ed. Bayamón, Puerto Rico: Impresos Quintana, 1983.

Deiros, Pablo A. and Carlos Mraida, *Latinoamérica en llamas.* Buenos Aires: Editorial Caribe, 1994.

Detweiler, J. F. "The Spanish-American Baptist Seminary: A Brief History." In *Seminario bautista hispano-americano: Reglamento y plan de estudios, 1930–1931.* Los Angeles, 1930.

Díaz, Samuel. *La nave pentecostal: Crónica desde el inicio de las Asambleas de Dios y su travesía por el noreste hispano de los Estados Unidos.* Grand Rapids: Vida, 1995.

Díaz-Paja, Fernando. *History of Spain.* New York: Leon Amiel, 1977.

Dickinson, Edward. *Music in the History of the Western Church.* New York: Charles Scribner's Sons, 1902. Reprint, New York: Greenwood Press, 1969.

Dolan, Jay P. and Allan Figueroa Deck, eds. *Hispanic Catholic Culture in the U.S.: Issues and Concerns.* Notre Dame: University of Notre Dame Press, 1994.

——— and Gilberto M. Hinojosa, eds. *Mexican Americans and the Catholic Church, 1900–1965.* Notre Dame: University of Notre Dame Press, 1994.

Drachman, Diane. "Immigration Statuses and Their Influence on Service Provision, Access and Use." *Social Work* 40, no. 2 (March 1995).

Bibliography

Elizondo, Virgilio. *The Future is Mestizo*. Bloomington, IN: Meyer Stone, 1988.

———. *Galilean Journey: The Mexican-American Promise*. Maryknoll, NY: Orbis, 1983.

———. "Mestizaje as a Locus of Theological Reflection." In *Frontiers of Hispanic Theology in the United States*, edited by Allan Figueroa Deck, S. J., 106–23. Maryknoll, NY: Orbis, 1992.

Elliot, J. H. *Imperial Spain: 1469–1716*. New York: Penguin, 1963.

Ellis, Ivan Cheever. "The Origin and Development of Baptist Churches and Institutions in Southern California." Ph.D. diss. University of Southern California, 1938.

Espinosa, Gastón. "Borderlands Religion: Los Angeles and the Origins of the Latino Pentecostal Movement in the U.S., Mexico, and Puerto Rico, 1900–1945." Ph.D. diss. University of California, Santa Barbara, 1999.

———. "Your Daughters Shall Prophesy: A History of Women in Ministry in the Latino Pentecostal Movement in the United States." In *Women and Twentieth-Century Protestantism*, edited by Margaret Lamberts Bendroth and Virginia Lieson Brereton. Urbana, IL: University of Illinois Press, 2002.

Estrada, Isabel A., Ruby H. Vargas, and Judith L. Bishop. *Fieles al Maestro: Bordadoras del diseño misionero*. Dallas: Woman's Missionary Union of Texas, 1992.

Failde, Augusto. *Éxito latino*. New York: Simon & Schuster, 1996.

Ferguson, Marianne. *Women and Religion*. Englewood Cliffs, NJ: Prentice Hall, 1995.

50 aniversario de la Asamblea Apostólica. Rancho Cucamonga, CA: AAFCJ, 2000.

Fontánez, Santiago Soto. *Misión a la puerta*. Santo Domingo: Editora Educativa Dominicana, 1982.

———. "Mensaje a la diáspora hispana." Address, National Convention of Baptist Leaders in New Jersey, November 2, 1981.

Franco, Simón R. "Remembranzas." *La luz apostólica* (January 1972): 7.

Fuentes, Carlos. *The Buried Mirror: Reflections on Spain and the New World*. New York: Houghton Mifflin, 1992.

Gamio, Manuel. "The Leader and the Intellectual." In *The Mexican Immigrant: His Life Story*. Chicago: University of Chicago Press, 1930. Reprinted as *The Life Story of the Mexican Immigrant: Autobiographical Documents Collected by Manuel Gamio*. New York: Dover, 1971. Page references are to the 1971 edition.

———. *Mexican Immigration to the United States: A Study of Human Migration and Adjustment*. Chicago: University of Chicago Press, 1930. Reprint, New York: Dover, 1971. Page references are to the 1971 edition.

Gardner, Richard. *¡Grito! Reies Tijerina and the New México Land Grant War of 1967*. Indianapolis and New York: Bobbs-Merrill, 1970.

Garza, Minerva N. "The Influence of Methodism on Hispanic Women." *Methodist History* 34:2 (January 1996): 78–89.

Gaxiola, Maclovio, ed. *Himnos de suprema alabanza a Jesús*. 2nd ed. Hermosillo, Sonora: 1939.

———. *Historia de la Iglesia Apostólica de la Fe en Cristo Jesús*. Mexico DF: Librería Latinoamericana, 1964.

Gaxiola, Manuel J. *La serpiente y la paloma*. Pasadena: William Carey Library, 1970.

Gibson, Charles. *Los aztecas bajo el domino español: 1519–1810*. Mexico: Siglo XXI, 1978.

Glick, Thomas F. *Islamic and Christian Spain in the Early Middle Ages: Comparative Perspectives on Social and Cultural Formation*. Princeton: Princeton UP, 1979.

Goff, James R., Jr. *Fields White unto Harvest: Charles F. Parham and the Missionary Origins of Pentecostalism*. Fayetteville, AR: University of Arkansas Press, 1988.

Bibliography

Goizueta, Roberto. "A Christology for a Global Church." In *Beyond Borders: Writings of Virgilio Elizondo and Friends,* edited by Timothy Matovina. Maryknoll, NY: Orbis, 2000.

González, Juan. *Harvest of Empire: A History of Latinos in America.* New York: Viking, 2000.

González, Justo. *The Changing Shape of Church History.* St. Louis: Chalice Press, 2002.

———, ed. *En nuestra propia lengua: Una historia del metodismo unido hispano.* Nashville: Abingdon, 1991.

———. *Santa Biblia: The Bible Through Hispanic Eyes.* Nashville: Abingdon, 1996.

———. *The Theological Education of Hispanics.* New York: Fund for Theological Education, 1988.

Grado, Pedro, ed. *Pequeña colección de himnos.* Laredo, TX: 1905.

Greely, Andrew. "Is Ethnicity Unamerican?" *New Catholic World* (May/June 1976): 106–12.

Grijalva, Joshua. *A History of Mexican Baptists in Texas.* Dallas: Baptist General Convention of Texas, 1982.

Gutiérrez, Felipe, ed. *Nuevo himnario de melodías evangélicas selectas.* Brownsville: Latin American Council of Christian Churches, 1944.

Gutiérrez-Lee, Adalia and Miriam Gutiérrez, eds. *Dios también me llama a mí.* Valley Forge, PA: National Ministries, n/d.

Harwood, Thomas. *History of the New Mexico Spanish and English Missions of the Methodist Episcopal Church from 1850–1910.* 2 vol. Albuquerque: El Abogado Press.

Haven, Gilbert. *Mexico: Our Next-Door Neighbor.* New York: Harper and Bros., 1875.

Hernández, Bernardo. *Estatutos acordados en 1a convención mexicana de la Iglesia de la Fé Apostólica Pentecostés.* Los Angeles: Bernardo Hernández, 1926.

Hill, Samuel S. and Robert G. Torbet. *Baptists North and South.* Valley Forge: Judson Press, 1965.

Hoffman, Abraham. *Unwanted Mexican Americans in the Great Depression: Repatriation Pressures, 1929–1939.* Tucson: University of Arizona Press, 1974.

Holland, Clifton L. *The Religious Dimension in Hispanic Los Angeles: A Protestant Case Study.* Pasadena: William Carey Library, 1974.

Huegel, Juan E. *Apostol de la cruz: La vida y labor misionera de Federico J. Huegel.* Mexico, DF: Transformación, 1995.

Hull, Eleanor. *Women Who Carried the Good News: The History of the Woman's American Baptist Home Mission Society.* Valley Forge: Judson Press, 1975.

Iglesia de Dios en Cristo, Menonita. *Alabanzas favoritas, no. 2.* Moundridge, KS: Gospel Publishers, 1993.

Inman, Samuel Guy. *Evangelicals at Havana.* New York: Committee on Cooperation in Latin America, 1929.

Isasi-Díaz, Ada María. *En la lucha: Elaborating a Mujerista Theology.* Minneapolis: Fortress Press, 1993.

——— and Fernando Segovia, eds. *Hispanic/Latino Theology: Challenge and Promise.* Minneapolis: Fortress Press, 1996.

——— and Yolanda Tarango. *Hispanic Women: Prophetic Voice in the Church.* New York: Harper and Row, 1988.

Jenkins, Philip. *The New Christendom? The Coming of Global Christianity.* New York: Oxford UP, 2002.

Jenks, Philip E. "Elizabeth Conde-Frazier: Preparing the Prophets." *American Baptist in Mission,* 191 (Winter 1992–1993).

Bibliography

Kahl, Willi. "Bolero." In *The New Grove Dictionary of Music and Musicians*, edited by Sir George Grove and Stanley Sadie. London: MacMillan, 1980.

Kaiser, O. "Seminario Bautista Hispano Americano." In *Libro de oro del cincuentenario, 1923-1973*. Southwest American Baptist Hispanic Convention, 1973.

Kendrick, Klaude. *The Promise Fulfilled*. Springfield, MO: Gospel Publishing House, 1999.

Lamberts Bendroth, Margaret and Virginia Lieson Brereton, eds. *Women and Twentieth-Century Protestantism*. Urbana: University of Illinois Press, 2002.

Latourette, Kenneth Scott. *A History of the Expansion of Christianity*. 7 vols. Grand Rapids: Zondervan, 1970.

Leavenworth, Lynn and Milton Froyd. "The Spanish American Baptist Seminary and Its Tasks." Mimeograph evaluation presented to the Directive Body of the Spanish American Baptist Seminary, Southern California. April, 1954.

León-Portilla, Miguel. *Los antiguos mexicanos*. Mexico: Fondo de Cultura Económica, 1983.

——. *La filosofía Náhuatl*. Mexico: Universidad Nacional Autónoma de México, 1966.

——. *Visión de los vencidos: Relaciones indígenas de la conquista*. Mexico: Universidad Autónoma de México, 1984.

Lerma, Rosario V. *Marcial de la Cruz: Himnos del pasado*. Pasadena: Rosario V. Lerma, 1985.

Lockwood, Manuel. "Recent Developments in U.S. Hispanic and Latin American Protestant Church Music." D. Min. project, Claremont School of Theology, 1981.

Lozano, Nora O. "Ignored Virgin or Unaware Women: A Mexican-American Protestant Reflection on the Virgin of Guadalupe." In *A Reader in Latina Feminist Theology*, edited by María Pilar Aquino, Daisy L. Machado, and Jeanette Rodríguez, 204-16. Austin: University of Texas Press, 2002.

Luce, Alice E. "The Latin-American Pentecostal Work." *The Pentecostal Evangel* (June 25, 1927).

Luna, David. "Patterns of Faith: Woven Together in Life and Mission." *American Baptist Quarterly* 5, no. 4 (December 1986).

Lynch, James R. "Baptist Women in Ministry Through 1920." *American Baptist Quarterly* 13, no. 4 (December 1994).

Lyon, Ruth. "Latin American District Leads the Nation." *The Pentecostal Evangel* (May 26, 1960).

Machado, Daisy. "Latinos in the Protestant Establishment: Is There a Place for Us at the Feast Table?" In *Protestantes/Protestants: Hispanic Christianity within Mainline Traditions*, edited by David Maldonado, Jr. Nashville: Abingdon Press, 1999.

Madsen, Paul O. "Appendix 2." In Luis Fidel Mercado, *Theological Education for the Present and Future American Baptist Hispanic Pastor: Its Context and Content*. Los Angeles, May, 1972.

Maldonado, Jr., David, ed. *Protestantes/Protestants: Hispanic Christianity within Mainline Traditions*. Nashville: Abingdon, 1999.

Marini, Stephen. "From Classical to Modern: Hymnody and the Development of American Evangelicalism." In *Singing the Lord's Song in a Strange Land: Hymnody in the History of North American Protestantism*, edited by Edith L. Blumhofer and Mark A. Noll, 1-38. Tuscaloosa: University of Alabama Press, 2004.

Martínez, Juan F. "Origins and Development of Protestantism Among Latinos in the Southwestern United States 1836-1900." Ph.D. diss. Fuller Theological Seminary, 1996.

Bibliography

———. *Sea la Luz: The Making of Mexican Protestantism in the American Southwest, 1829–1900.* Denton, TX: University of North Texas Press, 2006.

Martínez, Raquel Mora. "*Mil voces para celebrar—Himnario metodista.*" *The Hymn* 49 (April 1998): 25–29.

Matovina, Timothy, ed. *Beyond Borders: Writings of Virgilio Elizondo and Friends.* Maryknoll, NY: Orbis, 2000.

McCombs, Vernon. *From Over the Border: A Study of the Mexicans in the United States.* New York: Council of Women for Home Missions, 1925.

———. "Spanish and Portuguese District." *Journal of the Southern California Annual Conference, Methodist Episcopal Church, Forty-Second Annual Session,* 1917.

McDannell, Colleen. *Material Christianity: Religion and Popular Culture in America.* New Haven: Yale UP, 1995.

Melgarejo, José Luis. *Antigua historia de México.* Mexico, DF: Secretaria de Educación Pública, 1976.

Mendoza, Vicente, ed. *Himnos selectos.* Mexico: 1905.

Menéndez y Pelayo, Marcelino. *Historia de los heterodoxos españoles.* 2nd ed. Vol. 63. Santander: Consejo Superior de Investigaciones Científicas, 1948.

Menzies, William W. *Anointed to Serve.* Springfield, MO: Gospel Publishing House, 1971.

Methodist Episcopal Church South. "Cuba Mission." In *Annual Report of the Board of Foreign Missions.* Nashville: Methodist Episcopal Church South, 1907.

———. *El evangelista mexicano* (Chihuahua, Mexico, época 2) 10, no. 17 (May 1, 1928).

———. "Rev. P. A. Rodríguez." In *Annual Report of the Board of Foreign Missions.* Nashville: Methodist Episcopal Church South, 1909.

Miller, Elizabeth. "Retreat to Tokenism: A Study of the Status of Women on the Executive Staff of the American Baptist Convention." Division of Christian Social Concern. Valley Forge, PA: American Baptist Convention, 1970.

Miranda, Jesse. "Mensaje de instalación de superintendente." June 15, 2002.

Morales, Adam. *American Baptists with a Spanish Accent.* Valley Forge: Judson Press, 1964.

Mummert, Gail, ed. *Fronteras fragmentadas.* Zamora, Michoacán: Colegio de Michoacán y CIDEM, 1999.

Náñez, Alfredo. *History of the Rio Grande Conference of the United Methodist Church.* Dallas: Southern Methodist University, 1980.

Náñez, Clotilde Falcón. "Hispanic Clergy Wives." In *Women in New Worlds: Historical Perspectives on the Wesleyan Tradition,* edited by Hilah F. Thomas and Rosemary Skinner Keller, 161–77. Nashville: Abingdon, 1982.

Nava, Antonio C. *Autobiografía: 100 años.* Rancho Cucamonga, CA: AAFCJ, 1994.

———, ed., *Himnos de consolación.* 2nd ed. Los Angeles: A. C. Nava, 1932.

Niebuhr, H. Richard. *Christ and Culture.* New York: Harper and Row, 1951.

Ortega, José A. *Mis memorias en la Iglesia y la Asamblea Apostólica de la Fe en Cristo Jesús.* Indio, CA: José A. Ortega, 1998.

Ortegón, Samuel M. "Religious Thought and Practice among Mexican Baptists of the U.S., 1900–1947." Ph.D. diss. University of Southern California, 1950.

Ortiz, Manuel. *The Hispanic Challenge.* Downers Grove, IL: InterVarsity Press, 1993.

Page, Frederic B. [A. Suthron, pseud.] *Prairiedom: Rambles and Scrambles in Texas, or, New Estrémadura.* New York: Paine and Burgess, 1845. Quoted in de León, *They Called Them Greasers.*

Bibliography

Parham, Sarah E. *The Life of Charles F. Parham, Founder of the Apostolic Faith Movement.* Tri-State Printing, 1930. Reprint, Birmingham: Commercial Printing Co., 1977. Page references are to the 1977 edition.

Parra Herrera, Santos, Josefina Huerta de Parra, and César Rodríguez Cámara, eds. *Himnos de victoria.* Mexico, DF: Iglesia Evangélica Independiente, 2000.

Peña, Manuel. *The Mexican American Orquesta: Music, Culture, and the Dialectic of Conflict.* Austin: University of Texas Press, 1999.

———. *The Texas-Mexican Conjunto: History of a Working-Class Music.* Austin: University of Texas Press, 1985.

Petersen, Douglas. *Not by Might nor by Power: A Pentecostal Theology of Social Concern in Latin America.* Oxford: Regnum, 1996.

Ramírez, Daniel. *Antonio C. Nava: Charisma, Culture, and Caudillismo, Portraits of a Generation.* Fayetteville, AR: University of Arkansas Press, 2002.

———. "Borderland Praxis: The Immigration Experience in Latino Pentecostal Churches." *Journal of the American Academy of Religion* 67, no. 3 (Fall 1999).

Ramos, Tomás Rosario. *Historia de los Bautistas de Puerto Rico.* 2nd ed. Santo Domingo, Dominican Republic: Editora Educativa Dominicana, 1979.

Rembao, Alberto. *Discurso a la nación evangélica.* Argentina: La Aurora, 1949.

Richey, Russell E. *Early American Methodism.* Bloomington: Indiana UP, 1991.

Riggs, George A. *Baptists in Puerto Rico: Brief Historical Notes of Forty Years of Baptist Work in Puerto Rico, 1899–1939.* Ponce: PRE, 1939.

Rodríguez, Baldemar. *Antología de guerra: 40 años de ministerio.* Rancho Cucamonga, CA: AAFCJ, 2000.

Rodríguez, Jeannette. *Our Lady of Guadalupe: Faith and Empowerment among Mexican-American Women.* Austin: University of Texas Press, 1994.

Rodríguez, Primitivo A. *Himnario cristiano para uso de las iglesias evangélicas.* Nashville: Smith and Lamar, 1908.

Russell, Olive, ed., "From Ocean to Ocean: 1936–1937. A Brief History of Sixty Years and the Sixtieth Annual Report of the Missionaries: Medical, Educational, and Evangelistic of the Woman's American Baptist Home Mission Society." Publication of the American Baptist Churches.

Ryerson, Charles Anthony, III. "Meaning and Modernization in Tamil India: Primordial Sentiments and Sanskritization." Ph.D. diss. Columbia University, 1979.

Salazar, Lorenzo. *This is My Story.* CA: Salazar Family, 1993.

Santiago, Carmelo. "Los Angeles Baptist City Mission Society y el ministerio hispano." In *Libro de oro del cincuentenario, 1923–1973.* Southwest American Baptist Hispanic Convention, 1973.

Scherer, James. *Gospel, Church, and Kingdom.* Minneapolis: Augsburg, 1987.

Schipani, Daniel. "La Iglesia y la liberación femenina." *Boletín teológico*, 13–14 (1984).

Schmidt, Jean Miller. *Grace Sufficient: A History of Women in American Methodism 1760–1939.* Nashville: Abingdon, 1999.

Scott, Lindy. "La conversión de inmigrantes mexicanos al protestantismo de Chicago." In *Fronteras fragmentas,* edited by Gail Mummert. Zamora, Mexico: Colegio de Michoacán y CIDEM, 1999.

Sellers, Jeff M. "You Can Take the Boy Out of the Barrio. . ." *Christianity Today* 46, no. 10 (September 9, 2002). http://www.christianitytoday.com/ct/2002/september9/3.56.html?start=1.

"75 años de pentecostés en México." *Nueva Visión* (Mexico DF) 2, no. 3 (Fall 1989).

Bibliography

Sharry, Frank. "Myths, Realities, and Solutions." *Spectrum: The Journal of State Government* 67, no. 1 (Winter 1994).

Solivan, Samuel. "Sources of a Hispanic/Latino American Theology: A Pentecostal Perspective." In *Hispanic/Latino Theology: Challenge and Promise*, edited by Ada María Isasi-Díaz and Fernando Segovia. Minneapolis: Fortress Press, 1996.

Spann, E. Edward. "A Tale of Two Hymnals: The Brazilian Baptist *Cantor Cristão* (1891) and *Hinário Para o Culto Cristão* (1991)." *The Hymn* 43 (April 1992): 15–21.

Stafford, Tim. "Here Comes the World." *Christianity Today* 39, no. 6 (May 15, 1995).

Stols, Eddy. "México en la época colonial." In *México, 3000 años de historia, civilización, y cultura*, edited by Jacques Groothaert. Mexico: Grupo Noriega, 1994.

Tijerina, Reies López. *Mi lucha por la tierra*. México: Fondo de Cultura Económica, 1978.

———. *They Called Me "King Tiger": My Struggle for the Land and Our Rights*. Houston: Arte Público Press, 2000.

Tillich, Paul. *A History of Christian Thought from its Judaic and Hellenistic Origins to Existentialism*. New York: Touchstone, 1967.

Torbet, Robert G. *A History of the Baptists*. 3rd ed. Valley Forge: Judson Press, 1978.

Troyer, L. E. *The Sovereignty of the Holy Spirit*. Los Angeles: Students Benefit Publishing Co., 1934.

Villafañe, Eldin. *El Espíritu liberador: Hacia una ética social pentecostal hispanoamericana*. Grand Rapids: Eerdmans, 1996.

———. *The Liberating Spirit: Toward an Hispanic American Pentecostal Social Ethic*. Lanham, MD: University Press of America, 1992.

Villegas, Daniel Cosío, coord. *Historia general de México*. Mexico: Colegio de México, 1981.

Wagner, Peter. *Churchquake: How the New Apostolic Reformation is Shaking Up the Church as We Know It*. Ventura, CA: Regal Books, 1999.

Walls, Andrew. *The Cross-Cultural Process in Christian History*. Maryknoll, NY: Orbis, 2002.

———. *The Missionary Movement in Christian History*. Maryknoll, NY: Orbis, 1996.

Wilhoit, Mel R. "'Sing Me a Sankey': Ira D. Sankey and Congregational Song." *The Hymn* 24, no. 1 (January 1991): 13–18.

World Christianity Encyclopedia. New York: Oxford UP, 2000.

Yo soy chicano. VHS. Directed by Jesús Salvador Treviño. Los Angeles: NLCC Educational Media, 1997.